A DANGEROUS IDEA

Also by Debbie Levy

Becoming RBG
The Year of Goodbyes
This Promise of Change (with Jo Ann Allen Boyce)
Imperfect Spiral

A DANGEROUS IDEA

THE SCOPES TRIAL,
THE ORIGINAL FIGHT
OVER SCIENCE IN SCHOOLS

DEBBIE LEVY

BLOOMSBURY
CHILDREN'S BOOKS

NEW YORK LONDON OXFORD NEW DELHI SYDNEY

BLOOMSBURY CHILDREN'S BOOKS
Bloomsbury Publishing Inc., part of Bloomsbury Publishing Plc
1385 Broadway, New York, NY 10018

BLOOMSBURY, BLOOMSBURY CHILDREN'S BOOKS, and the Diana logo
are trademarks of Bloomsbury Publishing Plc

First published in the United States of America in January 2025
by Bloomsbury Children's Books

Bloomsbury books may be purchased for business or promotional use. For information on bulk purchases
please contact Macmillan Corporate and Premium Sales Department at specialmarkets@macmillan.com

Library of Congress Cataloging-in-Publication Data
available upon request
ISBN 978-1-5476-1221-5 (hardcover) • 978-1-5476-1222-2 (e-book)

Book design by John Candell
Typeset by Westchester Publishing Services
Printed and bound in the U.S.A.
2 4 6 8 10 9 7 5 3 1

To find out more about our authors and books visit www.bloomsbury.com
and sign up for our newsletters.

For Rick

CONTENTS

CHAPTER 1
THE DRUGSTORE PLAN   1

CHAPTER 2
THE REAL TARGET   10

CHAPTER 3
CLARENCE AND WILL   21

CHAPTER 4
BOY ORATOR OF THE PLATTE   27

CHAPTER 5
"WHATEVER DEGRADES ANOTHER DEGRADES ME"   38

CHAPTER 6
TWO TALL MEN, TALKING   48

CHAPTER 7
PROOFS AND PERVERSIONS   60

CHAPTER 8
DARWINISM GOES TO SCHOOL   68

CHAPTER 9
BETTER TO DESTROY   75

CHAPTER 10
"WHAT ARE MOTHERS TO DO"   82

CHAPTER 11
THE ROAD TO DAYTON   88

CHAPTER 12
THE CIRCUS COMES TO TOWN   97

CHAPTER 13
IN THE BEGINNING   111

CHAPTER 14
TO STRANGLE PUPPIES   122

CHAPTER 15
PRAYERS AND CHAIRS   134

CHAPTER 16
FOUR WITNESSES AND A TEXTBOOK   142

CHAPTER 17
SPEECHLESS   151

CHAPTER 18
THE GREATEST SPEECH   157

CHAPTER 19
SOMETHING BRAND NEW   171

CHAPTER 20
ANY QUESTION THEY PLEASE   177

CHAPTER 21
"I AM NOT AFRAID"   187

CHAPTER 22
VERDICTS   195

CHAPTER 23
AFTERLIVES AND LEGENDS   204

CHAPTER 24
A VICTORY   220

CHAPTER 25
THE EVOLUTION OF EVERYTHING   224

EPILOGUE   233

ACKNOWLEDGMENTS   237

TIMELINE   239

SOURCE NOTES   247

SELECTED BIBLIOGRAPHY   261

PHOTOGRAPH CREDITS   266

INDEX   268

A DANGEROUS
IDEA

CHAPTER 1
THE DRUGSTORE PLAN

It was a warm afternoon in early May, perfect for a friendly game of tennis. John Thomas Scopes was batting the fuzzy ball back and forth with some of his students on the clay court at the high school. He'd just finished his first year as a teacher, and was hardly much older than the kids he taught.

Another boy—a little boy, not one of the tennis players—approached the court. He waited for a point to end.

"Mr. Robinson says, if it's convenient," the boy said to John, "for you to come down to the drugstore."

Frank Earle Robinson—"Doc" Robinson, some called him—owned the drugstore. But he was more than a shopkeeper. He was also chairman of the Rhea County school board.

John was curious, but he didn't hurry off the court. When the game was over, he walked downtown in his sweaty shirt to Robinson's Drug Store on Main Street to see what was up.

Doc Robinson gave John a chair. The boy who worked behind the

Inside Robinson's Drug Store, Dayton, Tennessee, where town leaders hatched the plan for the prosecution of John Scopes.

fountain brought John a soda. And what was up was a gathering of the leading citizens of the tiny burg of Dayton, Tennessee.

"John, we've been arguing," said one of them. That was George W. Rappleyea, who worked for the company that owned the nearby, and failing, iron and coal mines. He was young, thirty-one, originally from New York.

"I said that nobody could teach biology without teaching evolution," George continued.

"That's right," John responded. He could not imagine where this conversation was headed. George went to the shelf where Doc

Robinson displayed for sale the textbooks used in the local schools. He picked one up: *A Civic Biology*.

"You have been teaching 'em this book?"

It was the standard biology textbook in public high schools across Tennessee—in high schools across the country, for that matter. The book included a brief section on evolution, the scientific theory that animals, plants, and people have developed over time from earlier species. Although neither biology nor evolution were his fields—John had been hired to teach physics and math, and, especially, to coach football—he had been filling in for the regular biology teacher, who'd been out sick all semester.

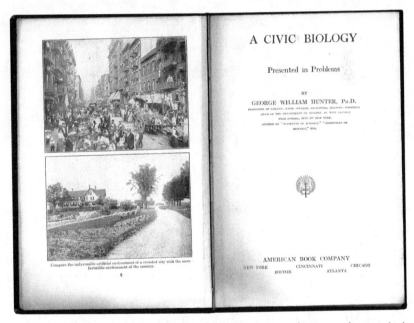

Title page of *A Civic Biology*, the textbook authorized by the state of Tennessee for use in high schools, and used by John Scopes in his biology class at Rhea Central High School.

"Yes," John said. He'd used *A Civic Biology* in class. How else was he supposed to know what to teach?

Now Doc Robinson joined the conversation. "Then you've been violating the law," he said.

Everyone around the table—two lawyers, the school superintendent, Robinson, and Rappleyea—agreed. John had broken the law.

Now would have been a good time for someone to slap John on the back and tell him this was a joke. After all, teaching from *A Civic Biology* hadn't been his choice; he'd been following the statewide curriculum, trying to do whatever the regular biology teacher—who was also the principal!—would have done.

Anyway, since when was teaching a unit in biology class a crime?

Since seven weeks earlier.

On March 21, 1925, the governor of Tennessee signed into law House Bill 185—more commonly known as the Butler Act, after John Washington Butler, the state legislator who introduced it. In the words of the Butler Act, educators in Tennessee's public schools were barred from teaching "any theory that denies the story of the Divine Creation of man as taught in the Bible." The law went on to prohibit any instruction "that man has descended from a lower order of animals."

In other words, no evolution.

The amount of time that John had spent on evolution with his students—well, he couldn't remember, but it was hardly any. The men around the table didn't care. Whatever it was, it was enough. John had broken the law.

But this was, in fact, a far friendlier conversation than it might seem.

Before the men had summoned John, they'd been discussing something that George Rappleyea had seen in the *Chattanooga Daily Times*. The American Civil Liberties Union (ACLU), a group formed a few years earlier with the mission of protecting individual rights, wanted to bring a legal challenge against the Butler Act. But the

organization couldn't do that until a teacher was charged with breaking the new law. "Distinguished counsel have volunteered their services," the ACLU announced in a press release that was printed in the
newspaper. "All we need now is a willing client."

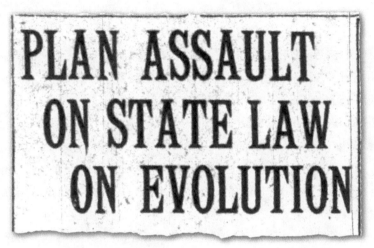

The headline in the *Chattanooga Daily Times* on May 4, 1925, that got George
Rappleyea's attention.

George Rappleyea could not stand the new anti-evolution law. He
had some scientific training and was offended by the law's implication
that a person could not believe in God and acknowledge evolution at
the same time—of course you could! Yes, evolution was a scientific
explanation for how all living things, including humans, could trace
their lineages back over eons. Evolution described how life changed
over those ages from simple to complex forms. And yes, the scientific
explanation upended the biblical story of a literal six-day creation told
in the book of Genesis. But George, and many people of faith, agreed
that the theory of evolution was perfectly consistent with religious
belief. Perhaps the Supreme Being's greatest creation was the evolutionary method of metamorphosis by which species were always
changing. Perhaps the Bible's six days of creation meant something

other than six days of twenty-four hours each—perhaps they were "days" of extraordinary length, each lasting millions of years. Perhaps the creation story was a literary device. But if some people thought that evolution wasn't consistent with religion—well, the theory of evolution was science, and schools should be in the business of teaching science in their science classes, not religion.

Unlike George, Doc Robinson and the other town leaders didn't detest the Butler Act. Walter White, the school superintendent, for one, thought the law was a fine idea and the theory of evolution a godless notion that would corrupt America's youth. But George knew how to get them interested.

"Mr. Robinson," he'd said before the group sent for John, "you . . . are always looking for something that will get Dayton a little publicity."

True. Dayton's bigwigs wanted to put their town on the map. Its coal mines, blast furnaces, and button factories had closed. There just wasn't much going on in this eastern Tennessee borough, and that was not good for townspeople who wanted steady jobs. It was not good for small businesses that needed townspeople with money to spend. People had tried all sorts of things—a factory to make crates in which to pack the strawberry crop that fruited every spring, a hosiery mill, a cotton ginning company. But Dayton remained in the doldrums.

"I wonder if you have seen the morning paper?" George continued.

Robinson had seen the newspaper, had seen the ACLU's plea— but hadn't seen what it had to do with Dayton. George shared his brainstorm: Dayton should accept the ACLU's offer to challenge the Butler Act. They should enlist the biology teacher at Dayton's own Rhea Central High School. Surely he'd taught evolution. The city attorney should prosecute the teacher under the Butler Act. A trial would be held in the local court. The ACLU would come in to defend

Main Street, downtown Dayton, Tennessee, 1925.

the teacher. The town would make sure that no harm came to the accused teacher; his job would not be endangered and he would not incur any legal expenses.

The eyes of the nation, maybe the world, would be drawn to the case—which meant they would be drawn to Dayton. Hundreds of people, especially newspaper reporters, would come to town for the trial. These people would need to eat and drink and sleep; this would all be a windfall for the local restaurants and hotels. Even more importantly, the event would show off Dayton's many fine qualities—hardworking people, paved streets, nearby railroad connections, beautiful land, freshwater springs. The scenic mountains nearby! Chickamauga Lake—excellent fishing!—and countless cool swimming holes, not to mention the meandering Tennessee River. All these fine qualities might attract some important new industry to set up shop in the faltering town.

So when John T. Scopes sat down with his soda, the first thing George and the others needed to know was whether he'd taught evolution. In Chattanooga, for example—an hour's drive to the southwest—the school superintendent told a reporter that teachers in schools there didn't teach evolution. The head of schools in Knoxville, the city eighty miles to the northeast of Dayton, dismissed the idea of teaching evolution, explaining, "Our teachers have a hard enough time teaching the children how to distinguish between plant and animal life."

But John said yes, he had taught evolution. Sort of. Maybe. He might have. He did use the textbook with its explanation of evolution. The men happily told him he'd broken the law. And next Doc Robinson asked him the question that would create a circus in Dayton and a frenzy beyond. It would create history, as well as legends. It would highlight rifts between city and country people, modernists and traditionalists, religious adherents and nonbelievers. It would entice two of the most famous personalities in the country to come to Dayton to settle scores in a battle that had been years in the making.

"John, would you be willing to stand for a test case?"

John was known to be mild-mannered. Mild-looking, too: lanky, with straw-colored, thin hair and horn-rimmed glasses that gave him a scholarly appearance. He was quiet, but he wasn't a pushover. Still, he didn't need to think too long about Robinson's question.

Yes, he answered. Yes, he would challenge the anti-evolution law.

So a justice of the peace came to the drugstore and issued a warrant for John's arrest.

A constable "arrested" him.

Frank Robinson picked up the telephone and called the Chattanooga newspaper. "This is F.E. Robinson in Dayton," he said. "I'm chairman of the school board here. We've just arrested a man for teaching evolution."

John Scopes, left, and George Rappleyea, who came up with the idea of prosecuting John to bring attention to Dayton, Tennessee.

George Rappleyea sent a telegram to the American Civil Liberties Union in New York informing them that Dayton had that "willing client" they were looking for.

And John, after draining his soda, returned to the tennis court for another game.

CHAPTER 2
THE REAL TARGET

The pages in George William Hunter's book *A Civic Biology* that were dedicated to the science of evolution numbered no more than six, in a volume of 400-plus pages. But although *A Civic Biology* was the source of John's supposed wrongdoing, the target of the Butler Act was a different book and a different author—two different books, really, both written by an English naturalist named Charles Darwin.

The first was titled *On the Origin of Species*. It grew out of a five-year, life-altering ocean journey the naturalist took nearly a century before the drugstore clique gathered in Dayton. Darwin was hired in 1831 by the captain of a little ship called the HMS *Beagle*. The captain's main task was to survey and map the coast of South America, taking a westward route across both the Atlantic and Pacific oceans. Darwin's job, as naturalist and geologist, was to investigate and take detailed notes on the landforms and life encountered on the globe-circling voyage. When he set out on this exciting and dangerous journey, Darwin didn't imagine himself writing a book that would jolt the world. But that is what he ended up doing.

Once back home in England in 1836, Darwin began working through his data: thousands of pages of notes and a vast collection of animal and plant specimens, all pointing to the amazing diversity of life. He had detailed notes on the size and structure of birds. On beaks and claws. On fossils of giant armadillos and llamas and rhinoceros-sized rodents. There were lists of specimens, zoological diaries, and geological journals. He conducted experiments in his garden and backyard dovecotes. He consulted with fellow scientists.

From 1836 to 1858—more than twenty years—Darwin compared and contrasted, considered and reconsidered. Slowly, slowly, he was becoming convinced that mountains of evidence pointed to one con-

clusion: life on Earth had evolved over millions of years. Borrowing a term from the work of animal breeders, he called the process of this evolution "natural selection."

Natural selection: two words to capture many. Relentless, random mutations in offspring lead to small transformations of traits. Some of those traits end up being better suited to

Charles Darwin, around 1854, a time when he was working on his book *On the Origin of Species*.

constantly changing environments. Compared to animals that lack those traits, the offspring with the mutated traits are more likely to survive and have offspring of their own. This leads to gradual shifts in populations, and eventually species—it leads, that is, to *evolution*—toward the traits that allow for survival, and are therefore passed on to more offspring.

The idea didn't occur to Darwin in one sudden burst. In 1844, midway through his twenty-year process, Darwin wrote to his friend and fellow British scientist Joseph Hooker: "I am almost convinced (quite contrary to [the] opinion I started with) that species are not (it is like confessing a murder) immutable."

It is like confessing a murder. The idea of some type of evolution was already circulating among scientists. But the long-held view, in science as well as religion, was that all species were created long ago by God, as described in the Bible's book of Genesis. These God-created species were "immutable"—that is, unchanging. Darwin was finding, however, that species were in fact changeable. Modern species had mutated from earlier species. They had, in fact, changed.

This was, to many, a darkly subversive view. And Darwin even had to convince *himself* that everything he'd been taught to believe about the history of life on Earth had been missing the very nature of change, and the changing of nature. Before this, he had clung so closely to a book called *Natural Theology* by William Paley, an English churchman, that he could recite its lines by heart. Lines like:

> The marks of *design* are too strong to be got over. Design must have had a designer. That designer must have been a person. That person is God.

But now, he had to follow the evidence.

A few years before he made his confession to his friend Joseph

Hooker, Darwin published an account of his journeys on the *Beagle*. In it, he noted, for example, that finches from the different islands he'd visited in the Galápagos were similar in many ways—but their beaks were markedly different in shape. The various beaks were well suited for eating the particular seeds and other foods available on the different islands where the finches made their homes. "Seeing this gradation and diversity of structure [of beaks] in one small, intimately related group of birds," Darwin wrote, "one might really fancy that . . . one species had been taken and modified for different ends."

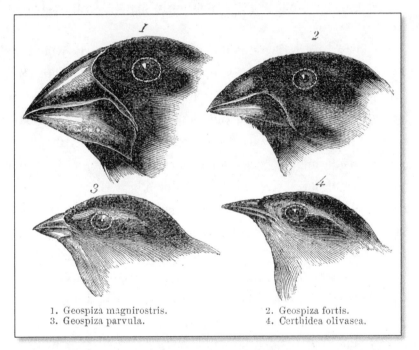

1. Geospiza magnirostris.
2. Geospiza fortis.
3. Geospiza parvula.
4. Certhidea olivasea.

Drawings of beaks of finches from Charles Darwin's book, *Journal of Researches*, also known as *The Voyage of the Beagle*, originally published in 1839.

Might the birds' beaks have transformed over time? Might these birds have shared ancestors that started in one location and then dispersed to separate islands, where their beaks, over countless years, changed in ways that reflected their particular environments? The very questions challenged the long-held view, central to the faith of so many people, that God had created all animal species once and forever.

Besides Hooker and other British friends, Darwin reached out repeatedly to Asa Gray, a professor at Harvard University and the most prominent botanist in the United States. The two engaged in a flurry of correspondence. "My dear Sir," Darwin began in April 1855, "I want to beg a great favour of you, for which I well know I can offer no apology. . . . I have the greatest curiosity about the alpine Flora of the U.S."

He knew he was directing his questions to a man who would find them irresistible. Whatever there was to know about plants in 1855, Gray probably knew it. "I rejoice in furnishing facts to others to work up in their bearing on general questions," he responded. The two naturalists sent blizzards of enthusiastic missives across the Atlantic.

In considering the beaks of the finches, Darwin had been pondering striking *differences* among birds that otherwise seemed closely related. Now, he was trying to tease out an explanation for his observations of *similarities* among plants that grew in far-flung locales. They were different species, but shared characteristics that suggested they had descended from the same ancient ancestors. Which eventually led to the big question: faced with these strong similarities, was it reasonable to continue to assume that every single variety of plant was specially, independently created by God? Or was it more reasonable to conclude that these varieties had common ancestors?

Although Darwin hadn't admitted it outright, he wasn't only trying to explain flowers and trees. He was trying to work out the puzzle of life itself. Finally, in a letter dated July 20, 1857, the British naturalist spilled the beans to his Harvard friend:

But as an honest man I must tell you that I have come to
the heteredox conclusion that there are no such things
as independently created species—that species are only
strongly defined varieties. I know that this will make you
despise me.

Darwin knew that Asa Gray, a man of science, was also a man
of God. In the textbook that he published that very same year,
First Lessons in Botany—which became the leading schoolbook on
the topic—Gray instructed students that "the Creator established a
definite number of species at the beginning, which have continued
by propagation, each after its kind." But Gray did not despise Darwin, and his response to his friend revealed the open mind of a
scientist: "No one can have worked at systematic botany as long as
I have, without having many misgivings about the definiteness of
species."

Later in 1857, in his next letter to Gray, Darwin outlined his
bombshell theory of natural selection. It contradicted what his friend
had so recently written in his textbook; it contradicted so much of the
thinking that scientists and non-scientists alike had accepted for so
many centuries. There was *not*, according to Darwin, a definite number of species formed once and for all time at the beginning. Each
creature was *not* distinct and unchanging over the ages. Rather, species were changing all the time.

By now, Darwin was working diligently on what he called his "big
book"—a book that would reveal his findings and theory to the public.
He wanted to make it as perfect and convincing as possible. By the
summer of 1858, he'd written about 250,000 words. He figured he
needed another 250,000 to complete it.

Half a million words: that would be a long book. A very, very long book, more like a multivolume set. And he'd already been at work for two decades.

Just at this same time, Darwin received a letter from a fellow British naturalist, Alfred Russel Wallace. Wallace had also been investigating natural selection, and in his letter he shared his conclusions about evolution. They were remarkably similar to Darwin's. The two men immediately wrote a scientific paper together.

Wallace's emergence as a fellow evolutionist provided the spark that Darwin needed to release his theory into the larger world. Publish your book already, his other friends urged him! It's been twenty-plus years, and if you don't, someone else will beat you to it! So, finally, Darwin decided to unleash his ideas on the public. Rather than the gargantuan "big book" he'd been planning, he would publish what he considered only an "abstract" of that larger work. Maybe so, but it was still 502 pages. *On the Origin of Species* was published in England on November 24, 1859, to much excitement and controversy. (Wallace didn't publish a book of his own on the theory of evolution, but in *Origin of Species* Darwin prominently stated that "Mr. Wallace, who is now studying the natural history of the Malay archipelago, has arrived at almost exactly the same general conclusions that I have.")

Immediately Darwin sent a copy to Asa Gray. It arrived by Christmas. In the margins, Gray wrote such notations as "Well put" and "Yes" and "!!!" Yes to evolution—or "transmutation of species," or "descent with modification," as the scientists put it. Yes to natural selection.

And yes, still, to God. Gray saw evolution itself as the work of God, and revised his high school botany textbook to include both Darwin's theory and a Supreme Being. All living things *and* the workings of natural selection, Gray wrote, are "the conception of One Mind."

Darwin sent early copies of his new book out widely, including to another luminary on Harvard's faculty, Louis Agassiz. Agassiz was the most famous zoologist in the United States. He was also a racist through and through, believing in the superiority of white people over Black people and other people of color. He took white supremacy to an even more odious level when he decided, and taught, that Black and white people did not belong to the same species.

So it was not surprising that when this Harvard professor scribbled in the margins of his copy of *Origin of Species*, it was to complain: "This is truly monstrous." "The mistake of Darwin . . ." "A sentence likely to mislead!" This was, after all, a man who was scientifically certain that God had not only separately created every species, but had also specially created the species of white people, superior to and different from the species of Black people.

While Harvard professors such as Asa Gray and Louis Agassiz debated the merits of *Origin of Species*, ordinary people in the United States had a few other things on their minds in 1860—like the bitter debate over slavery. Like the divisive presidential election, which elevated Abraham Lincoln to the White House, which led to the dissolution of the nation and civil war.

Still, when an American publisher made Darwin's book available to bookstores and libraries in January of that year, intellectuals, academics, religious leaders, and the just plain curious dug in. Many embraced the book. To anti-slavery advocates, Darwin's theory uncovered the noxious nonsense behind the notion that Black people and white people belonged to different species. The theory of evolution said that all people had common ancestors. It was not a stretch to say that, therefore, all were equal.

Over the next decade, debate around Darwin's ideas bubbled and frothed—in the pages of magazines and journals, in drawing rooms, in auditoriums and lecture halls. Unlike Agassiz, many if not most scientists came to accept evolution. However, there were serious differences among them in how exactly they thought species evolved. Was it through Darwin's "natural selection"—that is, through the slow accumulation of random modifications? Did species evolve through changes that were not random, but rather that came about in response to some need of the organism? (Did the giraffe have a long neck because its ancestors were reaching high in trees for food?) Did species change through a supernatural mechanism—that is, through the work of God? Darwin himself did not pretend to know how exactly traits were passed down from one generation to another—he was only certain that they *were* passed down, somehow.

And what about human beings? *Origin of Species* contains not a single word about the evolution of humans. This was an intentional omission. As Darwin explained in a letter to Alfred Russel Wallace in 1857, "I think I shall avoid the whole subject, as so surrounded with prejudices, though I fully admit that it is the highest & most interesting problem for the naturalist."

But Darwin could not leave that "highest & most interesting problem" alone. "Our ancestor," he wrote in a letter to Scottish geologist Charles Lyell,

> was an animal which breathed water, had a swim-bladder, a great swimming tail, an imperfect skull & undoubtedly was an hermaphrodite! Here is a pleasant genealogy for mankind.

This didn't disturb Darwin, but he feared many of his fellow human beings would be appalled. He couldn't help himself, though: in 1871 he published this theory for all to see. His follow-up book, *The Descent of Man*, set out the evidence that human beings, like every other species, descended from earlier forms of living creatures. The origins of mammals, including primates, were sea creatures. People— *homo sapiens*—were a type of primate. We, too, could count sea creatures in our family tree, and our prehistoric ancestors were related to other primates, like gorillas and chimpanzees.

"Man," Darwin wrote, "still bears in his bodily frame the indelible stamp of his lowly origin." The skeletons of mammals, including humans, were similar to birds, amphibians, and reptiles. When Dar-

win compared the embryos of various species, he was even more convinced of his conclusion. At various stages in their developments, human embryos appear nearly identical to the embryos of other vertebrates. Darwin

Darwin's book *The Descent of Man* piqued public interest and also became fodder for numerous editorial cartoons. Clockwise, from below right, are images from an 1882 issue of *Punch*, an 1887 issue of *Punch*, and an 1871 issue of *The Hornet Magazine*.

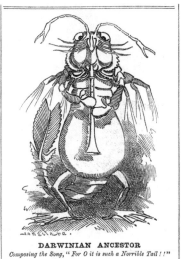

DARWINIAN ANCESTOR
Composing the Song, "For O it is such a Norrible Tail ! !"
"Our ancestor was an animal which breathed water, had a
swim-bladder, a great swimming tail, and an imperfect skull."—
Darwin to Lyell.

PUNCH'S ALMANACK FOR 1882.

MAN·IS·BVT·A·WORM·

also identified parts of human anatomy that no longer serve any purpose—"rudiments," he called them, such as a particular point on the outer ear—as leftovers from earlier stages of human evolution.

People were appalled, as Darwin anticipated, but they were also fascinated. In the United States, hundreds of publications spread the news. As one popular journal noted soon after the book was published, its sales were "almost unprecedented in scientific literature." Editors at *Harper's New Monthly Magazine* predicted "there is no doubt that it will exercise a very powerful influence upon the science of the day." The most widely read American women's magazine anticipated that *The Descent of Man* "will call forth discussion and dissent among the masterminds of the age."

Two of those "masterminds" were still children.

CHAPTER 3
CLARENCE AND WILL

When *On the Origin of Species* was published in the United States in 1860, a little boy named Clarence was growing up in a house full of books, kids, and two freethinking parents. Christianity was central to the lives of most people in America at the time, and certainly in Clarence's hamlet of Kinsman Township in the northeastern corner of Ohio. Many viewed their religion and their country's government as intertwined. But Amirus and Emily Darrow, Clarence's parents, were not among these faithful.

The Darrows were part of the emerging freethinkers' movement, and they believed in the power of reason and debate over the dictates of religion and authority. Amirus and Emily supported women's rights, even though the customs and laws of the day kept women firmly under the control of their husbands and powerless to steer the government that made those laws. Amirus and Emily opposed slavery and advocated for its abolition, even while much of the nation insisted that the enslavement of Black people by white people was right, just, and godly. In the Darrow home, fellow abolitionists could find a bed and a meal as they traveled from town to town to build a movement they hoped would end the abomination of slavery.

This fizzy mix of agitation and opposition didn't just passively filter down to the Darrow children. It was in the air, in nightly read-alouds around the dining table and enthusiastic talk about such activists as Frederick Douglass, Sojourner Truth, Wendell Phillips, and John Brown. It was in their names: three of the six sons, including Clarence, were named in honor of famous opponents of slavery. Clarence's parents chose "Seward" as his middle name, for William Seward, the prominent anti-slavery activist who, after the election of 1860, became President Abraham Lincoln's secretary of state.

And, most flagrantly, this culture of questioning and doubting was arranged on shelves and piled on tables. For while Amirus Darrow built furniture and coffins for a living, he lived for books. The house was bursting with them. Everyone in town knew about the vast trove of volumes at the Darrow home; the family had the biggest library in the county. Ipso facto, as little Clarence Seward Darrow might say in thirty years' time when he was a lawyer, that big library made the Darrows rather strange.

So once *Origin of Species* reached American bookstores, Amirus Darrow obtained a copy for his personal library and let the drumbeat of evidence for a new way of thinking shake the foundation of his unusually progressive home. Eleven years later, when *The Descent of Man* came to America, that volume, too, found its way into the Darrow home and the hands of its inhabitants, including fourteen-year-old Clarence.

———◆•◆———

Meanwhile, two states over, in southern Illinois, another family

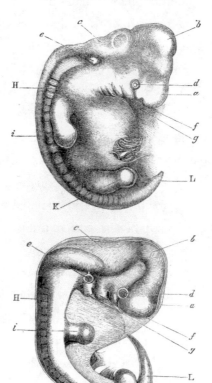

Fig. 1. Upper figure human embryo, from Ecker.   Lower figure that of a dog,
from Bischoff.

_a._ Fore-brain, cerebral hemispheres, &c.
_b._ Mid-brain, corpora quadrigemina.
_c._ Hind-brain, cerebellum, medulla ob-
longata.
_d._ Eye.
_e._ Ear.
_f._ First visceral arch.

_g._ Second visceral arch.
H. Vertebral columns and muscles in
process of development.
_i._ Anterior ⎱
K. Posterior ⎰ extremities.
L. Tail or os coccyx.

A page comparing human and dog embryos in Darwin's _Descent of Man_,
a book that was on the Darrows' bookshelf when Clarence was a boy.

was locked in an embrace with the religion that the Darrow family rejected. Christianity and church were central to the Bryan family: Silas and Mariah and kids, including a little boy, born in 1860, named William. Christianity anchored the Bryan family to their hometown of Salem. So did their belief in neighborliness, democracy, and equality— for white people. The guest room in the Bryan home was for traveling churchmen and pro-slavery politicians, not roving abolitionists.

A pillar of his community, Silas Bryan was a successful lawyer, state senator, and circuit court judge. He became a wealthy man. No one was likely to tag the Bryan family as strange. And no one was likely to see Charles Darwin's books on a bookshelf in the Bryan home. The notion that people descended from other animals through a process just the same as any other living thing on Earth—this violated the very core of the Bryan family's tenets. People were sacred, imbued with a special design and purpose. This idea had been passed down for generations.

No matter what books graced the shelves inside the Darrow and Bryan homes, the children were not going to be learning about Charles Darwin's new theory in school. Both Clarence and Will attended public elementary schools, which by 1860 were common in many parts of America. They were fed a steady diet of *McGuffey's Readers*, a popular series written by a Presbyterian minister. There was definitely no evolution in those books. No science at all, really, although Charles Darwin, after all his research into beaks and claws, might have been interested in *McGuffey's* story of little Rose and Willie, brother and sister, who find a bird's nest:

How does the bird make the nest so strong, Willie?
The mother bird has her bill and her claws to work with, but she would not know how to make the nest if God did not teach her.

McGuffey's Readers were unavoidable in the mid-1800s, as was their strong Protestant sensibility, as was Bible study, even in public schools. Most everyone in America was one version or another of Protestant. If infidels (which is how his neighbors labeled Amirus Darrow), or Catholics, or Jews, or Muslims were uncomfortable with the pervasive Protestant ethics or culture, they could go ahead and be uncomfortable. Majority ruled.

The Darrow and Bryan boys also learned the basics in their elementary schools: reading, writing, arithmetic. And from there both Clarence and Will, unlike most American teenagers at the time, continued their education. They attended private academies, where they studied such subjects as algebra, history, and Latin. Unlike elementary schools, these academies also offered courses in science, styled "natural philosophy" or "natural history." Here, too, the glow of religion and God's presence did not dim. Educators taught that the natural world illuminated God's handiwork. Young scholars learned that God was the Designer. Charles Darwin wasn't the only student to absorb William Paley's arguments in *Natural Theology*.

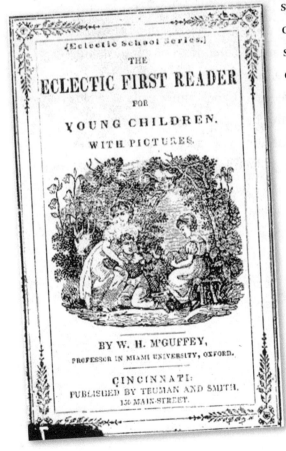

[Eclectic School Series.]

THE

ECLECTIC FIRST READER

FOR

YOUNG CHILDREN.

WITH PICTURES.

BY W. H. M'GUFFEY,

PROFESSOR IN MIAMI UNIVERSITY, OXFORD.

CINCINNATI:
PUBLISHED BY TRUMAN AND SMITH.
150 MAIN-STREET.

One of the *McGuffey's Readers* used at the time Clarence Darrow and William Jennings Bryan were schoolchildren.

So Clarence and Will's school experiences weren't very different, despite the differences in their lives at home. And they shared another experience—more than experience, really, it was a talent, a genius—that would propel them toward each other in a few decades' time: these two were talkers. Speechifiers. Sermonizers. Americans flocked to hear good orators in the nineteenth and early twentieth centuries. A thrilling oration was the blockbuster movie of the time.

At a young age, Will thought he might grow up to be a preacher, mesmerizing a congregation from his place in the pulpit. He loved to stand on the steps outside his house and make speeches in front of the neighborhood kids. He may not have had anything sensible to say, but that didn't stop him, even at the age of four, from mimicking his elders—ministers, politicians, lawyers in his father's courtroom.

Clarence bloomed later as an orator. His childhood ambitions ran more toward the baseball diamond than the church dais. Still, like most schoolboys, Clarence was expected to develop the art of delivering "pieces"—that is, short speeches. It took him a while to decide that he had something worth saying, but when he did, he caught up to the boy two states over. As if by destiny—not exactly an evolutionary concept—Clarence Darrow and William Jennings Bryan set off on paths that eventually brought them to a fiery collision.

CHAPTER 4
BOY ORATOR OF THE PLATTE

D on't go in there!"
     The farmer left his plow to warn off two women who were walking toward the woods.

"There is a man over there shouting and waving his hands," he continued. "I think he must have escaped from the asylum."

It was May of 1880. A man in the woods shouting and waving his hands? Sermonizing to the trees? The two women weren't alarmed. They knew it had to be Will Bryan, practicing one of his speeches.

Will's ardor for speechmaking, already burning when he was a small child, had only grown warmer as he grew older. While still schooled at home, he had regularly climbed up on the tiny table in the Bryans' back sitting room and lectured on his lessons to an appreciative audience of one: his mother. But Will wanted to make speeches that made everyone, not just his mother, stop and listen.

This took some work.

At fifteen years old, in 1875, Will went off to Jacksonville, Illinois, about 150 miles northwest of Salem. There he attended Whipple Academy, a college preparatory school, and then Illinois College. As a student, he was competent. Diligent. Conscientious. But his eyes were on one particular prize: he wanted to win the declamation contest—a speechmaking competition. He applied himself earnestly, attending lectures by some of the renowned speakers of the day. He studied Latin and Greek, the languages of ancient orators.

For his first attempt, he delivered a speech about another speech—American patriot Patrick Henry's "Give Me Liberty or Give Me Death" oration. It did not go over so well. "The judges did not seem to regard me as especially promising," he later recalled. Still, he kept plugging away, as he advanced from prep school to college. He lived, breathed, and dreamed speechmaking—yes, dreamed, as when, during Will's freshman year in college, he dreamed that he was awarded second place in that year's contest. In his waking hours a day or two later—he won second place.

Nice, but not what Will was after. He practiced and practiced. He excelled at committing lines, and eventually entire speeches, to memory. He was known for going off into the woods to lecture to the trees—as he did on that May day in 1880 when he was a college junior and the two women out for a stroll laughed off the farmer's warning of a dangerous shouting man.

The declamation competition that year took place a few days after Will talked to the trees. He won first place.

He also won over Mary Baird, one of those two women walking by Will's woods. When Mary and Will first met, she was a student at the Jacksonville Female Academy, down the road from Illinois College. She noticed his dark hair and eyes, his impressive height, his broad smile. "My classmates in boarding school sometimes warned me that he was too good," she later wrote, "but after considering the matter, I decided that I preferred marrying a man who was too good rather than one who was not quite good enough."

How good was Will Bryan? He didn't drink liquor or wine. He didn't play cards. You might find him around campus carrying a Bible—which he read frequently. Outside of school, his main "diversions," Mary observed, were "Sunday school, church, prayer meeting, an occasional church social." That's how good Will Bryan was.

Will lived in Chicago for two years to attend law school, a logical choice for a young man who enjoyed public speaking. After he and Mary got married, they made their home back in Jacksonville. Will joined a law firm with three other lawyers. Most of his work was for clients who were owed money by others; basically, Will served as their bill collector. It wasn't the type of work that demanded a silver-tongued orator, or even a highly skilled lawyer, but it did call for other qualities that Will cultivated: patience and empathy. Yes, he was demanding payment from people on their debts, but he went out of his way not, as he put it, to "make men mad" while doing this unenviable job.

But whether he was a kind bill collector or a mean bill collector, he was a bill collector in a small town. On a business trip to Lincoln, Nebraska, Will decided to make a change. That city had four times as many people, friends from law school, and a fine university. By the summer of 1888, the Bryans were living in a newly built house in Lincoln.

There was still lawyering in Lincoln. It paid better than the lawyering in Jacksonville, and it wasn't all bill collecting. More significantly, there was politics. And so much of politics was about Will Bryan's first love: speechifying.

Like his father before him, Will belonged to the Democratic Party—also known as the Democracy. After the Civil War, as Will was entering politics, the party attracted a hodgepodge of supporters. It was known for representing farmers over city folks and poor people over rich people. But it drew supporters in cities, too, especially in the North, where the Democratic Party appealed to white immigrants who looked to it for jobs and other favors. The Democracy was also known, especially but not exclusively in the South, for its embrace of white supremacy.

Lincoln was a Republican Party town, so Will had plenty of people to try to convince of the correctness of the Democratic Party line. He embraced people of the working classes, who found themselves squeezed out of opportunities to advance because of the growing concentration of wealth in the hands of powerful men and giant corporations. Will railed against high tariffs imposed by the U.S. government on goods imported from foreign countries. Such tariffs, supported by the Republican Party, protected American industrialists (who were generally Republicans) from competition from lower-priced foreign imports. But tariffs hurt ordinary Americans by raising the prices of the goods they needed to buy. Tariffs also hurt American farmers when foreign countries retaliated by slapping their own import taxes on American corn and wheat, making those grains more expensive and therefore less attractive in overseas markets.

Corporations and tariffs: these subjects might not seem likely to arouse passions, much less passionate oratory. But Will had a way about him.

It was 1887, and Will had traveled to a town in the western part of Nebraska to make a speech. He took an overnight train back to Lincoln, arriving home at dawn. He sat on the edge of the bed and woke his wife. He needed to tell her something.

"Mary," he said, "I have had a strange experience. Last night I found that I had power over the audience. I could move them as I chose. I have more than usual power as a speaker. I know it. God grant I may use it wisely."

He was twenty-seven years old. His power to move people—to laughter, to tears, to cheering—was taking off.

"Boy Orator of the Platte," people called him, referring to the river that runs through Nebraska. Even those who disagreed with the content of his speeches had to admit that the instrument through which that content was delivered—Will's voice—was splendid. It was pleasant and full, crisp and comprehensible. He could bring up its volume to incredibly loud levels, reaching the far corners of large auditoriums without any perceptible strain.

His speeches, while about political topics, frequently had the feel of sermons. He was proudly a Christian, and he wove biblical rhythms, quotations, and belief into his public addresses.

Nebraska Democrats chose Will as their candidate for the U.S. Congress in 1890. And even though Will was a Democrat running in a Republican congressional district, he won the election handily, and went to Washington, DC, as U.S. Representative William Jennings Bryan. And from there, awareness of his oratory prowess spread beyond Nebraska.

When he delivered his first major speech—about tariffs—in Congress, Will's audience was spellbound. He spoke for an hour. Then another hour. Legislators and locals rushed to the House of Representatives to witness the show. His hometown newspaper, setting aside its own editorial opposition to Will on the tariff question, gushed, "Where is the Nebraskan with soul so dwarfed by what he falsely imagines to be politics that he cannot rejoice in the merited popularity . . . of our young congressman? Bryan is worth more to us than an advertising train."

After he was elected to office, William Jennings Bryan quickly earned a reputation as a powerful speaker.

Invitations to make speeches poured in. Newspaper reporters found him irresistible; they often made a point of describing his dress (string tie and plain boots), his firm jawline, his easy smile. Will became known for his talks on another hot topic of the day: money, and whether it should be based strictly on the nation's gold reserves or also on silver. Will was a "free silver" man, because it would benefit the working classes, while the gold standard favored big business. After he gave a three-hour speech in Congress on this issue, a weekly newspaper in Missouri cooed: "That was one of the most wonderful speeches that ever emanated from a human brain that ever passed the lips of men."

The more popular he became, the more Will also attracted detractors. To them, his beautiful rhetoric and dramatic delivery, so often weaving Christian ethics with public policy, were a lot of show and little substance. A satirical poem made the rounds in anti-free-silver newspapers:

> I am Bill,
> Bill the Metaphor manipulator,
> When I talk the universe listens,
> And the little stars
> Stand on their heads in ecstasy.

The poem continued for quite a few lines. Here are some of the more tasty ones:

> My morning repast is fricasseed
> Dictionary;
> My noonday meal is a plate of
> Hashed-brown similes

With the quotation marks extracted;

And at eventide I dine

Upon a pot-roast of English language,

Served with

Pea green exclamation points.

The universe may not have been listening to Will (Will, he called himself, not Bill), but plenty of people were. His star ascended. He positioned himself as the champion of regular working people, poor people, small-town and country people. It was them against the city elites who were running the country. Against moneyed interests who wanted all the country's wealth to be siphoned upward to the bosses and the bankers and the corporate bigwigs. This is what Will told his audiences, anyway.

Will's concern for the downtrodden and the forgotten was sincere. But it left out a significant segment of the American population: people of color. Mostly he ignored them. Listening to his speeches, you would never know, for example, that Black Americans experienced race discrimination wherever they turned—walking down the Main Streets that Will championed, traveling on trains, seeking decent work and wages and education and housing. You would never know that violence against African Americans was soaring. This blindness on Will's part was baked into his personality; he was a man who later began his memoirs with this statement: "I was born a member of the greatest of all the races—the Caucasian Race."

Will left the House of Representatives to try for the U.S. Senate in 1894. He lost that election, but continued to gain audiences throughout the country. He didn't return to lawyering. His new career as an orator earned him enough money to support his family nicely. Speaking from the East Coast to the West, he took the stage at debates, conventions, under big tents. His fee of $100 per appearance equaled what he used to earn for two weeks of work as a lawyer.

By the time the Democratic Party met in Chicago for its nominating convention for the presidential election of 1896, Will was a force. Various candidates jostled for the nomination. The new Chicago Coliseum—the biggest venue in the world, with a capacity of 20,000 and acoustics that only an extraordinary speaker could conquer—played to Will's strengths. Lesser orators' words couldn't be deciphered beyond the first few rows; the sound just bounced around. When it was Will's turn to address the conventioneers, he gave a speech that not only could be heard throughout the Coliseum, but that also soon would be reprinted and quoted throughout the country.

The scene inside the cavernous hall at the Democratic National Convention of 1896.

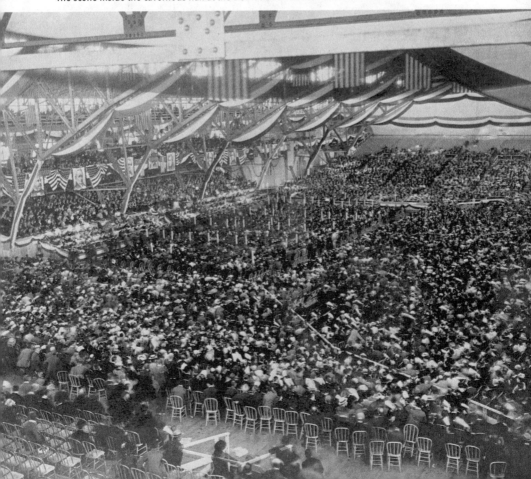

Fervently he spoke of the "producing masses"–the working people. His focus was on the money supply–on rejecting the gold standard as a policy that oppressed "the laboring interests, and the toilers everywhere." Speaking for twenty minutes, Will challenged those who said that government policies such as taxing the rich and making

money more easily available would disturb "business interests." "Business interests," he preached, had to be redefined to include workers who made the employer's business possible. Farmers in overalls who grew food were as important as the men in suits who sold that food. Miners who dug minerals and metals out of the earth deserved the same consideration as the financiers who traded those minerals and metals.

The crowd applauded and cheered repeatedly. Then Will came to a thundering proclamation: "You shall not press down upon

William Jennings Bryan as candidate for president of the United States, 1896.

the brow of labor this crown of thorns. You shall not crucify mankind"—and he stretched his arms out to his sides, mimicking a crucifixion—"upon a cross of gold."

He held the pose, channeling Jesus Christ himself. Shocking. Twenty thousand people went silent.

He left the stage.

"The whole convention sprang to its feet, and twenty thousand throats roared," the *Indianapolis News* reported. "Men shouted like maniacs." Cheer after cheer rose up for Will. People waved their hands, their handkerchiefs, their hats. They opened umbrellas, if they had them. They cried. The celebrations lasted longer than Will's speech.

Among the 20,000 people in the Chicago Coliseum was a Democratic Party activist who also had a reputation as a gifted orator. "I have enjoyed a great many addresses, some of which I have delivered myself," this activist later wrote, "but I never listened to one that affected and moved an audience as did that."

Even while surrounded by a crowd wild with excitement, this other Democrat was highly unlikely to have been among the 20,000 throats that were roaring. Throw his hat? Not his style. Wave his hands? No. At most what he probably did with his hands was applaud.

This lukewarm listener was Clarence Darrow.

CHAPTER 5
"WHATEVER DEGRADES ANOTHER DEGRADES ME"

While young Will Bryan was working on his passion for stirring speechmaking, young Clarence Darrow was working on his passion, too. He was working on his running, throwing, and hitting. As a boy in elementary school in Kinsman, Ohio, a teenager at the Kinsman Academy, and at Allegheny College in Pennsylvania, Clarence later wrote, "Never has life held for me anything quite so entrancing as baseball."

And while Will read and reread his Bible stories, Clarence's holy book was more along the lines of *The Story of a Bad Boy*, a novel by Thomas Bailey Aldrich. Not that Clarence was a bad boy. He just wasn't notably good. There was a lot about school that he didn't like. He hated taking Latin classes. And Greek. He hated the study of history—just a bunch of names and dates to memorize. He hated learning grammar. Geometry, too.

And yet, for all the distaste he voiced about school, Clarence learned. He learned the subjects that he said he hated. He learned at home, too, where history wasn't about names and dates, but tales of bold people who stood up for justice, like his middle-name namesake, William Seward. He absorbed grammar through the books the family read aloud around the dining table. He was drawn to scientific topics, like zoology and geology. His father encouraged him to question the ideas that others held dear. "My instinct," Clarence later wrote, "was to doubt the majority view."

While Clarence didn't set out to be an orator, unlike a certain boy who lived over in Salem, Illinois, he was drawn to speechmaking and debate. Clarence couldn't help noticing that the best orators, at least in his view, were lawyers. On public holidays and at political rallies, lawyers came to Kinsman from nearby towns to entertain and educate local audiences. Across the street from the Darrows' octagonal-shaped house was the tin shop. The tinner also served as Kinsman's justice of the peace, an official who heard minor disputes. Clarence liked the sharp exchanges between lawyers: "I enjoyed the way the pettifoggers abused each other." Clarence soon joined in his small town's declamation contests. His specialty was taking the unpopular view of the issues of the day and somehow winning the contests even while promoting ideas that most people rejected.

After Kinsman Academy, Clarence completed a year of prep school at Allegheny College. The Darrows didn't have money for him to continue. Perhaps it was just as well, as he didn't seem to place much more value on his college coursework than on his elementary school classes: "I came back a better ball player for my higher education," Clarence wrote. "I abandoned further school life and began my education."

Back in Kinsman, Clarence became a teacher in one of the country schools outside of town. The students hadn't had an instructor quite like him before. He told them he would not hit them, breaking with the widespread tradition of corporal punishment in schools. He expanded both lunchtime and recess time—why not? They'd been his favorite parts of the school day. They still were, it seemed. Clarence played games, especially baseball, right along with his students.

But Clarence knew he couldn't earn a living by playing games forever. He wanted to make more money. And he continued to think about the "pettifoggers"—those lawyers who talked circles around one another before the justice of the peace. A good lawyer, he figured, could spend his days arguing and get paid good money for it.

So Clarence started reading law books when he was done teaching for the day. And when he was twenty years old, he quit his teaching job to attend law school at the University of Michigan in Ann Arbor. He did not distinguish himself there, and gave it up after a year. A law degree, though, wasn't the only way to become a lawyer in those days. Clarence apprenticed with a law firm in Youngstown, Ohio, for a year. He passed the exam to become a full-fledged lawyer, came back to Kinsman, and married his sweetheart, Jessie Ohl. They lived above a store in tiny Andover, Ohio, not far from their hometown.

Not many law clients came to Clarence at first. The business he did get was largely bill collections work—echoing the experience of that other young lawyer whom Clarence hadn't yet met. But—again mirroring Will Bryan's experience as a spanking-new lawyer—Clarence received speaking invitations. He appeared at the usual patriotic gatherings, public holidays, and small-town picnics. He wasn't orating about much of substance yet, but in a Memorial Day speech in 1886, he did venture a rather extreme idea: that women should be allowed to vote in elections. But he wasn't yet one of those nimbly argumentative lawyers he'd admired in the tinsmith's courtroom.

Clarence was always reading something. By his late twenties he was devouring books that deeply affected him and his political ideas. His reading and observations confirmed many of the values he was raised with. He became appalled at the inequality in American society, and at ever-increasing concentrations of wealth among the privileged few. He was disgusted at the dreadful working conditions of so many laborers—including children. People became criminals, Clarence concluded, largely because of their social conditions, not because they were intentionally evil. He became more and more open about his agnosticism—his questioning, if not disbelief, of the existence of God.

Clarence drew inspiration not only from books of political philosophy and economy, but also from works of literature. Walt Whitman was a favorite author. "Each of us limitless—each of us with his or her right upon the earth," the poet wrote. "Whatever degrades another degrades me." Before long, Clarence was writing essays and lecturing on Whitman and on the poet's relevance in the everyday world. "It is a sad mistake to believe that injustice and wrong can injure only the poor and the weak," Clarence wrote, taking Whitman's observations as his credo. "Every mean word and narrow thought and selfish act degrades the aggressor, leaves its mark upon his soul and its penalty in his life." Injustice damaged not only its victims but also society as a whole and even the oppressors themselves. This conviction would shape Clarence's life and work.

To fire up his law career, Clarence moved with Jessie and their baby boy to the larger Ohio town of Ashtabula. He attracted more interesting cases, leaving the collections work behind. Three years after that, restless for more, Clarence moved his family to the big city: Chicago. It was 1887. Clarence was thirty years old. And it was in the Windy City that his career and reputation took flight.

Clarence joined all kinds of clubs in Chicago—the Land and Labor Club, the Personal Rights League, the Secular Union—which gave him all kinds of opportunities to hone his oratory. The Secular Union, a gathering of freethinkers who wanted to keep religion out of public life, offered Clarence a forum in which to develop his ideas. At an Easter gathering of this group, Clarence gave a talk with a theme that definitely would not have worked in a more typical Easter celebration: "The religion for which we are struggling and which must prevail in the future is not based upon . . . a Supreme Being," he said. Rather, the "religion" that was meaningful to Clarence and his like-minded friends was based on "a foundation deep in human reason."

Despite being named for one of the founders of the Republican Party, William Seward, Clarence became active in the Democratic Party. Clarence's political views didn't neatly line up with all the Democrats' positions. He rejected, for example, the southern Democrats' politics of white supremacy. Not only did he favor political rights for African Americans; he believed in and practiced social equality as well. Unlike most white people, whatever their political affiliation, whether Southerners or Northerners, Clarence socialized with African Americans. He promoted Black resistance to white supremacy. For that matter, he embodied white resistance to white supremacy. "Now and then," he said in a speech before the Men's Club in Chicago,

> we find some statesman who proposes to solve the Negro question by wishing to send them off to themselves somewhere, as if the Lord made one country for white people and another for black people, and he forgot to sort them out, and as if we should do the sorting—but the South does not propose to send the Negroes away, for if they sent the Negroes away they would be obliged to work themselves.

But compared to the Republican Party's consistent support for big business interests, the Democratic Party's concern for the laboring classes aligned with Clarence's views. He was most comfortable in the more radical wing of "the Democracy," eventually embracing the view that only drastic changes in the economic system could make a difference in the lives of workers. Campaigning for Democratic candidates, Clarence became a familiar headliner, appreciated for his sense of humor. "The people who heard Clarence Darrow of Chicago at the opera house last Saturday night will be pleased to know that

he is billed for another address on the evening of Nov. 7," announced the Decatur, Illinois, *Daily Review* in late October 1892. "He is one of the brightest men in the state and it is a treat to hear him. He will have one of the biggest audiences of the campaign."

As his reputation in politics expanded, so did Clarence's law practice. Clients came to him with cases that drew public attention, and he took those that

Clarence Darrow

raised issues he was passionate about. One of these issues was the inhumanity and fecklessness of the death penalty.

In 1894, a mentally ill young man named Patrick Eugene Prendergast was convicted and sentenced to hang for the murder of the mayor of Chicago. After the conviction, Clarence represented Prendergast in a special trial conducted to review his death sentence. Clarence had worked for the slain mayor earlier in his career and deeply mourned his death. But for Clarence, the taking of a life for a life was a travesty that outweighed his personal feelings—especially when the murderer suffered from mental illness. "Here is Prendergast," he pleaded with the jury, "the product of the infinite God, not of his own making. . . . I beseech of you, gentlemen"—there were no women on juries in 1894—"do not visit upon this poor boy the afflictions which God Almighty placed upon him for some inscrutable reason unknown to us."

He concluded:

> This poor, weak, misshapen vessel, I place in your protection and your hands. I beg of you gentlemen take it gently, tenderly, carefully. Do not, I beseech you, do not break the clay, for though weak and cracked and useless it is the handiwork of the infinite God.

Clarence, the agnostic, invoking God? This was his first big closing argument, and maybe he thought it was his best approach. As a nonbeliever, he was in the minority. He was arguing for a man's life and needed to speak to the jury in terms its members would understand. His argument did move the jurors; it brought tears to the eyes of some of them.

But they still sentenced Prendergast to hang.

In the career that lay ahead of him, of the 102 cases in which Clarence fought against a sentence of capital punishment, this, the Prendergast case, was the only one in which his client was put to death.

Clarence was equally passionate about the rights of workers to join labor unions and strike against big business for better pay and working conditions. In his first case representing the interests of the working class, he defended Eugene V. Debs, the famous union leader and political activist. (Debs also went on to run for president five times.) The legal proceedings against Debs centered on his activities during a combative strike and boycott in 1894 against the company that made Pullman railroad cars. As Clarence saw it, the prosecution of Debs was a case of the government doing the bidding of powerful business interests. Clarence achieved only a partial victory for Debs. But his advocacy for workers' rights drew attention from Democratic politicians.

So by 1896 Clarence was a well-known courtroom litigator, a favorite speechmaker, and a political activist. And that was why he attended the Democratic National Convention at the Chicago Coliseum on July 9 of that year, when Will Bryan stunned and excited the 20,000 attendees with his "Cross of Gold" speech. There the two orators from America's heartland met for the first time.

During the speech, Clarence sat with his good friend and mentor John Altgeld. Altgeld, who was governor of Illinois, did not applaud. He did not cheer. Clarence thought he looked sad. The next day, after Will clinched the nomination to run as the Democratic candidate for president, Altgeld and Clarence were talking about what happened. "It takes more than speeches to win real victories," Altgeld warned. "Applause lasts but a little while."

Altgeld continued: "I have been thinking over Bryan's speech. What did he say, anyhow?"

After the convention, Clarence became the Democratic candidate for the U.S. House of Representatives from Illinois's third congressional district. He also campaigned for Will. Like Will, Clarence believed that the government should rein in capitalists who only chased profits, never considering the well-being of employees or communities. He favored limiting the workday to eight hours to protect workers. He opposed high tariffs and advocated a silver-backed money supply as beneficial to farmers and debtors.

1896 presidential campaign button for William Jennings Bryan after his "Cross of Gold" speech at the Democratic National Convention.

But on Election Day, November 3, Will lost the presidency to the Republican Party candidate, William McKinley. Clarence lost his congressional race to his Republican opponent. Governor Altgeld lost his gubernatorial race.

Clarence kept turning over Altgeld's comments in his mind.

What did he say, anyhow?

So many words, so little meaning. So much religion, so little reason. Clarence saw Will as a big talker, but not a thinker. As hollow. Will hadn't read widely enough—what did he know of science, literature, philosophy? He found all his answers in the Bible. He should not be a political leader. He enthralled audiences, but he didn't educate them.

A few months after the election, Clarence and Will were together at a Democratic Party gathering.

"You'd better . . . study science, history, philosophy and quit this village religious stuff," Clarence said. "You're head of the party before you are ready and a leader should lead with thought."

"Darrow's the only man in the world who looks down on me for believing in God," Will commented to the others gathered around.

The quarrel between Clarence Darrow and William Jennings Bryan had begun. It would simmer, grow, make headlines, entertain, and explode—ending only when one of them lay down for his afternoon nap in a guest house in Dayton, Tennessee, twenty-eight years later.

CHAPTER 6
TWO TALL MEN, TALKING

U nlike Clarence Darrow, the Democratic Party did not give up on Will. In 1900, and again in 1908, he won the party's nomination for president.

Both those times, too, he lost the elections.

It wasn't for want of talking. Will was the first presidential candidate to take his case directly to voters. Candidates before him had others speak for them; campaigning was viewed as beneath the dignity of a future president. For his identification with ordinary citizens, Will became known as the Great Commoner. It was a moniker that stayed with him for the rest of his life. In 1901, after his second presidential loss, Will founded a newspaper he called *The Commoner*—and it was all about publishing the thoughts of William Jennings Bryan.

While Will evoked mockery from some for his emotional style and his appeals to Christian morals, he attracted the love and admiration of millions of Americans. In the 1896 election alone, Will rode the rails for three months, reaching twenty-six of forty-five

William Jennings Bryan outside the office of his newspaper, *The Commoner*, 1905.

states and speaking in person to some five million people. During that presidential run, girls joined "Bryan Clubs" and complained that they could not have voted for Will even if they'd been adults. (The Nineteenth Amendment to the Constitution, giving women the right to vote, wasn't adopted until 1920.) In a school in New Jersey, all the third graders informally adopted "Bryan" as their middle name. So did their teacher. Parents named their children "Bryan" in his honor.

For those who could not get to a Bryan speech—no problem! Thanks to the recent invention of the record player, "Bryan Speaks Rain or Shine," announced an advertisement in a Nebraska newspaper in 1908. "Have you heard him speak? You can if you will come to our store.

> He is speaking here every day on
> the Genuine Edison Phonograph.
> To-day he speaks on An Ideal Republic,
> The Tariff Question,
> The Railroad Question,
> Swollen Fortunes,
> and six other favorite Subjects.

"You get the full effect of his sonorous voice and his wonderful tricks of voice and manner," the ad continued. "It is also so natural and life-like you are apt to find yourself applauding the speaker."

Will's speaking career only expanded after his election losses. So did his braiding together of religion and politics. He wrote and spoke—preached, really—about the Christian duty to "do good" in both private and public life. This was a distillation of the Social Gospel movement, which had been developing since the late 1800s as a reaction against the unbridled capitalism and materialism of the era Mark Twain dubbed the Gilded Age.

Again, for Will, applying Christian morals to politics and government excluded Black Americans. Will seemed indifferent to racism and the rise of "Jim Crow" laws in the South, which oppressed African Americans and denied them voting rights. (This was in spite of the explicit guarantee of Black voting rights in the Fifteenth Amendment, added to the U.S. Constitution in 1870, when Will was ten years old.) In an article headlined "Mr. Bryan on the South," *The Commoner* explained, "Mr. Bryan's views on southern race problems are sane. His feeling for the negro is kind; his interest in the white comes first."

The editors of *The Appeal*, an African American–owned newspaper, countered:

> One of the most stupendous frauds of the present day is the so-called political reformer . . . among whom we have no hesitation in including the much-lauded William Jennings Bryan. Mr. Bryan is . . . a mixture of "bigotry" and "bumptiousness."

In 1912, Woodrow Wilson, an overt racist and lukewarm adherent of the Social Gospel movement, was elected president. The new president tapped Will as his secretary of state, in charge of the nation's foreign policy. In Europe, war broke out in August 1914—a ruinous conflict that ultimately ensnared more than thirty nations. Wilson, and many Americans, sided with the Allies (which included Great Britain, France, and Russia) against the Great Powers (which included Germany, Austria-Hungary, and the Ottoman Empire). Will, unlike his commander in chief, strongly opposed American involvement in this or any foreign war, and in 1915 he resigned as secretary of state rather than remain part of an administration that joined the conflict later known as World War I.

Back he went on the lecture circuit. He took up new causes. Will favored Prohibition—a national ban on alcoholic beverages—and worked for the adoption of the Eighteenth Amendment, which in 1919 made Prohibition the law of the land. He supported women's right to vote, secured by the Nineteenth Amendment in 1920. He continued to advocate for decent working conditions, wages, and respect for laborers. He spoke, passionately, personally, about his Christianity.

A 1908 campaign poster for William Jennings Bryan, who supported the right of women to vote.

And it was this fervent religiosity that brought Will to Charles Darwin's theory of evolution. Or, at least, to Will's version of Darwin's theory.

Here he is, melodious and gently humorous, under a big tent bursting with admirers, or inside a packed auditorium:

> I am not yet convinced that man is a lineal descendant of the lower animals. I do not mean to find fault with you if you want to accept the theory; all I mean to say is that while you may trace your ancestry back to the monkey if you find pleasure or pride in doing so, you shall not connect me with your family tree without more evidence than has yet been produced.

Of course, Darwin's theory does not say that humans trace their ancestry "back to the monkey." But Will is setting up a classic straw man argument: distorting the actual meaning of the thing he doesn't like into something extreme or ridiculous, and arguing against this distortion rather than against the reality of the thing. Humanity's supposed "monkey ancestor" is an easy target, much easier than Darwin's more complex theory of descent with modification. Will isn't out for scientific accuracy. He is out to confirm the divinity of Jesus Christ and the presence of God and miracles in the world. Science does not confirm miracles.

Further, Will explains, because Darwin and other scientists cannot with certainty pinpoint the moment life began, the whole theory is unconvincing—and certainly not more convincing than the story of divine creation. "But there is another objection," Will continues:

> The Darwinian theory represents man as reaching his

> present perfection by the operation of the law of hate—the merciless law by which the strong crowd out and kill off the weak. . . . I prefer to believe that love rather than hatred is the law of development.

This is Will at his most Will-ful. He really does believe in the power of love. He really does believe that through love, and the love of God, humanity can progress.

But the theory of evolution is not about hate, or about killing off the weak. Will has set up another straw man to knock down.

The speech is long—forty-five pages. It is rambling yet also riveting. Will knows how to hold an audience. He pokes fun at science: "Unless you can explain a watermelon, do not be too sure that you can set limits to the power of the Almighty." He dismisses the importance of scientific knowledge: "Water has been used from the birth of man; we learned after it had been used for ages that it is merely a mixture of gases, but it is far more important that we have water to drink than that we know that it is not water."

Will gave this speech, titled "The Prince of Peace," over and over and over again. Audiences could not get enough of it. **This Is the Address for Which There Is the Most Demand on the Chautauqua Circuit, and It Is the One Which Obtained for Him His Reputation as a Lecturer,"** read the supersized headline at the top of the *New York Times* spread that published the lecture in full. Will traveled the country as part of the Chautauqua circuit—hugely popular gatherings, often taking place under large tents, in which crowds enjoyed entertainers, musicians, singers, and orators. Leading speakers of the day went on national tours to enthrall their fans, who received them as celebrity performers. Will was one of the top draws, up there with Helen Keller (interpreted by Anne Sullivan), Alexander

BRYAN'S MOST FAMOUS LECTURE, "THE PRINCE OF PEACE"

This Is the Address for Which There Is the Most Demand on the Chautauqua Circuit, and It Is the One Which Obtained for Him His Reputation as a Lecturer.

By William Jennings Bryan.

The *New York Times* dedicated generous space to William Jennings Bryan's "The Prince of Peace" lecture.

Graham Bell, and Eugene Debs. According to some estimates, Will's ticket sales were exceeded only by Helen Keller's.

There was another top draw at Chautauqua events. He, too, advocated for the underdog, the laborers, the have-nots against the bankers, railroad magnates, the corporate titans. But he did not speak of miracles or Jesus Christ or the duties of a Christian.

Of course, it was Clarence Darrow.

———————

After he lost his congressional race in 1896, Clarence focused on his law career. While Will was sermonizing about the rights of the laboring classes and underprivileged, Clarence was going to court to defend those rights. He represented labor unionists and accused murderers and alleged conspirators. He represented women who dared to publish sex education materials.

As a courtroom lawyer and orator, Clarence didn't put on airs. If you were his witness in a trial or his audience in an auditorium, he was likely to start out talking in a conversational tone as if the two of you were the only ones in the room. His language was unaffected yet also intellectual. He might appeal to your sense of humor or empathy. He might openly cry. You probably would, too.

A typical Darrow client was the union man on trial for criminal conduct while striking against a woodworking mill in Oshkosh, Wisconsin. With provocative metaphor, Clarence reminded the jury of the factory rules that led his client and other workers to strike:

> The poor devil who works there for six or seven dollars
> a week cannot speak loud except in case of fire, and he
> cannot go out excepting he raise his hand like a little boy
> in school, and he cannot speak to his neighbor because it

hinders him in his work. When the poor slaves go in there at a quarter to seven in the morning they lock the door to keep them there; and when the whistle sounds at twelve they send their guards around to unlock the doors. And when one o'clock comes again, this high priest of jailers sends his turnkey back to lock up his American citizens once more so that they cannot leave the mill until nighttime comes.

"This is really not a criminal case," Clarence said. "It is but an episode in the great battle for human liberty." He explained that when the union asked the owner of the mill to negotiate, the owner refused. There would be no bargaining between equal human beings. No, Clarence recounted, rather, "He desired that these poor slaves should come to him and . . . beg him as individuals, as Oliver Twist in the almshouse held out his soup bowl."

Clarence's argument went on for eight hours. He spoke without notes. It took the jury less than an hour to find his client not guilty.

As his reputation grew, people crowded courthouse doors for a chance to see the great Darrow, to learn, to laugh. What they saw was a tall man, rangy, with big shoulders. His suits were generally shabby. Threads might hang from his shirts. His fingernails might not be as clean as they could be. A lock of his hair insisted on falling over on his forehead, no matter how he wet it down. He didn't usually stand up as straight as he could, and he slouched in his chair as if to not call attention to himself, although by his very lack of posture, he was calling attention to himself.

In 1903, Clarence represented coal miners on strike from the anthracite mines of Pennsylvania, one of the most significant labor disputes in U.S. history. Again he delivered his closing argument over the course of eight hours. As usual, he spoke without notes.

"They have come in here with broken arms, and disfigured faces, and broken legs, and with one eye and with no eyes," he said.

> If the civilization of this country rests upon the necessity of leaving these starvation wages to these miners and laborers or . . . upon the labor of these poor little boys from twelve to fourteen years of age who are picking their way through the dirt, clouds and dust of the anthracite coal, then the sooner we are done with this civilization and start over anew, the better.

After he concluded, the hundreds of spectators burst into applause. The miners won a significant increase in pay, an eight-hour workday, and measures to prevent the exploitation of child labor.

Clarence had become the most famous lawyer in the United States. Newspapers called him the "Great Defender." A decade later he stopped taking labor union cases after he was charged with (and acquitted of) bribing a juror in a notorious case involving a union in Los Angeles. He focused on criminal cases, representing all manner of accused murderers and felons. Clarence was more interested in the conditions that could lead a person to crime than in the labels "good" and "evil." "The man who owns a sweatshop or a department store may not be to blame himself for the condition of his girls, but when he pays them five dollars, three dollars, and two dollars a week, I wonder where he thinks they will get the rest of their money to live," he said in a talk before the prisoners of the Chicago jail in 1902. "The only way to cure these conditions is by equality."

In his talks on the Chautauqua circuit, while Will Bryan was preaching "The Prince of Peace," Clarence was lecturing on the Russian writer and philosopher Leo Tolstoy. This may not sound like a big crowd-pleaser, but on this topic he was in fact considered a "Great Attraction," as a Kansas newspaper put it in 1905. He was, the gushing headline proclaimed, "A Giant in Height, With an Eloquence Unsurpassed."

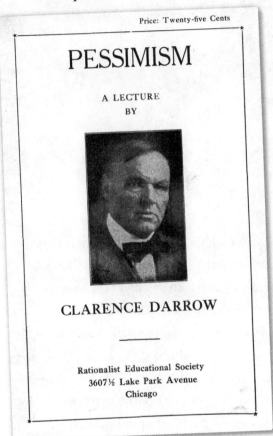

Price: Twenty-five Cents

PESSIMISM

A LECTURE
BY

CLARENCE DARROW

Rationalist Educational Society
3607½ Lake Park Avenue
Chicago

So there they were, two tall men wowing audiences across the country. Will began his campaign against the theory of evolution. Clarence became "a close observer," he wrote, "of Mr. Bryan's campaign against knowledge." Mr. Bryan would not have characterized his campaign that way. But he may not have minded the attention.

One of Clarence Darrow's lectures bore the thought-provoking title "Pessimism."

CHAPTER 7
PROOFS AND PERVERSIONS

While the Great Commoner and the Great Defender were growing in their reputations and influence, so too was Charles Darwin's theory of evolution. Most American scientists, religious or not, accepted evolution as a fact. The American Library Association recommended both *On the Origin of Species* and *The Descent of Man* on its 1895 *List of Books for Girls and Women and Their Clubs*. Around the same time, the *New York Times* reported that *The Descent of Man*—twenty-five years after publication—was still one of the most popular titles in the Manhattan branches of the New York public libraries. In 1900, *The Outlook*, a widely read national magazine, asked ten men who were "well-known in the world of thought and letters" to name "the ten books which have influenced thought most this century." The publication reported, "Every one of the ten give Darwin's 'Origin of Species' as belonging in the list." It was the only book on which all agreed.

Outside the pages of *Origin of Species* and *The Descent of Man*,

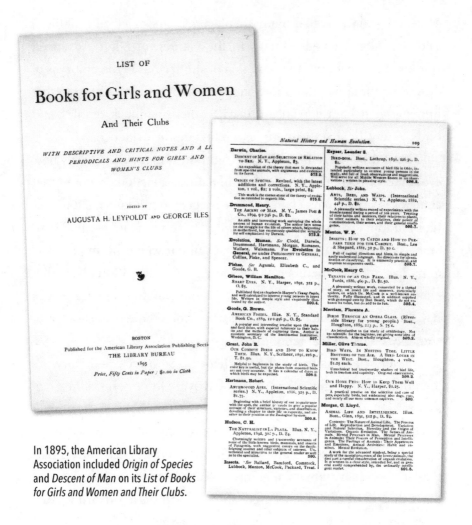

In 1895, the American Library Association included *Origin of Species* and *Descent of Man* on its *List of Books for Girls and Women and Their Clubs*.

science marched on. Paleontologists discovered fossils that connected prehistoric reptiles to birds. They uncovered fossils that revealed the evolution of horses in North America. (Fossils of humanity's ancestors would not be uncovered in significant numbers until the 1920s and after.) The geologist Charles Lyell, a friend of Darwin's, published a study, almost as radical as *Origin of Species*, setting forth the geological evidence of humanity's long, long tenure on Earth—eons before

4004 B.C., the year that many theologians (who rejected evolution) said that God created humans in the Garden of Eden. Advanced studies of comparative anatomy, and of similarities in the embryos of different animals, added more support for Darwin's conclusion that humans share common ancestors with other mammals, reptiles, and birds. Scientific investigations kept piling up the evidence.

This didn't mean the scientific community agreed on exactly how evolution worked. Darwin's theory of natural selection proposed that changes in an animal's characteristics occurred randomly. If a particular random change—such as the ability to run fast and escape predators—helped an animal survive, that animal would be more likely to outlive another member of the same species that didn't have that characteristic. The animal with the helpful random change would have babies, who would have babies, who would have babies—all, presumably, enjoying that random change.

Other scientists had different theories. Some rejected Darwin's idea that random mutations were the driving force behind the great and varied tapestry of life. Some emphasized the role of an animal's environment in creating changes in the animal's body, skeleton, strengths, weaknesses. Some focused on whether, over time, a particular part of an animal's anatomy was used or not used; anatomical parts that were useful, and used, were passed on to offspring. Anatomical parts that fell into disuse withered away.

And how was a beneficial mutation, such as speed or the ability to eat certain foods, passed down from one generation to another? How did baby critters inherit traits from their parents? Darwin and his scientific colleagues . . . didn't really know. While Darwin was doing his research and writing, an Austrian monk named Gregor Mendel was experimenting with pea plants in his abbey garden. Raising generation after generation of peas, Mendel discovered that the plants transmitted their traits—flower color, for example—through what had to be separate and distinct units of inheritance. A pea plant inherited these units from both its "parent" plants.

Eureka! But not quite. Mendel knew Darwin's work; he'd marked notes all over his German-language copy of *Origin of Species*. But it does not seem to have occurred to Mendel that his units of inheritance—eventually to be dubbed "genes"—were responsible for carrying the variations in traits that Darwin observed from one generation to the next. And Darwin did not know of Mendel's work—how could he? Mendel lived in a monastery, cut off from most of the world. His work was revealed only after his death in 1884—two years after Darwin died.

So Darwin and scientists of his time were fuzzy about the mechanics. But they were not fuzzy about the fact that evolutionary change happened, and they knew that inherited traits played a role. And by the turn of the twentieth century, thanks to Mendel's work, scientists were beginning to understand how traits passed from parent to offspring, whether pea plants or people.

———◆◆———

Unfortunately, other mutations—the man-made kind—were simultaneously warping Darwin's theory to make it far less scientific and far more sickening. Leading intellectuals and scientists perverted the theory of evolution into the notion that some people were more worthy of life than others. They started with a phrase that Darwin did not invent: "survival of the fittest."

An English philosopher named Herbert Spencer—who lived around the same time as Darwin—came up with "survival of the fittest" as another way to express Darwin's concept of natural selection. "This survival of the fittest," he wrote after reading *Origin of Species*, "is that which Mr. Darwin has called 'natural selection,' or the preservation of favored races in the struggle for life."

Spencer and his followers decided that natural selection and the "survival of the fittest" applied to society as a whole. The strongest, most intelligent, and most "civilized" were the most worthy: for Spencer, that meant white Europeans. It was only natural and right that they should take charge of society. Indeed, it was only natural and right that they should dominate other societies, as England was doing in building its empire. It was natural and right that they should control industry and the economy and amass great amounts of wealth. This was "survival of the fittest." A scientific theory about biological evolution became a social policy: Social Darwinism.

It was only a short step from Social Darwinism to even more repugnant ideas about how to treat the "unfit." Charles Darwin's own cousin, Francis Galton, took Herbert Spencer's notions to the next level in 1883 when he made up the word "eugenics"—derived from the Greek word "eugenes," meaning "well-born" or "good in stock"— and spun a new type of "science" around it.

The problem with humanity, Galton decided, was that evolution wasn't working quite as it should. That is, sure, there were the "fittest," and sure, they survived, at least sometimes, but so did the unfit. The lower classes—who were unfit, in Galton's scheme—had higher birth rates than the upper classes. As a result, the excellence and intelligence of humankind was being diluted. Society needed to take steps to ensure that the unfit lower classes didn't have so many babies. That was eugenics.

Unlike some later eugenicists, Galton didn't advocate sterilizing or jailing or killing off those he deemed unfit, poor, or unbrilliant. He just wanted eugenics to become a "religious dogma among mankind," as he wrote in 1904, accepted "as a hopeful and most important study."

It may not have become a religious dogma, but the idea of eugenics definitely caught on. Around the world, people formed eugenics societies to promote this "hopeful" science that was not really science. In Germany in 1905, scientists and others formed the Society for Racial Hygiene, which was not really hygiene. Thirty years later, "racial hygiene" and the superiority of the "Aryan race"–not really a race– became a deadly obsession of Germany's Nazi Party.

Just as not every titan of industry turned Darwin's theory of evolution into a justification for society's gross inequality, not every scientist, social scientist, or public official twisted evolution into a blueprint for discriminatory social engineering. But many did. Public officials became convinced that by taking evolution into their own hands, they could cleanse society of the "unfit." And so in 1907, Indiana became the first state to enact a law requiring the sterilization of people who were found to be "idiots" or "imbeciles," as well as women– but not men–who were "feebleminded" or "promiscuous." In the two decades that followed, nearly thirty states adopted similar laws.

It would be lovely to be able to say that Charles Darwin bore no responsibility for these atrocious lines of thinking. Lovely but not entirely true. In *Origin of Species*, Darwin avoided the question of human evolution, limiting himself to plants and animals. When he did address human evolution in *The Descent of Man*, Darwin was clear that all humankind had descended from a common ancestor. This put him at odds with the popular racist theory of his time that the "better" white or Caucasian race came from the best ancestors, and "lesser" races–basically, all people of color–came from their own inferior ancestors. Darwin did not suggest that his theory of natural selection should be applied to society, or the economy, or politics.

But–he did say some other stuff. Even if unintentionally, he did give the Social Darwinists and the eugenicists grist for their mills.

The great scientist included some problematic and unscientific statements in *The Descent of Man*. Most notably, in his efforts to explain "the several so-called races of men," as he put it, Darwin repeatedly demeaned Africans, people of African descent, and Indigenous people. As a matter of evolutionary development, he contended, they were inferior intellectually, culturally, and morally to European whites. This was classic white supremacy. Similarly, in Darwin's view, men were superior to women, in physical strength, intelligence, and creativity—but he did conclude that women beat men in their moral capabilities.

Darwin presented these conclusions without a social or political agenda. But his ideas were like candy to those who were looking to build their own scientific-sounding theories of Social Darwinism and eugenics.

You see, they would explain with conviction, *Darwinism shows that savages cannot be expected to govern themselves properly. How fitting for a great white nation like Great Britain to build an empire to rule over them.*

You see, they would say, *in Nature the strong outcompete the weak. How fitting for us to grow ever more wealthy and ever stronger, and for the weaklings to get the leftovers.*

You see, they would say, *when we coddle the weak in society, we're going against the laws of Nature. Better that we should withdraw supports for the needy, who are drags on our evolutionary development.*

You see, they would insist, *since females are the weaker, less capable sex, of course a husband should rule over his wife, and a girl need not be educated to the same level as a boy. It's only natural!*

Darwin died in 1882. By the time these perversions of his theory gained ground, he was gone. Had he lived longer, perhaps he would have pressed the purveyors of these false ideologies to remember that his goal had been only to prove the fact of evolution. Not to suggest social policy. Not to justify the British Empire. Not to defend wealth inequality. He might have noted that natural selection is not about progress and has no goals. It's simply a thing that happens. In introducing *The Descent of Man*, he even acknowledged that it was possible he had "exaggerated" the power of natural selection, but "I have at least, as I hope, done good service in aiding to overthrow the dogma of separate creations."

Thanks to Darwin, evolution became bedrock science by the early twentieth century. For sure, there were religious people who rejected it and adhered instead to literal readings of the biblical stories of creation and the Garden of Eden. And yes, Will Bryan started complaining about evolution in the early 1900s, but he wasn't terribly heated. Not yet.

Then came the invention of the public high school.

CHAPTER 8
DARWINISM GOES TO SCHOOL

Turn back the calendar, back to the 1870s: Fifteen-year-old Will Bryan was away from home at the Whipple Academy. He felt lucky to be there; he knew his parents were paying a pretty penny for his private high school education.

Around the same time, young Clarence Darrow had a different attitude toward the Kinsman Academy. "I cannot avoid a feeling of the appalling waste of time," he wrote, looking back on his experience. "Schools were not established to teach and encourage the pupil to think . . . their effort was to cement the minds of pupils according to certain moulds. The teachers were employed to teach the truth, and the most important truth concerned the salvation of their souls." Clarence wasn't wrong about the soul-saving efforts that went on in high schools. Christian-centered teaching did not end with *McGuffey's Readers*.

Whether a high school student of the late 1800s fit the "mould" of a Will Bryan or a Clarence Darrow, they would have been among the few Americans who advanced beyond elementary school. Public high schools offering free education were rare. Private academies, like those attended by Will and Clarence, were not free. Even by 1890, only around 200,000 kids nationwide were enrolled in high schools—amounting to less than four out of every 100 teenagers. This was about to change dramatically.

If you were to believe Clarence Darrow, "Schools probably became general and popular because parents did not want their children about the house all day." There are other, less cynical, explanations for the explosion of public high schools in America. Between 1870 and 1920, a growing number of jobs, whether on factory floors or in offices, required workers with more education than elementary school. The ranks of doctors, lawyers, and teachers were also expanding; they, too, needed learning beyond grammar school.

From 2,500 public high schools in 1890, the total grew to 14,300 in 1920. Not only did states get busy building schools—on average, a new school opened every day between 1890 and 1920—they also made attendance mandatory. By 1918, all forty-eight states had compulsory education laws. At least some lawmakers hoped to reduce child labor. If the law required parents to put their children in school, those kids would have a chance of avoiding dangerous work in mines and factories. Here was a reason for the expansion of public education that even Clarence Darrow could embrace.

So by 1920, if you were between the ages of six and sixteen, you were probably attending school. You'd go to high school at least for a couple of years. And if you were in high school, one of the subjects you were likely to take was biology. And if you were taking biology, one of the subjects likely to be covered in your class was Charles Darwin's theory of evolution, by then a component of generally accepted scientific knowledge.

And this got some people seriously disturbed.

They became disturbed about teaching evolution to their children. And to other people's children. When it came to shielding young minds from harmful ideas, the adults evolved into exceptionally agitated organisms. "Strange how anxious old folk are apt to be over 'the children,'" Clarence later wrote, reflecting on the anti-evolution movement.

But what was harmful about teaching evolution?

It was, in a word, godless. Or this is how the newly emerged Christian movement known as Fundamentalism saw it. Many Christians, those known as "modernists," could hold both evolution and a belief in God in their hearts and minds, so they did not consider the science "godless." But to Fundamentalists, the Bible was the unerring word of God. The story of creation, Adam and Eve in the Garden of Eden, the miracles of Christ, were not to be questioned. They were truths, not allegories. Evolution denied these truths. It was a godless notion, which must be rejected.

Evolution didn't suddenly become godless once it started popping up in America's high schools. But when evolution leaked out of the academic journals that children didn't read and welled up in the school textbooks that children did read—that's when it became a big problem for Fundamentalists.

In 1916, a professor from Bryn Mawr College published a study that found that young people started college as faithful Christians, but by the time they graduated, "40 to 45 percent" denied or doubted Christian dogma. This horrified Will Bryan. He concluded that Darwinist drivel was responsible for the decline of religious devotion among America's youth—not just college students, but high schoolers as well. A decade earlier, he had only mildly rebuked Darwin's theory. Now he viewed it in a much darker light.

And if evolution was a problem for William Jennings Bryan, whose weekly newspaper column was published in a hundred newspapers, and whose admirers flocked to his speeches and bought his pamphlets—it was going to be a problem the whole country knew about.

For Will, evolution was not only contrary to the literal word of the Bible and the special creation of human beings, which was bad enough. He also believed that the cruel precepts of Social Darwinism had influenced the leaders of Imperial Germany to conduct the brutal, bloody conflict in World War I. The actual scientific theory of evolution and the perversions of Social Darwinism were all the same to him. He blamed the idea of "survival of the fittest" for encouraging the extreme inequality of the so-called Gilded Age, too. Darwinist thinking, Will became convinced, was at war with humanity.

The country had changed, was changing still—and not for the better, by Will Bryan's lights. Modernism was overtaking old-time religion, time-honored ways of life, and traditional values, all the foundations of Will's beliefs. A new culture was on the rise. It took hold in cities, where new music and literature—the sounds and stories of the Jazz Age—caught on. It challenged the familiar morality and customs of the nineteenth century. New ideas rooted in racial and ethnic diversity, science, and sexual freedom competed with the conservative Christianity that had been the American norm, and that had been the core of Will's life.

In the face of these changes, Will's priorities changed. Evolution, he decided, was far more dangerous than he had acknowledged in his "Prince of Peace" speech. He was going to have to save the souls of America's children. He was going to have to write a new speech.

———◆◆◆———

The Grand Opera House in Wausau, Wisconsin, was packed on the evening of May 12, 1919. "The greatest need of the world today is a whole-hearted belief in God," the esteemed speaker, Will Bryan, told his audience. It was an audience inclined to agree with him; the speech was sponsored by the Biblical Alliance, a group dedicated to the inclusion of Bible study in schools. "I believe in higher education," Will continued, "but I feel that we are paying men to undermine the faith of our own children." Everyone knew he was talking about how state governments used money they raised from their citizens in the form of taxes to pay teachers who were teaching evolution to their children.

Will worked in some monkey business, as usual: "I don't want to take any pleasure from the men who think that they are descended from a monkey," he said, "but I do not want them to include me in their family tree." And he assailed nonbelievers—working in a typical clever turn of phrase. "The first question usually asked by the atheist is, 'Where do you begin?'" he said. "My answer is 'In the beginning God created the heavens and the earth.' In return I ask the atheist, 'Where do you begin?' He has no answer." And then, Will injected the slick quotable quote: "I would rather begin with God and work down than to begin with a piece of dirt and work up."

"It is time for the world to challenge the unbeliever," Will told his crowd. The speech was titled "Back to God." Afterward, envelopes were passed around the auditorium to collect donations to support that challenge. It was a good night for the Biblical Alliance. And Will was just getting started.

———◆◆———

But first, Will had another speech to make, one of great importance to its audience but not so much to the rest of the world. Four days after his outing in Wausau, Will was in his hometown of Salem, Illinois, to deliver the commencement address to the twenty-two graduating seniors of the local public high school, class of 1919. Although he now lived in Florida, Will frequently returned to Salem to speak. The graduation ceremonies were held on Friday morning, May 16, at the Methodist church. It was a big day for the twenty-two young people in the graduating class.

Will started speaking. Presumably he shared some encouraging and inspiring words for the seniors who, as the local newspaper put it, "will soon be turned into the world." Presumably these young people and their families hung on the hometown hero's every word. As one of them later wrote, "He was one of the most perfect speakers I have heard; he was nearly always flawless in every way." And yet. The Great Commoner made "a minor slip," this graduate

12 BOYS, 10 GIRLS IN CLASS OF 1919

Class of 1919 of S. H. S. Will Soon Be Turned Into World. Bryan to Deliver the Address.

The graduating class of the Salem High School enjoys a rather unique reputation, in that for the first time in the history of the school, the number of male graduates is greater than the females. Out of a class of twenty-two, only ten of them are young ladies. The members of the class are as follows:

Misses Bessie Barenfanger, Ethel Estes, Ruby Huser, Aretae Jones, Anna Morton, Dorothy Murphy, Nora Radloff, Irma Schwartz, Inez Tate and Nellie Townsend, Earl Bruce, Quinn Charlton, John Davidson, John Doolen Charles Edwards, Lewis Huser, Raymond McLain, Jean McMackin, Robert Mercer, John Morris, John Scopes and Elbridge Telford.

The Commencement exercises will be held on Friday morning, May 16, at 10:30 o'clock at the Methodist church and Hon. W. J. Bryan will deliver the Commencement address. The baccalaureate sermon will be given on next Sunday night at the Methodist church by Rev. P. R. Glotfelty.

A May 8, 1919, article in the local newspaper in Salem, Illinois, announced the upcoming Salem High School graduation. John Scopes is listed as one of the graduates and William Jennings Bryan as the speaker.

said. "He made a pronounced whistling effect"—as in, "s-s-s-s" at the end of a word ending with "s." It prompted a burst of laughter from this senior, and three of his friends, all sitting in the front row. It was not their finest moment; they just could not control themselves. The giggling was, as giggling can be, contagious. Soon chuckles and chortles bounced around the room. The audience, this student said, "was jolted out of the spell Bryan had woven."

Will stared at the guilty foursome, two boys and two girls. They did their best to get themselves together. The audience quieted. As he continued with his speech, Will shot these front-row disrupters a look now and then—a warning to keep quiet. One of the kids, the one who wrote about the incident, was a lanky boy with wispy blondish hair.

That was John Scopes.

CHAPTER 9
BETTER TO DESTROY

Will was on a roll. His "Back to God" speech was a hit: "William Jennings Bryan thrilled one of the largest audiences which ever assembled in Ford's Opera House yesterday afternoon in what has been designated by many who heard him as one of the greatest addresses he has ever made," declared the *Baltimore Sun* in early 1919.

But Will didn't stop at just one new speech. He composed an entire suite of speeches to attack Darwinism's influence on children and young adults, and brought them to audiences throughout the country.

There was "In His Image": "William Jennings Bryan was given a hearty welcome Tuesday morning at Nebraska Wesleyan university, where he spoke to a large audience of students, faculty, and friends," the *Nebraska State Journal* reported in late 1920. "The adress [*sic*] . . . was intended to explode the Darwinian theory of descent of man."

There was "The Menace of Darwinism": "'**THE MENACE OF**

DARWINISM' GIVEN NATIONAL ATTENTION," shouted the double-decker all-capital-letters headline in the *Miami Herald* in early 1921.

"The Bible and Its Enemies": "William Jennings Bryan, speaking to an audience which filled the Municipal Tabernacle last night, characterized believers in the 'guesses of Darwin' and adherents of a 'man-made Bible' as the greatest menaces to the peace of the world," reported the Louisville *Courier-Journal* in the fall of 1921.

Will's speeches were long, passionate, entertaining, mesmerizing— and studded with nonsense. "How can teachers tell students that they came from monkeys and not expect them to act like monkeys?" he asked. Fact-check, again: evolutionary theory did not say that people "came," or descended, from monkeys. Rather, humans and chimpanzees (who are a type of ape, not monkey) share a common ancestor.

Will hammered away at a few common themes. "All the ills from which America suffers," he said in one speech, "can be traced back to the teachings of evolution. It would be better to destroy every other book ever written, and save just the first three verses of Genesis."

Will did not merely assert the superiority of biblical teachings over scientific learning. He went further, insisting that the theory of evolution wasn't even really science. "There is not a single fact in the universe," he claimed, "that can be cited to prove that man is descended from the lower animals. Darwin does not use facts; he

William Jennings Bryan's audience at a Bible class in Miami, Florida, in 1921.

uses conclusions drawn from similarities. He builds upon presumptions, probabilities and inferences."

With this, Will was objecting to the modern scientific method that had come into existence by the twentieth century. Science takes evidence in the natural world and formulates explanations—also called hypotheses, or theories—as to what that evidence means. A hypothesis is tested repeatedly. It is challenged. It is revised in light of new evidence and discoveries. A hypothesis predicts occurrences in nature. It is not a casual guess. The theory of evolution was (and is) a strong example of a scientific hypothesis, supported by profound evidence and not contradicted by credible proofs.

But Will rejected all of this:

> The word hypothesis is a synonym used by scientists for the word guess; it is more dignified in sound and more imposing to the sight, but it has the same meaning as the old-fashioned, every-day word, guess. If Darwin had described his doctrine as a guess instead of calling it an hypothesis, it would not have lived a year.

As always, Will laced his speeches with entertaining turns of phrase: "It is better to trust in the Rock of Ages," he declaimed, "than to know the age of the rocks." And, "It is better for one to know that he is close to the Heavenly Father, than to know how far the stars in the heavens are apart." It all made for a grand experience for those who

heard the great William Jennings Bryan at a Bible conference or a Chautauqua gathering. And the many others who couldn't witness a live performance could read "The Menace of Darwinism" in booklet form for five cents a copy.

Will's campaign against evolution was as spirited and intense as any of his campaigns for political office. And more to the point—his campaign quickly became political. Will was not content merely to alert the nation to the perils of this most dangerous idea. "The parents who pay the salary," Will argued, "have a right to decide what shall be taught." Put another way, he said, "The hand that writes the pay check rules the school." The hand that wrote the paycheck for public schools was, and still is, taxpayer-funded state governments. So Will's campaign against evolution became a campaign to pressure state legislatures to outlaw the teaching of evolution in public schools.

He did face pushback. But none of it stopped or discouraged Will; it seemed to energize him. At a speech before an audience of 6,000 in New York City in the spring of 1922, a heckler disrupted the event. Will heckled back: "Why don't you establish your own school and teach your doctrine? But don't come here and take my audience."

The more he talked, the more opposition he attracted—from scientists, from modernist clergymen, from academics and professors and journalists and educators, and from students themselves. After Will gave a lecture called "Science v. Evolution" at Dartmouth University in January 1924, the school solicited feedback from students who attended. Those who considered themselves "evolutionists" offered comments like these:

"He seemed to be ridiculing evolution, not arguing against it."

"He is an old man firmly believing in the teachings of his youth. He thinks that because the trend is different nowadays society is going to the dogs."

Prohibition of Ideas.

The wisdom of the ostrich speaks in William Jennings Bryan's proposal to combat evolution by placing it under ban of law. Does the Commoner expect rational humans to imitate that bird and imagine themselves immune from scientific theories and discoveries merely by sinking their heads in the sands of ignorance?

If evolution is not true, and if the Commoner desires its falsity to be shown up, the best method would be its exposition—to the end that reasonable minds may catch its weak points. Restrictive legislation would accomplish nothing except to stimulate desire to learn what it is devised to suppress. If false, evolution will die. If true, it cannot be suppressed by law. Does Col. Bryan mean to apply prohibition to ideas?

In 1923, the editors of the *Washington Post* took William Jennings Bryan to task for suggesting that laws ban the teaching of evolution.

"Bryan did what I thought to be impossible. He talked for nearly two hours and didn't say anything."

He talked for nearly two hours and didn't say anything. This student could not have known that he was channeling Clarence Darrow's irritation nearly thirty years earlier with Will's "Cross of Gold" speech at the 1896 Democratic convention: *What did he say, anyhow?* Here it was again, the feeling that Will's mountain of words, for all their majestic heights, did not amount to much more than a pile of pretty phrases.

Clarence had been following Will's campaign against evolution ever since the "Prince of Peace" lecture. He tried to engage Will in debate. "Darrow Asks W.J. Bryan To Answer These," announced a *Chicago Daily Tribune* headline atop a list of fifty-five questions on its front page on July 4, 1923. Some were about science, some about theology—some seemingly designed just to poke fun. "Did

DARROW ASKS W. J. BRYAN TO ANSWER THESE

For Instance: "Did Noah Build Ark?"

Clarence S. Darrow, Chicago lawyer and writer, has sent The Tribune the following letter in reply to the letter from William J. Bryan recently pinted in this column. Mr. Bryan's letter upheld the position of the fundamentalists and contends for a literal interpretation of the Bible. Mr. Darrow asks Mr. Bryan a series of questions:

Editor of The Tribune: I was very much interested in Mr. Bryan's letter to THE TRIBUNE and in your editorial reply. I have likewise followed Mr. Bryan's efforts to shut out the teaching of science from the public schools and his questionnaires to various college professors who believe in evolution CLARENCE DARROW. and still profess Christianity. No doubt his questions to the professors, if answered, would tend to help clear the issue, and likewise a few questions to Mr. Bryan and the fundamentalists, if fairly answered, might serve the interests of reaching the truth—all of this assumes that truth is desirable.

Creation of the Earth.

For this reason I think it would be helpful if Mr. Bryan would answer the following questions:

Do you believe in the literal interpretation of the whole Bible?

Is the account of the creation of the earth and all life in Genesis literally true, or is it an allegory?

Was the earth made in six literal days, measured by the revolution of the earth on its axis?

Was the sun made on the fourth day to give light to the earth by day and the moon made on the same day to give light by night, and were the stars made for the benefit of the earth?

Did God create man on the sixth day?

Did God rest on the seventh day?

Garden of Eden.

Did God place man in the Garden of Eden and tell him he could eat of every tree except the tree of knowledge?

Was Eve literally made from the rib of Adam?

Did the serpent induce Eve to eat of the tree of knowledge?

Did the eating of this fruit cause Adam and Eve to know that they were naked?

Did God curse the serpent for tempting Eve and decree that thereafter he should go on his belly?

How did he travel before that time?

Did God tell Eve that thereafter he would multiply the sorrows of all women and that their husband should rule over them?

What About Flood?

Did God send a flood covering the whole earth, even the tops of the highest mountains and destroy "all flesh that has the breath of life," excepting the inmates of the ark?

Did God command Noah to build an ark for him and his family and to take on board a male and female of every living species on earth?

Did he build the ark and gather the pairs of all animals on the earth and the food and water necessary to preserve them?

As there were no ships in those days, except the ark, how did Noah gather them from all the continents and islands of the earth?

Did he then cause it to rain forty days and forty nights and destroy every living thing on the earth?

Did all these living things enter the ark on the second month and 17th day of the month?

Were all the high mountains on all the earth covered?

Did the waters prevail on the earth for 150 days?

Ararat and the Rainbow.

Did the ark rest on Mount Ararat in the seventh month and the tenth day of the month?

Did God set a rainbow in the heavens for a token that the world would not again be destroyed by flood?

Was this the first rainbow that ever appeared?

According to the old testament, was this not about 1,750 years B. C.?

Is not history full of proof that all colors and kinds of people lived over large and remote parts of the earth within fifty years after this time?

Were the pairs of animals sent to every quarter of the earth after the flood?

How could many species that are

(Continued on page 12, column 1.)

The *Chicago Daily Tribune* printed Clarence Darrow's questions to William Jennings Bryan on the front page.

God curse the serpent for tempting Eve and decree that thereafter he should go on his belly?" Clarence asked. "How did he travel before that time?"

Will did not respond. Why should he? Millions of people loved his lectures and pamphlets. Legislators introduced proposals to ban the teaching of evolution in Kentucky, North Carolina, Oklahoma, and Florida. They didn't succeed, but the ball was rolling. It was rolling toward Dayton, Tennessee. It was rolling, by pure coincidence, to the giggling boy in the audience at that high school graduation in Salem, Illinois, in 1919.

CHAPTER 10
"WHAT ARE MOTHERS TO DO"

In 1924, Will gave a major speech titled "Is the Bible True?" to a large audience in Nashville, Tennessee. Most of the state's officials attended. As usual, he drew ovations from the crowd. Laughs, too: Darwinists "don't even allow man to descend from a good American monkey," he said, but rather from some ape over in Africa. The audience ate it up.

After the speech, a group of anti-evolutionists sent copies of it to thousands of Tennesseans, including members of the Tennessee legislature. A year later, John Washington Butler of the Tennessee House of Representatives introduced House Bill 185 to outlaw the teaching of evolution. "I didn't know anything about evolution when I introduced it," Butler admitted later. But he'd heard "that boys and girls were coming home from school and telling their fathers and mothers that the Bible was all nonsense."

Actually, only the caption of Butler's bill used the word "evolution": "An Act prohibiting the teaching of the Evolution Theory," it

announced. The law itself con-
sisted of two sections. First, the
crime:

SECTION 1. BE IT
ENACTED BY THE GEN-
ERAL ASSEMBLY OF THE
STATE OF TENNESSEE,
That it shall be unlaw-
ful for any teacher in any
of the Universities, nor-
mals and all other public
schools of the State which
are supported in whole or
in part by the public school
funds of the state, to teach
any theory that denies the
story of the Divine Cre-
ation of man as taught in the Bible, and to teach instead
that man has descended from a lower order of animals.

In June 1925, the *Baltimore Sun* cartoonist took a dim view of the Tennessee anti-evolution law.

(A "normal" school was one specifically for training teachers.)

This was not the clearest piece of writing. It didn't say that it was
unlawful to teach "evolution" or "evolutionary theory," even though
that was the whole point. Rather, the law forbade instruction that
denied the biblical story of creation. It also separately went after
teaching human evolution—without mentioning "evolution"—by
forbidding instruction that humans came from "a lower order of
animals."

What if a teacher channeled Charles Darwin's old friend,

Professor Asa Gray, and taught that humanity's descent from "a lower order of animals" was part of God's work? Would that be a crime? The law didn't say.

What if a teacher shared the theory of human evolution but didn't suggest that it denied the creation story? Would that be criminal? The law didn't say.

Also—how were teachers to deal with the fact that the Bible contains two different stories of human creation? There's one in the first chapter of Genesis. There's another in the second chapter of Genesis. Chapter one has God creating male and female humans, seemingly at the same time, on the sixth day. Chapter two has God creating a male human first, settling the man in the Garden of Eden, and then deciding to make a counterpart for him, a female, formed out of the man's own body. These are not the same stories at all.

Once again, the law didn't say.

The Butler Act also didn't say that it was against the law to deny the story of the divine creation of dogs, or cats, or cows, or any other creatures—or of plants, the world's most abundant life-forms by biomass—although they, too, are included in the biblical accounts. Only man had to be kept under the protective umbrella of the story— or a story—of divine creation.

That was the crime. Next was the punishment:

SECTION 2. BE IT FURTHER ENACTED, That any teacher found guilty of the violation of this Act, shall be guilty of a misdemeanor and upon conviction, shall be fined not less than One Hundred ($100.00) Dollars nor more than Five Hundred ($500.00) Dollars for each offense.

The Butler Act passed the House easily, without debate, on an afternoon when the legislature churned through more than forty bills in a two-hour session.

Next, the proposal needed to pass the Tennessee Senate. This took a little longer, but not much. Newspaper editors wrote editorials, preachers preached sermons, and ordinary citizens wrote letters to newspapers and lawmakers. "What are mothers to do," one woman

The *Atlanta Constitution*'s editorial cartoonist depicted Tennessee lawmakers hacking away at a nonsensical notion of evolution.

The Family Tree

wrote, "when unwise education makes boys lose confidence in the home, the Bible, the government and all law?"

With that plaintive cry in their ear, an overwhelming majority of the Senate passed the Butler Act.

On it went to the governor, Austin Peay, for his signature. He heard from supporters and opponents, including leading academics in his state. The president of Fisk University, the most prestigious Black educational institution in Tennessee, urged the governor not

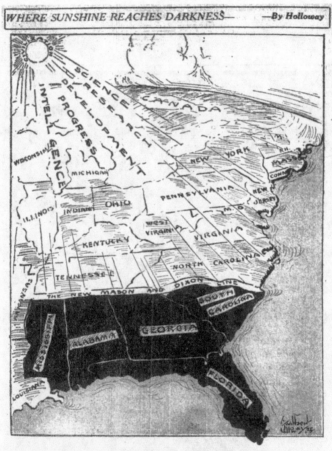

The nation's leading Black-owned newspaper in 1925, the *Pittsburgh Courier,* editorialized on the "darkness" engulfing southern states.

to sign the law. The governor did not hear from the president of the University of Tennessee, the state's major white public institution of higher education. Many students and faculty members there opposed the bill, but U-T's president—a scientist!—didn't want to endanger the school's funding. He remained silent.

Governor Peay signed the Butler Act into law on March 21, 1925. He didn't think he was doing anything of much significance. "I can find nothing of consequence in the books now being taught in our schools with which this bill will interfere in the slightest manner," he wrote. "Therefore, it will not put our teachers in any jeopardy. Probably the law will never be applied. . . . Nobody believes that it is going to be an active statute."

Nothing of consequence in the books now being taught?

The governor must not have looked very hard. What about Hunter's *A Civic Biology*, the textbook that Tennessee's public school teachers were instructed to use in biology class?

Probably the law will never be applied?

The governor's crystal ball was cloudy that day.

CHAPTER 11
THE ROAD TO DAYTON

Tennessee's Governor Peay might be excused for his failings as a seer. For how could he have predicted that the American Civil Liberties Union, an organization in New York City, would involve itself with Tennessee's law against teaching evolution? How could Governor Peay have anticipated a group of small-town boosters gathered around a drugstore table dreaming up a legal proceeding to test the Butler Act, purely out of a desire to draw attention to their little burg of Dayton?

And could the governor have foreseen a high school teacher, not so long out of high school himself, more or less saying to the drugstore clique, *Sure, yeah. Arrest me. I don't mind.*

There was an element of randomness to John Scopes's participation in the plan hatched at Robinson's Drug Store in May 1925, less than two months after the Butler Act became law. He had finished his teaching duties the previous week and intended to go home to see his parents, who now lived in Paducah, Kentucky. But he'd stuck around Dayton in hopes of getting a date with a particular young woman. (It never happened.) So there he was playing tennis, killing time, that fine morning when he was summoned to Robinson's.

Randomness also largely defined how John came to be a teacher in Dayton in the first place. After graduating from the University of Kentucky, John had spent the summer at his parents' home until a last-minute job offer from Rhea Central High School came his way. The football coach–who also taught algebra, physics, and chemistry– had resigned unexpectedly. John would take over as coach. He would take over the prior coach's teaching duties, too.

So John moved to Dayton and lived as a boarder with a local family. For fun, he went to the town's popular Saturday night dances. Like everyone else in Dayton, he went to church on Sundays.

Being "Coach Scopes" was definitely the most important role John played at Rhea Central High during his first year. "The Rhea High team, under the direction of Coach Scopes, and starting out with largely new material, has been growing better with each game," the *Chattanooga Daily Times* reported the month after John started his job. By Thanksgiving, he earned still more kudos in the sports pages: "Rhea High . . . is ever a dangerous foe to any team which strives to complete a season without treading the path of defeat," the *Daily Times* said.

Way to go, John! He led the Yellow Jackets to a record of four wins, four losses, and two ties.

In that first semester, John's responsibilities were football, algebra, physics, and chemistry. Not biology. And if not biology, then not evolution. But the principal, who was also the biology teacher, got sick during the second semester. Team player–and junior-most person–that he was, John became the school's substitute biology teacher. Which meant he taught out of the textbook mandated by state authorities, *A Civic Biology*. Which meant, in theory at least, John shared a few tidbits from the book about evolution.

So far, so random. But when the Dayton boosters sat John down in Robinson's Drug Store and coaxed him into his role as willing criminal, they may not have known that, in some ways, he was exactly

"Coach" Scopes filled in for Rhea Central High School's regular biology teacher in 1925.

the right guy for the job. "My father had read to me from Charles Darwin's *Origin of Species*, *Descent of Man*, and *The Voyage of the Beagle*, which I had then finished reading for myself," he later explained, "and, although not a trained scholar, I thought Darwin was right." In college at the University of Kentucky, one of John's favorite professors was Arthur McQuiston Miller—called "Monkey" Miller because he taught evolution. John approved when two of his other professors lobbied against a bill in the Kentucky legislature to prohibit the teaching of "Darwinism, Atheism, Agnosticism, or the theory of Evolution as it pertains to man." Kentucky lawmakers rejected the anti-evolution proposal.

But now, here in Tennessee, no fewer than six lawyers lined up to prosecute John. Leading the charge was the state's district attorney general, A. Thomas Stewart. There was retired state assistant attorney general Ben G. McKenzie, joined by his son, Gordon. There were two local lawyers who worked for the city of Dayton and who were also brothers, Sue and Herbert Hicks. Sue and Herbert—Sue was named for their mother, who died while giving birth to him—were friends with John. Sue had been one of the lawyers seated around the drugstore table when John agreed to become a criminal defendant. Another local lawyer, Wallace Haggard, rounded out the team whose aim was to prove John guilty of the crime of teaching evolution.

Half a dozen lawyers—why not add another? The World's Christian Fundamentals Association got the idea that the Dayton team should include the man who inspired the Butler Act: William Jennings Bryan, who had not tried a case in decades. Will Bryan, whose age and health had begun to take a toll on his once-imposing figure. (He was sixty-five, but struggles with diabetes made him seem older.) Will Bryan, who was still stomping the country spreading his anti-evolution gospel.

He also seemed to be growing harsher. During a recent speaking engagement at Brown University in Providence, Rhode Island, Will responded sarcastically to a student who asked a question. "I've come a long way to address you students at Brown University," he said, "but I shall certainly have to retire before this magnificent, bubbling fountain of wisdom on my right." Will then abruptly left the stage, to hisses, boos, and no applause.

Whether he was harsh or kind, fragile or hearty, the existing crew of prosecutors in Dayton wanted Will on their team. Sue Hicks reached out to him by letter, and he said yes. Will added one more lawyer: his son, William Jennings Bryan Jr., from Los Angeles.

On John's side, a well-known Tennessee law professor, John Randolph Neal, showed up in Dayton looking for the young teacher almost immediately after his arrest. They met at the Hotel Aqua, next to the drugstore: "Boy," Neal said to John, "I'm interested in your case and, whether you want me or not, I'm going to be here. I'll be available twenty-four hours a day."

But the ACLU wanted eminent, impressive attorneys on the case. As John noted, "Neal rarely impressed others favorably.... He seemed always in need of a shave; his graying hair usually needed cutting and brushing; often his clothes sagged or bagged or needed pressing." The ACLU had in mind several highly distinguished (and well-groomed) lawyers. Clarence Darrow, the nation's leading trial lawyer, was not on their list. But he was not the type of man to wait for an invitation.

Like Will Bryan, Clarence had some health problems and his age was showing. Also like Will, he'd grown, in some ways, harsher and sourer. This revealed itself in his surprising about-face on the Nineteenth Amendment to the Constitution, which in 1920 gave women the right to vote. Clarence had long supported women's rights—and yet he changed his mind when it came to their voting rights. It probably didn't help that the Eighteenth Amendment, which out-lawed the sale of alcoholic beverages across the United States, and which he thought was a terrible idea, had gotten significant support from women's groups.

But even an older (at sixty-eight) and curmudgeonly Clarence Darrow was a force. The previous summer, Clarence's reputation as America's greatest courtroom lawyer had grown ever more solid when he represented privileged teenagers Nathan Leopold and Richard Loeb in a high-profile murder trial in Chicago. The murderers had confessed their guilt of the horrendous and premeditated felony, and most observers expected the judge to impose the death penalty. Clarence brought his best game and his abhorrence of capital punishment, speaking for days on end, weaving poetry and psychiatry and philosophy into his arguments. Courtroom spectators cried. Clarence cried. And, ultimately, he obtained sentences of life imprisonment for his clients. It was a tremendous victory.

Now, nine months after Leopold and Loeb's case had absorbed the nation, news of John Scopes's prosecution blanketed the country. So did news of Will's participation in that prosecution. Immediately after that went public, the *St. Louis Post-Dispatch* editorialized:

> Obviously a towering figure is needed for the defense. Won't there be enough at stake in this case, and enough fun, to call Mr. Clarence Darrow back from his fishing haunts?

Clarence wasn't fishing—he was in New York when he heard that Will was joining the prosecution. "At once I wanted to go," he wrote. Along with Dudley Field Malone, a prominent New York lawyer with whom Clarence had worked before, Clarence sent a telegram to John

Randolph Neal offering to work on the case without charging a fee. He'd never offered his services for free before, but he was hankering for this fight.

The ACLU leadership wasn't on board with the idea. Yes, Clarence's legal skills were legendary. His history of working for the labor

Clarence Darrow, eager to participate in this high-profile trial, offered to represent John Scopes pro bono.

movement and objecting to government laws that stifled political dissent aligned with the ACLU's missions. Still, some in the organization's leadership feared Clarence would go too far if he went to Dayton. Everyone knew he'd been chomping at the bit to corner Will Bryan on his belief in the literal truth of the Bible. But a fight over whether Noah really did bring animals, two by two, on the ark—this was not what the ACLU was after. The organization's goal was to make the case that the state of Tennessee violated John Scopes's constitutional

rights by prohibiting teachers from sharing scientific knowledge with students. Assuming they would lose their challenge in the state courts, they planned to appeal the case all the way up to the U.S. Supreme Court.

Both Bryan and Darrow were satirized in the media leading up to the trial. The Memphis *Commercial Appeal* (right) compared teaching evolution to "bootlegging"—selling alcoholic liquor illegally during the nation's ban on alcohol—and took a dig at Darrow for his opposition to Prohibition. The *New Yorker* (below) placed Bryan in a lineup titled "The Rise and Fall of Man."

A couple of weeks after Clarence made his offer, the ACLU brought John to New York City for a series of meetings. Nearly every ACLU official and lawyer with whom he met advised against letting Clarence Darrow participate in John's defense. "The arguments against Darrow were various," John wrote, "that he was too radical, that he was a headline hunter, that the trial would become a circus." The discussions went on and on. At a final lunch to conclude John's two days in New York, someone finally thought to ask him to weigh in. He did not hesitate.

"I want Darrow," John said.

John got his lawyer. Dayton, and the nation, got the promise of a celebrity slugfest. After years of sparring from afar, William Jennings Bryan and Clarence Darrow would be brawling face-to-face.

CHAPTER 12
THE CIRCUS COMES TO TOWN

"Well," said Will after stepping down from the Southern Railway's Royal Palm train. "I'm here."

It was early afternoon on Tuesday, July 7, 1925. The Royal Palm's usual stop in this part of Tennessee was Chattanooga. For the Great Commoner, however, traveling from his home in Miami to take up duties in *The State of Tennessee v. John Thomas Scopes*, the railway made an unscheduled stop in Dayton.

Three hundred people flocked to the station to greet Will. News photographers climbed on top of automobiles to get their shots. Even if you were at the back of the crowd at the station, you could not miss Will in his big white cork helmet. When the applause died down, Will said, "Long have I looked forward to getting to Dayton. I am ready for anything that is to be done." He didn't speak much longer. It had been a long trip.

After a rest and lunch, Will strolled around Dayton, pith helmet on his head. He wore it, he explained, to protect his now-bald dome from

William Jennings Bryan posing with his welcoming crowd just after arriving in Dayton, Tennessee, July 7, 1925.

the summer sun. Will seemed in a fine mood, joking with reporters about his baldness and explaining that he inherited it from his father. (So close, so close, with this appreciation that traits are passed down from one generation to another, to treading on the basic stepping stones of evolution!)

The place Will toured was transformed from its sleepy self. A journalist from Chattanooga reported that "practically every home in Dayton has been thrown open for use of the visitors during the trial." The town set up tourist camps and temporary hospital facilities. Lights were strung around the ballpark for nighttime parking. For visitors arriving by airplane, the Morgan brothers' farm, two miles outside of Dayton, offered a landing area. "Two farm houses, equipped with telephones, are located near the field," the Chattanooga reporter added, "and arrangements have been made to meet the aroplanes [*sic*] when they land with automobiles so passengers can be taken to Dayton in a short time."

Once in Dayton, those passengers, like Will Bryan on his stroll around town, could not miss the banner that Doc Robinson had hung outside his drugstore: "Where It Started." Another local business deserved an award for most clever promotion, with its sign promising that "Darwin Is Right—Inside." This was Darwin's Dry Goods Store. Jim Darwin, who was indeed Charles Darwin's great-great-great nephew and a longtime resident of Dayton, really was right inside. One reporter visiting from New York wrote that there was "an

The sign outside Darwin's Dry Goods Store in Dayton announced the proprietor's familial connection to the notorious naturalist.

acre of hot dog stands," which sounds like an exaggeration, but if you combined the hot dog stands with all the booths selling fried chicken sandwiches, corn, watermelon, and lemonade near the Dayton court-house, and the pits dug to roast beef, you could probably come up with an acre or more of food vendors.

But clever banners and abundant snacks were only the beginning of Dayton's makeover. There were musicians singing hymns and pop-ular songs, peddlers offering shoes and calico. You could hardly go anywhere downtown without seeing a monkey or, to be precise, a pri-mate. Stores sold stuffed monkey dolls, neckties, umbrella handles, postcards, and pins. ("Your old man's a monkey," announced one pin.)

People and street vendors gathering in Dayton a few days before the start of the trial.

For sixty cents you could buy a commemorative medal, cast by the local Ford mechanic, with a carving of an ape and the words "Dayton,

Tenn. 1925." A live, trained chimpanzee named Joe Mendi, dressed like a proper gentleman, came to Dayton with his owner to entertain the gathering crowds. The Dayton Hotel installed a gorilla exhibit in its lobby. Robinson's Drug Store sold a soda dubbed "Monkey Fizz."

Chimpanzee Joe Mendi performed for children during his visit to Dayton during the trial.

Even before he came to Dayton to cover the trial, Baltimore-based journalist H.L. Mencken named the proceedings the "Monkey Trial." The label stuck. When trains pulled into the station, brakemen shouted, "All out for Monkeyville!" Over in Nashville, the manager of the Glendale Zoo reported a fifty percent increase in visitors wanting to take a look at the monkeys. "It has aroused the public's suspicions, evidently," he said, "and they are coming out to take at least another look before deciding if Darwin was right." Back in Dayton, Jim Darwin of the "Darwin Is Right—Inside" store reminded a journalist that his uncle never said that people evolved from monkeys. Most people had the wrong idea about the theory of evolution, he said, but he had his eye on business, not on changing minds. "I will probably be too busy to attend the trial," he said, selling clothing and shoes to customers regardless of their views on Darwinism.

If monkeys were everywhere in Dayton, so was religion. "Read Your Bible," commanded one huge banner. More signs: "Come to Jesus." "Prepare to Meet Thy Maker." "Be Sure Your Sins Will Find You Out." "You Need God in Your Business." Preachers from near and far set up booths to sell religious pamphlets and books. The Anti-Evolution League's offerings included, in addition to Will Bryan's books, a popular volume by leading anti-evolutionist T.T. Martin, *Hell and the High Schools*. One of Martin's leaflets showcased pictures of

A display of anti-evolution books for sale in Dayton at the start of the trial.

gorillas and the caption "Are These Your Ancestors?" Martin himself came in from Mississippi to sell his book and give lectures—and he had plenty of competition in that department. Everyone with an idea or two in his head, it seemed, came to Dayton to make a speech.

But none of these anti-evolution preachers and speakers could compete with the real deal: William Jennings Bryan. He was the anti-evolutionist who people came to see and hear. On his first night in Dayton, he did not let them down.

The Dayton Progressive Club welcomed Will with a banquet at the Hotel Aqua. It was, John wrote, "the social event of all Dayton's history." He was given a seat at the head table, across from Will. (How unusual was it for a criminal defendant and his prosecutor to enjoy a festive meal together on the eve of trial? Extremely unusual. Ridiculously unusual. Possibly unprecedented.) The dining room was filled with leading citizens, as well as anyone who could afford to buy a ticket.

"John," Will said, "I know you."

Oh yes, John remembered. But he wasn't expecting this great and famous man, who had met thousands and thousands of people in his life, to remember him.

"I think you're one of those high-school students who made a disturbance at that commencement address I delivered in Salem several years ago!" Will continued, laughing.

John smiled.

"John, we are on opposite sides this time," Will said. "I hope we will not let that interfere in any way with our relationship."

"Mr. Bryan, everyone has the right to think in accordance with the way he sees things and to act accordingly," John replied. "Believing differently on some issues should not influence the degree of respect and friendship one has for another."

"Good," Will said, "we shall get along fine."

They shook hands. Now they were friends—or at least friendly enough for Will to ask, before the plates were cleared, "John, are you going to eat your side dishes?"

"No, Mr. Bryan."

John wasn't much of an eater and hadn't touched his corn and potatoes. Will was known to have a considerable appetite. He gladly wolfed down John's leftovers.

After dinner, Will did what he did best: he gave a speech. "The contest between evolution and Christianity is a duel to the death," Will declared. "It has been in the past a death struggle in the darkness. From this time on it will be a death grapple in the light." His voice, that famous instrument, throbbed with emotion. He noted how fitting it was for the trial to defeat evolution to take place in the little town of Dayton—because Bethlehem and Nazareth, the locales central to the life of Jesus Christ, were also little towns. He complimented the audience's reputation: "I will put the character of the people of Tennessee against that of any people in the United States." Will was still a folksy, friendly, comfortable orator, at least when facing a welcoming audience.

The trial was scheduled to begin in three days, on Friday, July 10. Until then, Will's days and nights were filled with speaking engagements. He made news whenever he spoke. "Warns That if Defeated in the Courts the Bible Will Be Put into the Constitution," a front-page headline in the *New York Times* announced after he proposed a possible constitutional amendment to ban the teaching of evolution. But it wasn't all dinners and discourses. Will was hard at work writing the closing argument he intended to give at the end of the trial. "He has worked for two months on the speech," a reporter revealed. "It will undoubtedly be his greatest oratorical effort since his famous

THE CIRCUS COMES TO TOWN | 105

'Cross of Gold' speech, which lifted him from obscurity and made him a Presidential candidate for the first time."

Town leaders put on a separate banquet, on a different night, for the nation's most accomplished practitioner of the art of the closing argument: Clarence Darrow. Before coming to town, Clarence would not have won any popularity contests in Dayton. It wasn't only Darrow's godless reputation that marked him. It was also his image as a big-city Chicago lawyer come to their little village to lord his urban values over them. But there at the Hotel Aqua, in his after-dinner remarks, Clarence did what he did best: he won over an audience that started out against him. Big-city lawyer? Not at all! "I was born in a little town like this one. . . . I was one of the town loafers." As a writer from the *New Yorker* magazine put it:

> The old master who has won a hundred hostile juries won again. His ill-fitting clothes which he might have picked up at a second hand store on South Halsted Street, his lazy, ambling gait, his toothpick, his mannerisms, his homely, drawling speech—all this captivated the simple citizens of Dayton; the great man was one of them in half an hour.

Watching the "simple citizens" watch Clarence Darrow, watching Will Bryan, watching the monkeys, the hot dog stands, the soapbox preachers—taking it all in, to share with the world, was the largest phalanx of newspapermen, and two newspaperwomen, ever to descend on this corner of Tennessee. Some 200 reporters came to cover the trial of John Scopes. Not just any reporters, but "Newspaper Stars," as one headline noted. One train that rumbled into Dayton deposited newcomers to the world of journalism: announcers, engineers, and equipment from Chicago's WGN radio. Radio was a new technology,

John Scopes welcoming Clarence Darrow to Dayton, Tennessee, July 9, 1925.

and Daytonians received the WGN crew with reverence. The mayor moved out of his house so they could stay there. WGN would be broadcasting the trial live from the courtroom—a first in American history.

In addition to the mainstream—and largely white—press, the nation's vibrant and diverse Black newspapers found an irresistible story in Dayton. Their editors invited African American clergymen who held opposing views to write articles making the cases for creationism and evolution. But Black editors and correspondents also offered their own points of view. Journalist and intellectual William

Pickens reminded his readers of the science: "One of the greatest triumphs ever registered by the human mind was the discovery of the FACT of evolution of the forms of life," he wrote. "This law is witnessed by every blade of grass, by every leaf in the forests, by everything that walks or flies, and that creeps and crawls and increases—and even by the very cells of the one-sided brain of Bryan."

African American newspapers also pointedly called out the anti-equality element in some corners of the anti-evolution movement. The influential *Chicago Defender* introduced its readers to the trial in an editorial entitled "If Monkeys Could Speak":

> The Tennessee legislators who passed the law . . . probably never read the text themselves and all they know about the subject is that the entire human race is supposed to have started from a common origin. Therein lies their difficulty. Admit that premise and they will have to admit that there is no fundamental difference between themselves and the race they pretend to despise. Such admission would, of course, play havoc with the existing standards of living in the South.

All the reporters tumbling into Dayton were chasing stories—any stories that they could find. Sometimes this meant chasing down rumors. Celebrities were irresistible bait. "Thomas A. Edison, aged inventor and one of the most noted scientists in the nation, has offered his services as a witness for the defense in the Scopes evolution trial, it was announced by John R. Neal, leading defense counsel, Tuesday," the *Chattanooga News* reported. "Mrs. Thomas A. Edison, speaking for her husband, said Tuesday night over the telephone from Orange, N.J., that Mr. Edison had not offered to attend the Scopes trial and had no intention of being present," retorted the *Nashville Banner* the next day.

Sometimes the search for a journalistic scoop, or at least for enough words to fill up the newsprint columns, led to some distinctively non-newsworthy interviews. Walter White, the school superintendent who was part of the drugstore group, loved to talk to the press, and he gave colorful quotes. In an interview that ran in newspapers from California to South Carolina, White told a reporter why he had no trouble accepting the literal truth of every word in the Bible:

> Last summer I found a big black snake swollen near its stomach—if you'll pardon me mentioning it. I poked it and, if you'll pardon my mentioning it, up came a frog.

> Now, why would it have been any harder for the whale to keep Jonah, especially if the Lord His God were with him?

> None of these [biblical] stories are as hard to believe as radio.

The most famous reporter to come to Dayton was H.L. Mencken, who wrote for the *Baltimore Sun* and edited his own magazine, *The American Mercury*. Mencken was known for his sharp and satirical commentary about nearly everything, but especially about the South, and that would include Dayton, Tennessee. At least one local newspaper, the *Chattanooga News*, offered its readers a Jazz Age version of a trigger warning when it decided to run Mencken's coverage of the trial. "Editor's Note," the caveat began:

> The News, in our desire to present several viewpoints to its

readers, has at great expense, secured the rights to repub-
lication of the dispatches of H.L. Mencken, foremost living American iconoclast upon the trial. These dispatches
are in no way a reflection of the belief of The News as to
the issues involved. They are merely printed to afford our
readers a better insight into the attitude taken toward Dayton, Tenn., and the south by other sections of America. The
words of Mr. Mencken, brilliant, bitter, provocative, are typical of one viewpoint.

The editor had Mencken pegged. It wasn't long before local folks
were insulted by Mencken's descriptions of them as "morons," "hill-
billies," "yokels," and "peasants" fed a steady diet of "degraded nonsense" by "country preachers." And that was just what he served up
in a single article.

The *Chattanooga News* was also the journalistic home of Nellie Kenyon, one of the two women covering the goings-on in Dayton. Nellie
was only a few years older than John Scopes. It was Nellie who wrote
the feature on Jim Darwin and the "peculiar coincidence," as she put
it, of his family relationship with uncle Charles Darwin. Nellie followed this in late June by breaking the story of the drugstore clique—
that is, how the case against John was cooked up by town leaders in
Robinson's Drug Store. "Here is the 'inside story' of the origin of the
famous Scopes case," the exclusive report began, with a prominent
copyright notice displayed to scare off anyone tempted to steal it and
palm it off as their own work. "The arrest of the young Rhea County
high school professor for violating Tennessee's new anti-evolution act
didn't 'just happen.'"

A big scoop: check.

The nation's most prominent journalist: check.

A face-off between, take your pick, Good v. Evil, Knowledge v. Ignorance, Country Folk v. City Slickers: check.

Celebrity lawyers: double check.

And so all the boxes signifying a giant media event were ticked. Most attention focused on that double-checked box. "William Jennings Bryan and Clarence Darrow are in the ring; the rest are but shadows," wrote one columnist, who proceeded to describe Will's "mighty lion-like head" and "priestly air," and Clarence's "inquisitive eyes" and "wit like a cutting sword."

"As for John Thomas Scopes," this writer concluded, "he is there somewhere."

Yes, he was. He wasn't the center of attention, but the post office had no trouble finding John; the case was famous enough that he received mail simply addressed to "John T. Scopes, United States of America." One letter called him a "contemptible cur." Another from a local woman said he should be "burned at the stake." Another suggested that he should be hanged. It's fair to assume, if also strange to contemplate, that the letter writers' violent reactions to John were all prompted by their unshakable attachment to Christianity—as they understood it.

In an interview with Nellie Kenyon, John said, "I don't plan to teach next year. I may have a job looking through the bars of some jail."

No, he would not be looking through the bars of some jail next year. A criminal conviction under the anti-evolution law could result in a fine, but not imprisonment.

But one can forgive John for indulging in a bit of drama. After all, he was part of a circus.

CHAPTER 13
IN THE BEGINNING

Judge John T. Raulston issued his first ruling in *Tennessee v. Scopes* before he even got to the courthouse. "Coats off" would be the rule in his courtroom, he told reporters two days before the trial. It was too hot to require business attire—coats and collars and ties. (These were the days of removable shirt collars. These were also the days before air-conditioning.) Members of the press applauded this merciful decision—which, as things turned out, was pretty much the only brisk moment of the trial, which was about to unfold at its own unhurried, summery pace.

On Friday morning, July 10, the judge, rosy-faced and clean-shaven, made his way through the leafy fenced square of oak, elm, poplar, and sweet gum trees—and movie cameras and strolling musicians and food vendors—that surrounded the redbrick courthouse. He arrived with his wife, two daughters, his wife's mother, and, under his arm, a Bible. Judge Raulston told news reporters that he'd prepared for the proceedings by spending hours each day in his library

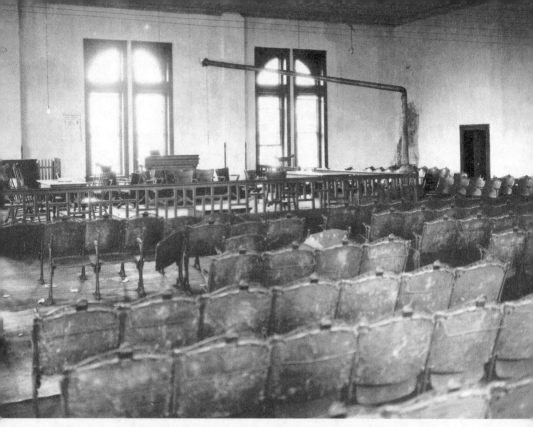

The empty second-floor courtroom in the Rhea County Courthouse before the trial of John Scopes.

reading law books and in his garden tending his vegetables. After posing for photographers and newsreel movie cameras, the judge and his family made their way up the wooden staircase to the large courtroom on the second floor. The space was already crammed, and stifling hot, with spectators and press people.

Judge Raulston was "beaming," the *New York Times* observed. "He is going to enjoy every minute of this trial." Maybe the judge was also smiling because, in anticipation of the big show, the courthouse had been repaired and renovated and the courtroom itself repainted, transformed from a dingy gray to a peaceful cream color. Maybe he was smiling because, as Nellie Kenyon reported, as part of this buffing up, he "has been provided with a new chair for his stand, which he has been wishing a long time."

Next through the big doors of the courtroom came Clarence Dar-row, his great shoulders bowed, face creased with deep wrinkles. With him came John Randolph Neal, the law professor who had attached himself to the case as soon as John Scopes had been arrested; Dudley Field Malone, the lawyer who had joined Clarence in offering their services pro bono to John; and Arthur Garfield Hays, an eminent New York civil liberties lawyer and ACLU leader.

Next came John. In his horn-rimmed glasses, open collar, and shirtsleeves rolled to his elbows, "he might be any college senior on vacation," the *New York Times* reporter wrote. Another newspaper columnist wrote that John looked like a "young man who so far for-got himself as to say 'darn' out loud in a Y.M.C.A. building." In other words, an upstanding, clean-cut youngster. John was accompanied by his father, Thomas Scopes, in from Paducah. George Rappleyea, the man who got John into this fix, sat next to John and his dad.

John Scopes and his father, Thomas Scopes, on the porch of the boarding house in Dayton where John lived.

Next came applause, which could mean only one thing: the arrival of the main attraction. "Here comes William Jennings Bryan," the WGN radio announcer intoned. "He enters now. His bald pate like a sunrise over Key West." Will heard, turned to look at the radioman, and laughed.

Judge Raulston wasn't immune to the Great Commoner's magnetic field; he walked over to shake Will's hand. Will and Clarence greeted each other, too, and talked for a while, their hands chummily on each other's shoulders. Photographers climbed on chairs and tables to capture the scene. It happened to be the anniversary of the day back in 1896 when Will had first been nominated to run for president. Mary Bryan, Will's wife, sat behind her husband in the wheelchair she used because of debilitating arthritis. Ruby Darrow, Clarence's wife (he and Jessie had divorced many years before), sat nearby.

Judge Raulston rapped his gavel. "The court will come to order," he said. "The Rev. Cartwright will open court with prayer."

And pray he did, the Reverend L.M. Cartwright. He prayed for eight long paragraphs—"interminably," in John's view. A wave of "amens" swept over the courtroom when he finished. Clarence Darrow, famous for his nonbelief in God, stood quietly.

The morning was taken up mostly by legal technicalities. Because John was accused of teaching "any theory that denies the story of the Divine Creation of man as taught in the Bible," Judge Raulston decided that he needed to read aloud the first chapter of the book of Genesis. "In the beginning," the judge began, "God created the heaven and earth."

People were shedding their outerwear. Clarence removed his suit jacket, revealing blue suspenders and a yellowish shirt. Will took off his black alpaca coat—a trademark element of his usual dress—his black tie, and the collar to his shirt. The other lawyers at the counsel tables, prosecutors and defense alike, also gave in to the heat—except for defense lawyer Dudley Field Malone. His double-breasted suit jacket remained buttoned. The temperature soared, and he remained suited up. Other mere mortals were in awe of his fortitude.

When the judge finished his lengthy Bible reading, he added a personal note. "I regard a violation of this statute as a high misde-meanor," he mused, "and in making this declaration I make no ref-erence to the policy or constitutionality of the statute, but to the evil example of the teacher disregarding constituted authority in the very presence of the undeveloped mind whose thought and morals he directs and guides."

Judge Raulston carried on in this vein for a bit longer before wrap-ping up with a few words about proceeding "with open minds." Com-ing after his assertion that John had set an "evil example," it seemed a little late—already—for that.

The courtroom was no cooler after the lunch break. Jackets stayed off—except for Dudley Malone's. Will, and many others in the court-room, tried to beat the heat with palm-leaf fans, some emblazoned with the "F.E. Robinson Co." logo (Doc Robinson did not miss an opportunity to promote business), some with a pressing question from a toothpaste company: "Do Your Gums Bleed?"

The pressing question for many people in Dayton was how they could snag ringside seats to the biggest show in town. Possibly the biggest show in their lives. The courtroom was large, but couldn't hold more than 300 people, including standing room, and the press presence left few places for ordinary citizens. One way to jump the line was to get on the jury. After all, jurors could expect to be in the room for every bit of the drama: opening statements by Bryan and

Darrow, examination of witnesses by Bryan and Darrow, objections and arguments by Bryan and Darrow, closing statements by Bryan and Darrow. What could be better?

Over the break, the sheriff had rounded up a hundred men from whom to draw a jury of twelve. The prosecution and defense lawyers would spend the afternoon questioning the potential jurors, one by one, until they filled out the jury box with twelve men whom neither side, nor the judge, had rejected because of perceived bias. It went like this:

"W.F. Roberson, number twelve," called out the sheriff, chewing on a toothpick as he spoke.

> Judge Raulston: Come around, Mr. Roberson. Are you a householder or freeholder in Rhea county?
> W.F. Roberson: Yes, sir.
> Judge: You are a householder?
> Roberson: Yes, sir.

A householder simply lived in a home. A freeholder was the legal owner of a house. Both were eligible to serve as jurors in Tennessee, unlike, for example, women or African Americans.

> Judge: Have you formed or expressed an opinion as to the guilt or innocence of this defendant, John T. Scopes?
> Roberson: Well, to some extent, judge.
> Judge: What do you base that opinion on, Mr. Roberson?
> Roberson: Rumor.

That might not seem entirely fair to John, assuming Roberson's opinion tended toward the guilt of defendant John T. Scopes, which was absolutely a fair assumption. W.F. Roberson might seem to be an excellent candidate to be dismissed by the judge for bias. But no.

"And do you think you can wholly disregard your opinion," Judge Raulston continued, "and go into the jury box, and try the case on the law and the evidence, and render a fair and impartial verdict?"

"Yes, sir," said Roberson.

"I think he is a competent juror, gentlemen," the judge said. "I will pass him to the state first."

The state—that is, the prosecution—was happy to have W.F. Roberson, with his rumor-based view of John's guilt, on the jury and had no further questions for him. Next came Clarence's opportunity.

> Clarence: Have you ever given any special attention to this case?
> Roberson: Well, no more than just reading the newspapers.
> Clarence: Are you satisfied that you could try it with perfect fairness to both sides?
> Roberson: Yes, sir, I think I could.
> Clarence: All right, we will take him.

And that was that for W.F. Roberson. What could Clarence do? You couldn't find a jury of twelve completely unbiased men in Rhea County for this case. W.F. Roberson might be as good a juror as John could get.

Clarence probed a bit deeper with another potential juror, Jim Riley. Riley, a tall man with gold-rimmed glasses who used to work in the mines, told Judge Raulston that he'd only heard rumors about the case—who hadn't?—but that he had not formed opinions about John's guilt or innocence.

"Do you know anything about evolution?" Clarence asked.

"No, not particularly," said Riley.

"Heard about it?"

"Yes, I have heard about it."

"Know what it is?"

"I don't know much about it."

Riley said he hadn't really talked to anyone about evolution and hadn't studied enough about it to have an opinion on whether it was wrong.

"Ever heard anybody preach any sermons on it?" Clarence asked.

"No, sir."

"Ever hear Mr. Bryan speak about it?"

"No, sir."

"Ever read anything he said about it?"

"No, sir," Riley responded. "I can't read."

"Well," Clarence said, "you are fortunate." He accepted Jim Riley as a juror.

Then came J.P. Massingill, a minister at not one, not two, not three, but four churches in the countryside.

"Ever preach on evolution?" Clarence asked him.

"I don't think so, definitely; that is, on evolution as a whole," Massingill responded.

That was rather a squirrelly answer. Clarence tried again: "Did you ever preach on evolution?"

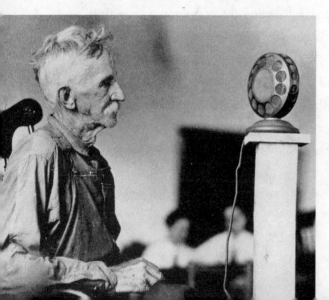

In the witness chair–and in front of a radio microphone–a man undergoes questioning to determine whether he will join the jury.

"Yes," Massingill said this time. "I haven't as a subject; just taken that up; in connection with other subjects. I have referred to it in discussing it."

"Against it or for it?" Clarence asked, as if he didn't know the answer.

"I am strictly for the Bible," Massingill said.

"I am talking about evolution," Clarence said. "I am not talking about the Bible. Did you preach for or against evolution?"

Massingill turned toward Judge Raulston. "Is that a fair question, judge?"

"Yes, answer the question."

"Well, I preached against it, of course," Massingill admitted.

Applause broke out in the courtroom.

At Clarence's request, Judge Raulston excluded Pastor Massingill from joining the jury.

And so it went. Judge Raulston chewed gum, looked at the headlines in the afternoon newspapers from Knoxville, and occasionally waved to familiar faces among the spectators. Will sat quietly, wiping his head with a handkerchief from time to time. The court didn't need anywhere near the 100 potential jurors who'd been summoned. The lawyers selected their twelve jurors, most of whom said that they read their Bible regularly and attended church regularly, all of whom swore they were not prejudiced against John Scopes. Jury selection over, the judge adjourned court for the weekend.

Nellie Kenyon's article on Saturday in the *Chattanooga News* provided mini-biographies of each of the jurors. She noted that one was a shipping clerk, one a school teacher, and the rest farmers. "There are eight republicans and four democrats," she also reported matter-of-factly.

The out-of-town press was more malicious than matter-of-fact.

A satirical cartoon by Clifford K. Berryman of the *Washington Star* shows a Dayton native bathing in the publicity of the trial, with William Jennings Bryan beaming down from the sky.

"The grade of intelligence also revealed by the attitudes . . . of the twelve indicates to this observer that at least nine of the Scopes jurors had never used a four syllable word in their lives until the term 'evolution' was crowded into the local vocabulary," sneered one correspondent whose dispatches went out to multiple newspapers. Another predicted, "Scopes is a convicted man, unless a miracle happens and the Lord

speaks in a way that the devout hill folk of Tennessee do not expect." Jury selection, he added, "was quite a study in suspenders and hickory shirts."

Some journalists wrote their accounts as if competing for a prize for the snarkiest: "There is no doubt that Scopes will be found guilty," a writer known for his wit opined, "and sentenced to read all of Bill Bryan's books. After that Darrow will protest the verdict on the grounds of cruel and unusual punishment."

No matter. These dozen jurors would not be reading sneering articles from Pittsburgh or San Francisco or Boston. Come Monday morning, they would be the lucky ones in their ringside seats, listening to the great William Jennings Bryan and the great, if infidel, Clarence Darrow.

That's what they thought, anyway.

Newspapers from coast to coast covered the trial in great detail, often on their front pages.

CHAPTER 14
TO STRANGLE PUPPIES

William Jennings Bryan may have disappointed spectators in the courtroom who had come to hear him speak on that first day. His only performance involved sweating and energetically waving his fan. His voice was not heard "beyond a cough," as one newspaperman put it. But over the weekend, Will made up for his silence. He spoke to a standing-room-only crowd at Dayton's First Methodist Church. He addressed a Sunday school class. (Judge Raulston was in attendance.) He gave a sermon on the courthouse lawn. (The judge attended that, too.) Clarence spent much of his time with the other lawyers for the defense, formulating legal strategies for the week ahead.

As for the defendant—John took some of the visiting journalists to one of his favorite swimming holes on the Tennessee River. He spent part of Sunday reading messages that were pouring in for him. "Messenger boys were kept busy delivering telegrams to the accused teacher at his home," reported the *Birmingham News*. John told the paper that many of them were supportive—an improvement over the you-should-be-burned-at-the-stake letters he'd received before the trial.

On Monday, July 13, court was delayed as Judge Raulston spent time with the press. He posed for photographs and for the movie cameras. (The newsreel film would be flown out of Dayton in time to be shown in movie theaters by the next day.) He entertained reporters with excerpts from his daily mail. "Dear Judge," he read from one letter. "What I want to know is, did Noah put on the ark flies, cockroaches, bedbugs, sheep, toads, scorpions, and rattlesnakes? If he did, he ought to have been hung as a horse thief or shot." Everyone got a laugh out of that.

After the leisurely pleasantries, court once again opened with a prayer. Everyone stood. "Oh, God, our Father, Thou Who are the creator of the heaven and the

1 2 2   ESTABLISHED MARCH 14, 1819   BIRMIN

SABBATH BRINGS MESSAGES OF PRAISE TO EVOLUTION TEACHER

—Photo by P. and A.

PROF. JOHN T. SCOPES

Sunday was a day of rest and quiet for Prof. John T. Scopes, evolution teacher of Dayton, Tenn. But messenger boys were kept busy delivering telegrams to the accused teacher at his home. Prof. Scopes says he has been given assurances of the moral support of many persons in all sections of the United States.

Alabama's *Birmingham News* front page shows John Scopes relaxing on the Sunday after the first day of his trial.

earth and the sea and all that is in them," the pastor began. It went on for a while. The reverend asked for the Almighty's blessings on the judge, the jury, the lawyers, the journalists, others inside the court, "and those on the outside to the ends of the earth." Since the court-room was overflowing, there were in fact plenty of people outside; for their benefit, WGN had installed a loudspeaker system to carry the sound of the proceedings to various gathering places in town. For those farther away—in Chicago, for example, which could be consid-ered the ends of the earth to some in Dayton—the radio announcer had pushed through the crowd to place his microphone up where the action was.

The prayer was concluding: ". . . we ask in the name of our Lord and Saviour, Jesus Christ." The pastor's "amen" echoed around the room, out in the courtyard, around the country.

Arthur Garfield Hays, distinguished Jewish lawyer for the defense whose lord and savior was not Jesus Christ, was quiet.

Court called to order, everyone blessed, microphones arranged, and—a new addition to the room—electric fans placed here and there, it was time for the jury to enter. Roll was called to make sure all twelve were there.

"What is your plea, gentlemen?" Judge Raulston asked John's legal team. Meaning: is John pleading innocent or guilty?

Neither. Not yet.

"May it please your honor," responded John Neal. "We make a motion to quash the indictment."

A *motion to quash the indictment.* To *quash* something in law is to nullify it—to make it go away. (Not the same as squashing something, but not so very different, either.) *Indictment* is the legal term for a for-mal criminal charge. So John's lawyers were asking Judge Raulston to dismiss the charges against John without going through a trial.

This was not unusual. Defense lawyers regularly ask judges to dismiss their clients' criminal cases before trial. John's lawyers had toted up more than a dozen reasons why the charges were legally insufficient and should be quashed. Now they would present their arguments in support of their motion—first John Neal, then Arthur Hays. Then the prosecutors would get to counter. And then Clarence Darrow would wrap up. The judge, spectators, people outside the courthouse, and the jury (the jury, the most important set of specta-tors), all would hear Clarence, the greatest trial lawyer in the country, cast his spell in the courtroom for the first time.

Except, no, the jury wouldn't.

"Mr. Officer," Judge Raulston said to the blue-uniformed police-man standing by his bench, "you may let the jury go."

Out they went, but not before some complaining by Clarence and his team. They wanted the jurors to hear their arguments about why the case should be dismissed. The judge, and prosecutors, wanted jurors shielded from discussions of law that might influence how they viewed the evidence they would eventually hear. "The court will be more at ease with the jury not present," said Judge Raulston.

"We will be less at ease," Clarence grumped.

Temperatures were soaring. The humidity and oppressive heat laughed at the electric fans spinning their blades uselessly. The judge removed his suit coat. The lawyers did, too, Clarence revealing blue suspenders and a shirt "with vague coloring," to quote the *New York Times*. Will Bryan sat in a collarless shirt, working his palm-leaf fan.

And there was Dudley Malone for the defense, once again but-toned up in his double-breasted brown suit, white shirt and blue knit-ted tie peering out the front. Everyone noticed.

Hours passed as John Neal, Arthur Hays, and prosecutors Ben McKenzie and Tom Stewart presented arguments.

The second-floor courtroom, filled to the brim as Tom Stewart, standing, speaks to the judge.

Finally it was the Great Defender's turn. "I will hear you, Colonel," Judge Raulston said to Clarence.

Clarence wasn't a colonel. But town leaders had given him the honorary military title when he arrived in Dayton. Will Bryan was a colonel by virtue of his noncombat service, a quarter century earlier, in the Spanish-American War, and he was frequently called "Colonel Bryan." So if the prosecutor was going to be addressed as "colonel," by golly, the defense attorney would also be called "colonel," keeping things fair and square.

"I shall always remember that this court is the first one that ever gave me a great title of 'Colonel,'" Clarence began, "and I hope it will

Clarence Darrow arguing before the judge and spectators during the trial, July 1925.

stick to me when I get back north." He knew it would not and should not, but that wasn't the point. He was just warming up his audience.

"I want you to take it back to your home with you, colonel," replied Judge Raulston.

Clarence, the not-really-a-colonel, began his assault with some plain words aimed directly at the opposing, and actual, colonel. William Jennings Bryan, he said, "is responsible for this foolish, mischievous and wicked act." Stretching out his arm as if brandishing a sword, Clarence boomed, "Here, we find today as brazen and as bold an attempt to destroy learning as was ever made in the middle ages." Eyes flashing, he added, "The only difference is we have not provided that they shall be burned at the stake, but there is time for that, Your Honor, we have to approach these things gradually."

Apart from this slash of sarcasm, Clarence mostly veered away from insults and worked his way through the reasons the judge should quash the charges against John. The Butler Act, he argued, violated the Tennessee state constitution's guarantee of religious freedom.

> That is what was foisted on the people of this state . . . that it should be a crime in the state of Tennessee to teach any theory of the origin of man, except that contained in the divine account as recorded in the Bible. But the state of Tennessee under an honest and fair interpretation of the constitution has no more right to teach the Bible as the divine book than that the Koran is one, or the book of Mormons, or the book of Confucius, or the Budda [sic], or the Essays of Emerson, or any one of the 10,000 books to which human souls have gone for consolation and aid in their troubles.

Next, Clarence argued that the law was impermissibly vague. *What did it even mean?* he asked. How was John Scopes, or anyone, to know what was allowed and what was forbidden under its ambiguous terms?

> Does this statute state what you shall teach and what you shall not? Oh, no! Oh, no! Not at all. Does it say you cannot teach the earth is round? Because Genesis says it is flat? No. Does it say you cannot teach that the earth is millions of ages old, because the account in Genesis makes it less than six thousand years old? Oh, no. It doesn't state that. If it did you could understand it.

Of course—if the Butler Act *had* said that you couldn't teach that Earth was millions of years old because it would contradict the Bible,

Clarence undoubtedly would have attacked that part of the law, too. But he was working with what he had, pulling at every loose string that he could find in the fabric of the anti-evolution law.

How else was the law impossibly vague, making it impossible to know whether a teacher's teachings violated it or not? Clarence noted that the Bible contained two different creation stories; which story of man's creation was the one a teacher must not contradict? He noted that the Bible was made up of sixty-six books; must a teacher master all of those books to make sure he didn't violate the Butler Act? That was not the way the criminal laws were supposed to work. And anyway,

> Who is the chief mogul that can tell us what the Bible means? He or they should write a book and make it plain and distinct, so we would know. Let us look at it. There are in America at least five hundred different sects or churches, all of which quarrel with each other and the importance and nonimportance of certain things or the construction of certain passages. All along the line they do not agree among themselves and cannot agree among themselves. They never have and probably never will.

With a thumb hooked under one of his suspenders, Clarence prowled the courtroom as he spoke. By turns whispering, booming, easygoing, stern, jovial, raging, he put on a show. He raised his shoulders up in a hunch, then dropped them down to shoot his big head forward. He stood, swaying gently and speaking slowly, and then he was on the move again, roaring. As he stalked and gestured, a small rip in the left elbow of his shirt grew bigger and bigger, until the sleeve was torn all the way around.

All eyes were on Clarence. Will Bryan sat, expressionless, his mouth drawn into a straight line, arms crossed for much of the time. Apart from Clarence's voice, the only other sound was the clicking of telegraph keys, as operators transmitted the scene they were witnessing to the outside world.

With those hundreds of Tennesseans watching him, Clarence was aware of his audience. Even as his arguments may have appalled these God-fearing people, he also acknowledged their beliefs. He would not tear them down.

> What is the Bible? Your Honor, I have read it myself. I might read it more or more wisely. . . . I know there are millions of people in the world who look on it as being a divine book, and I have not the slightest objection to it. I know there are millions of people in the world who derive consolation in their times of trouble and solace in times of distress from the Bible. . . . I haven't any fault to find with them at all.

But the Bible, Clarence insisted, was not meant to substitute for a book of science. Nor was the Bible at odds with acceptance of science, including the science of evolution. There were plenty of people, even right there in Tennessee, who believed in God and acknowledged evolution. And then, Clarence said, "along comes somebody who says we have got to believe it as I believe it. It is a crime to know more than I know. And they publish a law to inhibit learning."

He'd been talking for two hours. His argument was a journey. It might appear meandering—with visits to the far-flung territories of constitutional law, legislative drafting, the role of religion in modern life, the meaning of the Divine, the nature of the Bible—but Clarence had a map. Now he was going to bring it back home, back to the wickedness and foolishness that he laid on the Butler Act—and on Will, and on Fundamentalist Christians—in his opening lines. But not before he dangled a metaphor that seemed designed to make sure that everyone was still paying attention.

"To strangle puppies is good," he said, "when they grow up into mad dogs, maybe."

What?

Again, what looked like a meander was in fact full of meaning. Did Judge Raulston and the people of Tennessee think their anti-evolution law was a tame little puppy? Clarence did not; he believed it was going to lead to evil. It was going to grow into a mad dog. "I will tell you what is going to happen," Clarence said, "and I do not pretend to be a prophet, but I do not need to be a prophet to know.

> Your honor knows the fires that have been lighted in America to kindle religious bigotry and hate. . . . You know that there is no suspicion which possesses the minds of men like bigotry and ignorance and hatred.

> If today—

But for the judge, it was quitting time. "Sorry to interrupt your argument," he interrupted, "but it is adjourning time."

"If I may, I can close in five minutes," Clarence responded.

"Proceed tomorrow," the judge said.

"If today," Clarence proceeded, despite the clear command to stop. He leaned so close to the bench where Judge Raulston sat that the finger he was pointing almost touched the man's flushed face—

If today you can take a thing like evolution and make it a crime to teach it in the public school, tomorrow you can make it a crime to teach it in the private schools, and the next year you can make it a crime to teach it to the hustings or in the church. At the next session you may ban books and the newspapers. Soon you may set Catholic against Protestant and Protestant against Protestant, and try to foist your own religion upon the minds of men. If you can do one you can do the other. Ignorance and fanaticism is ever busy and needs feeding. Always it is feeding and gloating for more. Today it is the public school teachers, tomorrow the private. The next day the preachers and the lecturers, the magazines, the books, the newspapers. After a while, your honor, it is the setting of man against man and creed against creed until with flying banners and beating drums we are marching backward to the glorious ages of the sixteenth century when bigots ... burn[ed] the men who dared to bring any intelligence and enlightenment and culture to the human mind.

Now Clarence was done. His elbow was sticking out of the hole that had expanded as he prowled around his arena. It was a classic Darrow performance. He had navigated his audience down the slippery slope that led from the Butler Act, to book bans, to a society seething with bigotry and bloodshed.

"Wonderful speech," said more than one person to Clarence as he walked away from the courthouse.

There were other reactions. Reporters recorded hissing at the close of Clarence's argument. Another witnessed women emerging from the courtroom and looking at each other in horror. "The damned infidel!" exclaimed one of them. H.L. Mencken, the viperous columnist from Baltimore, wrote that Clarence's brilliance was wasted: "The net effect of Clarence Darrow's great speech yesterday seems to be precisely the same as if he had bawled it up a rainspout in the interior of Afghanistan. . . . The morons in the audience, when it was over, simply hissed it."

That night, oppressive heat gave way to a tremendous thunderstorm. Thunder crashed, lightning flashed, rain came down in buckets. The local electrical grid, not entirely reliable in the best of times, failed. Dayton went dark.

"I ain't agoin' to say just exactly that this is a judgment," said Buckshot Morgan of the blackout, "but it certainly is powerful mysterious."

Buckshot Morgan was an imaginary character invented by a nationally syndicated newspaper columnist, W.O. McGeehan. The joke spread among members of the press. Clarence's infidel speech had brought God's fury on Monkey Town.

CHAPTER 15
PRAYERS AND CHAIRS

Nine o'clock in the morning in the Rhea County Courthouse. Tuesday, day three of the trial. Stifling hot again; the previous night's storms had brought no relief.

Time for prayer.

Except: "I object to prayer," Clarence said just as the minister was about to launch into it.

Judge Raulston rejected Clarence's objection. "It has been my custom since I have been judge to have prayers in the courtroom when it was convenient," he said, "and I know of no reason why I should not follow up this custom."

Clarence pressed on. One prosecutor jumped in, then another. A defense attorney stepped up. Then another.

"Gentlemen," the judge pleaded, "do not turn this into an argument."

Too late for that. Clarence argued that the prayers would prejudice the jurors against the defense. Dudley Malone added that the types of prayers being offered were "argumentative," and they increased "the atmosphere of hostility to our point of view, which already exists in this community by widespread propaganda."

Tom Stewart retorted, "I would advise Mr. Malone that this is a God fearing country," to which Malone, a Catholic, snapped, "And it is no more God fearing country than that from which I came."

But the praying would proceed. Reverend Stribling invoked "reverence to the Great Creator of the world"—neatly making Clarence's and Malone's points about the tendencies of the prayers to undercut the defense. The reverend ended by asking for understanding and truth "in the name of our Blessed Redeemer, Jesus Christ." Arthur Hays once again remained quiet.

And that was it for the morning in court. Judge Raulston announced that, because the lights had been knocked out by the storm the night before, he'd been unable to finish writing his ruling on the defense's motion to quash. He was adjourning court until 1:00 p.m. But before he left the courtroom: "If you want to make any pictures, boys, make them now," the judge said to the photographers. "I will give you fifteen minutes." Judge Raulston was always in good humor with the press.

That good humor ended a few hours later. One o'clock came and went. Two o'clock. The judge came into the courtroom at 2:15, grim. He'd heard that his opinion on the motion to quash had been leaked to the press. No one was supposed to know how he was ruling. If, he said, any reporter published an article disclosing what was in the ruling before he, Judge Raulston, read it from the bench, "I will deal with them for contempt of court."

Again the judge left the courtroom. Three o'clock came and went. Hundreds of people remained, waiting for whatever came next. Spectators who couldn't find a seat crammed against the walls. The electric fans were even more useless than usual; the power was still out. The storm had also knocked out the town's drinking water; people refreshed themselves with soda pop, sold by boys who wriggled through the mass of humanity.

Finally, Judge Raulston returned. It was 3:45. Now he was hopping mad. But before the judge could vent, Arthur Hays broke his silence on the prayers he'd been enduring. He and the defense team had gathered a distinguished group of representatives from various religious organizations, asking the court to choose clergy who were not affiliated with Fundamentalist churches to present the devotions at the opening of court each day. As Hays stood to read the request, prosecutor Tom Stewart shot up.

"I submit, that is absolutely out of order," he said.

"Mr. Stewart–" Hays began.

Stewart cut him off.

The *Atlanta Constitution* offered a perspective on the goings-on in the courtroom.

Hays tried again.

"Will you please keep your mouth shut!" Stewart yelled.

And he wasn't even the one who came to court angry that afternoon.

Judge Raulston let Hays read the petition. Stewart objected "with all the vehemence of my nature." The judge decided that the Dayton pastors' association would choose the clergymen who would deliver the prayers for the rest of the trial. He would have no say in the matter, so no one could accuse him of influencing the jury.

Now he could get back to his own anger.

"I am now informed," Judge Raulston said unhappily, "that the newspapers in the large cities are being now sold, which undertake to state what my opinion is."

He'd been scooped!

The judge was so upset that he refused to issue his ruling. Nope. You could read about it in a big-city newspaper, but it wasn't real, because he hadn't formally ruled. He'd spent four hours writing it, he said, which "absolutely exhausted" him. He adjourned court for the day and appointed a committee of journalists to investigate who had stolen his thunder.

"Soda Pop Stands At Dayton Had Real Day," noted the drop head in this newspaper, reflecting the oppressive heat in Judge Raulston's courtroom on July 14, 1925.

The next morning, Wednesday, July 15, was as hot as the day before. Maybe even hotter. But Judge Raulston was no longer so steamed up. Attorney General Stewart, too, seemed to have cooled off, and apologized to Arthur Hays for telling him to shut his mouth. A Unitarian minister visiting from New York City to consult with the defense gave the opening prayer. It was about as un-Fundamentalist as a prayer could be: two sentences long, with no mention of the Creator. This didn't stop John Randolph Neal from renewing an objection to prayer in the courtroom and presenting his reasons in a little speech, which prompted Sue Hicks of the prosecution team to speak for the first time to reproach the defense for "this constant heckling every morning," which led the judge to muse that "any religious society that is worthy of the name should believe in God and believe in divine guidance," which induced Clarence to object.

At least nobody was shouting.

Judge Raulston asked for the findings of the investigating committee of journalists.

"It has been ascertained," began Richard Beamish, a well-known Pennsylvania journalist who headed the committee, that the reporter who sent out the bulletin divulging how the judge would rule did not obtain the information "in any improper or unethical manner."

That was . . . vague.

"I think the court is entitled to know how this information was had," Judge Raulston said.

This was delicate.

"Upon investigation," Beamish said, "we find that the information came from the court."

"Well," said the judge. The color drained from his face. He seemed dumbfounded. *He* was "the court." He'd outed himself? It wasn't some lawless reporter who broke into his office and sneaked a peek at the opinion?

No. There was no lawlessness. It happened like this: After Judge

Raulston adjourned court the day before, explaining that he'd been delayed by the power outage, John Scopes and a young reporter named William K. Hutchinson walked over to the Hotel Aqua to have lunch together. They strolled with the judge for part of the way. (No, it is not normal for a judge and a criminal defendant in his court to stroll and chat together on their way to lunch.) Gesturing toward a bundle of papers the judge was carrying, Hutchinson asked, "Is that your decision on the motion to quash?"

"No," said Judge Raulston, "that's being copied by the stenographer now."

"Will you read that decision this afternoon?" the reporter followed up.

"That is my intention."

"Then, after you adjourn until tomorrow, you'll take up the admissibility of expert testimony next?" Hutchinson asked.

"Yes," the judge responded.

And that's where he gave himself away. For if the judge had granted the defense's motion to quash the indictment, the case would be over. There would be nothing to "take up" next. The judge went on to his Tuesday lunch, completely unaware of what he had just divulged. William Hutchinson ran off to call in his scoop, arrived at by the power of inductive thinking, to his editors. Then he and John had their lunch.

Now it was Wednesday morning, and the mystery was solved. Judge Raulston recovered his composure. He was ready to issue the opinion whose conclusion was already known to the world, or at least to the newspaper-reading world. But first . . .

"If you gentlemen want to take my picture, take it now," he told the news photographers. Clearly he held no grudge against the press. Clearly he was—still—in no hurry to move things along. For five minutes, the judge posed as if reading the nineteen-page typed document on which he'd expended so much effort. And then he read it aloud, for real. Finally.

The Butler Act, Judge Raulston said, was a perfectly valid piece of legislation. It didn't violate a teacher's freedom of religion or speech or thought under the Tennessee Constitution. It didn't violate anyone's rights under the U.S. Constitution. If a teacher didn't want to abide by the Butler Act, "and if his conscience constrains him to teach the evolution theory," he could find other employment. So much for Clarence's warning about the slippery slope to chaos. The real trial could begin.

After a lunch break, that is.

"This has required quite a bit of energy, as you must know," said Judge Raulston, "for the court to read the opinion that has just been delivered in the atmosphere by which he was surrounded."

In the afternoon, the jury was finally brought in. The courtroom was so crowded that some of the newspaper reporters couldn't find seats. "Can we have chairs, judge?" one called out.

Prosecutor Ben McKenzie had a similar problem. "I wish at this time to ask the court to make the announcement to the people, and ask them that they not carry off the chairs of the attorneys," he said. "We are a necessary evil in the courtroom."

The official record of the trial reported the outcome: "The policeman announced that no chairs should be carried off from the attorneys, from either the state or the defense or the press."

Then another voice piped up. "I would like to make the request, the unanimous request of the jury," the jury foreman said, "to take up the matter of some electric fans here. This heat is fearful. While I think I could stand my part of it—"

The judge said he didn't have the authority to get more fans. Ben

McKenzie said that he didn't think Rhea County had the funds to install additional fans. Dudley Malone said he would buy some. The judge then said he would share his fan with the jury.

And at last: "What is your plea, gentlemen?" Judge Raulston asked. Guilty or not guilty?

CHAPTER 16
FOUR WITNESSES AND A TEXTBOOK

John Randolph Neal answered for John: "Not guilty, may it please your honor."

Now was the time for the two sides to make their opening statements. Attorney General Stewart's was all of two sentences: basically, he said, John taught evolution in a public school, which necessarily denied the biblical story of creation, and that was what they would prove, and that was against the law, the end.

Dudley Malone's opening statement was longer. He was setting the stage for the strategy the defense team had formulated: first, to educate the court—and, while they were at it, the larger world—on the meaning of evolution. "The prosecution has twice since the beginning of the trial referred to man as descended from monkeys," he said. "This may be the understanding of the theory of evolution of the prosecution"—a dig at their faulty scientific understanding. "No scientist of any preeminent standing today holds such a view."

The second prong in the defense's strategy was to show that

teaching evolution was not the same as denying the biblical story of creation. If, for example, you believed that a single "day" in the Genesis story meant something other than a twenty-four-hour day, you could reconcile an Earth on which life had been evolving for millions of years with the "days" of creation in the Bible.

"There might be a conflict," Malone admitted, "between evolution and the peculiar ideas of Christianity which are held by Mr. Bryan as the evangelical leader of the prosecution." But Will Bryan, Malone said, was not "an authorized spokesman for the Christians of the United States."

Malone hammered away at Will for a while, until Tom Stewart objected.

Judge Raulston agreed.

"I do not think Mr. Bryan's personal views are involved in this case," he said.

That was probably news to the people in the courtroom. It was likely news to anyone who knew anything about the case. It may even have been news to Will Bryan, who had promised a "duel to the death," and whose personal views were stamped all over the case. He spoke for the first time.

"I ask no protection from the court," Will said.

Loud applause broke out around the courtroom. Spectators stamped their feet, whistled, and cheered. The judge warned them he'd have to throw them out if they didn't settle down: "I cannot tolerate any expression of feeling on the issues in this case at all in the presence of the jury."

Malone finished up his statement, and the prosecution put on its first witness.

"Just state in your own words, Howard," said Tom Stewart, "what he taught you and when it was."

Howard Morgan, a student of John Scopes, testifying on Wednesday, July 15, 1925.

Howard Morgan, fourteen years old, had been a student of "Professor Scopes," as Stewart anointed John, in a freshman General Science class.

"It was along about the second of April," Howard began.

"Of this year," prompted Stewart.

"Yes, sir; of this year." Howard sounded nervous. In his white shirt, with top buttons opened, and white duck pants, he'd dressed as well as he could for the heat. But being in the hot seat—the witness stand was an oversized high-backed chair with a hard bench upon a square pedestal opposite the judge's seat—was intimidating. Wide-eyed, he carried on.

"He said that the earth was once a hot molten mass, too hot for plant or animal life to exist upon it; in the sea the earth cooled off; there was a little germ of one cell organism formed, and this organism kept evolving until it got to be a pretty good-sized animal, and then came on to be a land animal, and it kept on evolving, and from this was man."

"Go to the head of the class," interjected Arthur Hays.

"That is the theory that he taught you," Stewart prompted the teenager, "about a man being a little germ and sprouting in the sea, and so forth, and finally culminating and coming out on dry land."

Not really, but it was the sort of silly summary that could appeal to a roomful of anti-evolutionists.

Stewart moved on. "I ask you further, Howard," he said, "how did he classify man with reference to other animals; what did he say about them?"

"Well," said Howard, "the book and he both classified man along with cats and dogs, cows, horses, monkeys, lions, horses and all that."

"What did he say they were?"

"Mammals."

"Classified them along with dogs, cats, horses, monkeys and cows?"

"Yes, sir."

And so the prosecutor underscored John Scopes's offense: lumping man with other animals.

When Clarence's turn to cross-examine Howard came, he decided to have a little fun.

"He didn't say a cat was the same as a man?" Clarence asked the boy.

"No, sir; he said man had a reasoning power; that these animals did not."

Man's Place in Nature. — Although we know that man is separated mentally by a wide gap from all other animals, in our study of physiology we must ask where we are to place man. If we attempt to classify man, we see at once he must be placed with the vertebrate animals because of his possession of a vertebral column. Evidently, too, he is a mammal, because the young are nourished by milk secreted by the mother and because his body has at least a partial covering of hair. Anatomically we find that we must place man with the apelike mammals, because of these numerous points of structural likeness. The group of mammals which includes the monkeys, apes, and man we call the *primates*.

Although anatomically there is a greater difference between the lowest type of monkey and the highest type of ape than there is between the highest type of ape and the lowest savage, yet there is an immense mental gap between monkey and man.

Instincts. — Mammals are considered the highest of vertebrate animals, not only because of their complicated structure, but because their instincts are so well developed. Monkeys certainly seem to have many of the mental attributes of man.

Professor Thorndike of Columbia University sums up their habits of learning as follows : —

" In their method of learning, although monkeys do not reach the human stage of a rich life of ideas, yet they carry the animal method of learning, by the selection of impulses and association of them with different sense-impressions, to a point beyond that reached by any other of the lower animals. In this, too, they resemble man ; for he differs from the lower animals not only in the possession of a new sort of intelligence, but also in the tremendous extension of that sort which he has in common with them. A fish learns slowly a few simple habits. Man learns quickly an infinitude of habits that may be highly complex. Dogs and cats learn more than the fish, while monkeys learn more than they. In the number of things he learns, the complex habits he can form, the variety of lines along which he can learn them, and in their permanence when once formed, the monkey justifies his inclusion with man in a separate mental genus."

Evolution of Man. — Undoubtedly there once lived upon the earth races of men who were much lower in their mental organization than the present inhabitants. If we follow the early history

A Civic Biology (correctly) classified human beings as mammals, as Howard Morgan recalled in his cross-examination by Clarence Darrow.

"There is some doubt about that," Clarence countered wryly.

That drew a laugh from the audience.

Clarence asked Howard whether he remembered what made a mammal a mammal, but Howard didn't remember. No matter.

"But he said that all of them were mammals?" Clarence asked.

"All what?"

"Dogs and horses, monkeys, cows, man, whales, I cannot state all of them, but he said all of those were mammals?" Clarence repeated.

"Yes, sir," Howard started, "but I don't know about the whales; he said all these other ones."

More laughter.

"Well, did he tell you anything else that was wicked?"

Now everyone chuckled. The judge and prosecutors—even Will Bryan's face relaxed. After all, everyone who knew John Scopes knew that "wicked" was not a word that fit.

Howard shot his teacher a look and smiled.

"No," he replied, "not that I remember of."

"Now, that is about what he taught you?" Clarence said. "It has not hurt you any, has it?"

That got the room laughing again.

"No, sir."

"That's all."

The other student Stewart called to the witness stand was seventeen-year-old Harry Shelton. Harry—"Bud" to his friends—confirmed that John used George William Hunter's A *Civic Biology* textbook in his class. On cross-examination, he told Clarence that the only thing he remembered learning about evolution and biology was that all forms of life originated from a single cell.

"Did anybody ever tell you before?" Clarence asked.

"No, sir."

"That is all you remember that he told you about biology, wasn't it?"

"Yes, sir."

"Are you a church member?" Clarence asked.

"Sir?" The question seemed to surprise Bud.

"Are you a church member?"

"Yes, sir," Bud replied.

"Do you still belong?"

"Yes, sir."

"You didn't leave church when he told you all forms of life began with a single cell?"

That was the point. A student could learn about evolution—not that Bud Shelton seemed to have learned much about evolution—and still be an upstanding, churchgoing boy.

"No, sir," Bud said. He had not abandoned Christianity.

"That is all," Clarence said.

Hearing Howard's and Bud's testimonies, John thought, "If the boys had got their review of evolution from me, I was unaware of it. I didn't remember teaching it." Indeed, from his very first sit-down with town leaders at Robinson's Drug Store, John had waffled on this question. He waffled even as he confirmed that he used Hunter's *A Civic Biology* in class. But his shaky memory of whether he actually *taught* evolution hadn't stopped John from volunteering to be prosecuted. It hadn't stopped the drugstore clique from pressing him into service as part of their scheme to draw the world's attention to Dayton. And now, neither John nor his lawyers disputed the boys' claims that Professor Scopes had, in fact, taught the offending science. Clarence knew that a challenge to the Butler Act required John to say, or at least not to contradict, that he had taught evolution. After all, if John had not, there would be no reason to prosecute him, and without a prosecution, no one would be in Judge Raulston's court. The trial was something bigger than John and, as he later wrote, "That was all right with me." He opposed the Butler Act and was willing to be the face of the challenge.

The two adults called as witnesses by the prosecution were members of the drugstore group: Walter White, superintendent of schools, and Frank Robinson, school board member and drugstore owner. They both testified that, at the drugstore meeting where it all began, John admitted teaching evolution from Hunter's *A Civic Biology*. Attorney General Stewart submitted the book into evidence as Exhibit 1 in the case, marking in particular six pages.

There were pages 194 and 195. Page 194 had a section captioned, "The Doctrine of Evolution." Cross-examining Doc Robinson, Clarence read aloud from that page.

> Geology teaches that millions of years ago, life upon the earth was very simple, and that gradually more and more complex forms of life appeared, as the rocks formed latest in time show the most highly developed forms of animal life. The great English scientist, Charles Darwin, from this and other evidence, explained the theory of evolution. This is the belief that simple forms of life on earth slowly and gradually gave rise to those more complex and that thus ultimately the most complex forms came into existence.

Yes, Doc Robinson confirmed, that was what John said he'd taught in his biology class.

What else was in the offending pages that the attorney general had marked when he placed *A Civic Biology* in evidence to prove John's guilt? Page 195 asserted, "Although we know that man is separated mentally by a wide gap from all other animals," man also belonged to the group of mammals called primates—along with monkeys and apes. This was offensive, grouping man with monkeys. Attorney General Stewart also marked pages 252 and 253. Page 252 had a diagram of cell reproduction as part of an explanation of heredity; page 253 reintroduced the "great Englishman Charles Darwin" as one of the first scientists to realize that "this great force of heredity applied to the development or evolution of plants and animals." As the textbook explained it,

> In nature, the variations which best fitted a plant or animal
> for life in its own environment were the ones which were
> handed down because those having variations which were
> not fitted for life in that particular environment would die.

Not a terrible summary of Darwin's natural selection.

The last two pages the prosecution marked were 254 and 255, which focused on how plant cultivators could create new variations of crops—examples of artificial, as opposed to natural, selection. A photograph of four cobs of corn illustrated the improvements that might result.

The prosecution rested its case. Four witnesses and a textbook. Now it was the defense's turn.

Now the jury could hear John tell his story.

CHAPTER 17
SPEECHLESS

John's legal team had no intention of letting him tell his story.

Judge Raulston asked whether the defendant would be taking the witness stand to testify in his own defense.

"Your honor," Clarence said, "every single word that was said against this defendant, everything was true."

"So he does not care to go on the stand?" the judge asked.

"No," said John's defender. "What is the use?"

The defense lawyers did have a story they wanted to tell. It just wasn't John's story.

Clarence and his co-counsel had tapped twelve distinguished experts, all accomplished in their fields, to take the witness stand and tell this story. Among them was the rector of an Episcopal church in Knoxville who would testify that biblical stories were meant as allegories. A Methodist pastor from Chattanooga would point out that the Genesis story was silent on the process of the creation of human beings—yes, God created man, but the Bible didn't say *how*. Another expert witness was the dean of the divinity school at the University of Chicago, who would say that the two creation stories in Genesis were religious interpretations by ancient writers who used their best knowledge of the universe at the time.

Then there was a Jewish scholar who would remind everyone that because the Bible was originally written in ancient Hebrew, the English Bible was, by definition, an interpretation. Every translation is an interpretation. The King James Bible so popular among Protestant churches—and from which Judge Raulston read at the beginning of the trial—was riddled with translation errors, as well as interpretations, in the story of Genesis and elsewhere. Biblical literalists, then,

Clarence Darrow's telegram to twelve experts he asked to travel to Dayton, Tennessee, to testify at John's trial.

were choosing to take as fact an English interpretation of a text that was written in an ancient language full of ambiguities and unfathomable phrases.

There were zoologists, an anthropologist, a soil scientist. A psychologist. There was the state geologist of Tennessee!

One person there wasn't? The defendant.

"So I sat speechless," John later wrote in his memoir of the trial, "a ringside observer at my own trial, until the end of the circus."

Speechless, but not surprised. This defense strategy had been an open secret even before the trial started. Everyone knew that Clarence Darrow wanted to put creationism and biblical literalism on trial. Everyone understood that the ACLU wanted to advance freedom of thought, speech, and teaching. And frankly, the organization wouldn't cry too hard over a guilty verdict, because that would allow the ACLU to appeal the judgment to a higher court, even to the Supreme Court of the United States. A Supreme Court decision in their favor would create a rule of law that applied across the nation. A verdict out of a county courthouse in Tennessee wouldn't have nearly the same legal impact. And if John were found not guilty—that would get him off the hook, but it wouldn't get the ACLU the far-reaching ruling they wanted. Well before the trial started, observers mused that John was a scapegoat for a larger cause—"a sort of Scopes-goat," as one newspaper correspondent wrote.

After all the planning and strategizing, now at last the defense called its first witness to the stand: Maynard M. Metcalf, a scientist with expertise in biology in general, and zoology in particular. He was a professor at Johns Hopkins University in Baltimore, and had served on a federal government research committee. He was also, as Clarence made sure to bring out in his introductory comments, an active church member.

"Will you state what evolution is," Clarence asked, "in regard to the origin of man?"

Immediately Attorney General Stewart stood to object. "We except to that," he said. "We are excepting, your honor, to everything here that pertains to evolution or to anything that tends to show that there might or might not be a conflict between the story of the divine creation and evolution."

This was the prosecution's position: the jury didn't need to be schooled in either evolution or religion. There need not and should not be any expert discussion of whether a person could believe in the Bible and believe in evolution. As far as the Butler Act was concerned, teaching evolution was the crime. Whether the teaching did or did not also deny the story of creation was irrelevant.

After some back-and-forth, Judge Raulston decided that he would hear Dr. Metcalf's testimony, but the jury would not, at least not yet. He sent them out to the courtyard—warning them not to listen to the loudspeakers so they would not be tainted by evidence that he might ultimately decide was not valid. And so, out marched the twelve jurors—again. So much for their front-row seats to the show.

When they were gone, Clarence asked Dr. Metcalf once again: what is evolution?

The professor tutored the judge as best he could. It was late—going on 5:00 p.m.—and the courtroom was hot as ever. Evolution meant change, he said. When scientists spoke of the evolution of a plant or animal, they meant "the whole series of such changes which have taken place during hundreds of millions of years" from the organism's "lowly beginnings" to something "much more complex."

Judge Raulston leaned forward in his chair, interested. Dr. Metcalf was humble about the state of scientific knowledge; there was so much that scientists didn't know about how evolution worked. "There are dozens of theories of evolution, some of which are almost wholly absurd, some of which are surely largely mistaken," he conceded, "some of which are perhaps almost wholly true." But: "We are in possession of scientific knowledge to answer directly and fully the question: 'Has evolution occurred.'" The answer was absolutely yes.

How far back could scientists trace the existence of life on Earth? Clarence asked.

"Oh, that is an awfully hard question to answer in years," Dr. Metcalf replied. "No geologist talks years—it is ages."

"More than 6,000 years ago, wasn't it?" Clarence asked. He did not pull that number out of the air. Biblical literalists often insisted that God's creation occurred 6,000 years ago. Clarence's point was that fossil evidence proved such calculations to be fanciful.

"Well, 600,000,000 years ago is a very modest guess," Dr. Metcalf said.

Laughter erupted in the courtroom. Impossible! Six hundred million! People whispered in amazement and revulsion. "He is about as authoritative as an evening breeze," one skeptic said.

Interested as he may have been, Judge Raulston was also tired. "Colonel Darrow, will this extend very much further?" he asked. "It has been a pretty hard day for me."

This time Clarence didn't press on, and the judge adjourned court until the next morning.

As the lawyers were getting ready to go, Will walked over to Clarence, smiling. "A friend of mine sent me this and asked me to give it to you," he said. "It's carved from a peach pit, and it's so pretty I'd like you to keep it."

It was—what else?—a tiny monkey.

A friendly moment between antagonists Clarence Darrow, left, and William Jennings Bryan, inside the courtroom during a break in the trial, July 1925.

CHAPTER 18
THE GREATEST SPEECH

On the fifth day of creation, the Bible says God caused the waters of the earth to teem with living creatures. On the fifth day of John Scopes's trial—Thursday, July 16—the courtroom of Judge John T. Raulston teemed with living creatures, too. So many living creatures were teeming in his second-floor courtroom that the judge feared the floor might collapse. Do not make any "manifestations," he begged the spectators—no clapping or foot stomping. "I do not want to alarm you," he said. "I do not know myself, for I am not a mechanic, but I do know that the floor is heavily weighted and the least vibration might cause something to happen, and applause might start trouble."

The platform in front of the judge's bench also teemed with a particular species of living creatures on that fifth day: lawyers. They'd been sitting at their lawyers' tables all week, of course. Today, though, fully seven of them would enter the arena and make speeches. William Jennings Bryan Jr. for the prosecution. Arthur Garfield Hays for the defense. Sue Hicks for the prosecution. Ben McKenzie for the prosecution. William Jennings Bryan—the original—for the prosecution. Dudley Field Malone for the defense. And Tom Stewart for the prosecution.

It would be an oratorical extravaganza. The professed purpose was to argue the relevance, or irrelevance, of the defense's scientific and theological expert witnesses. In other words, should the judge let the jury hear the experts on evolution or not? As far as the court case was concerned, this was a technical legal issue. But with the whole country—except for the jury—listening, it was poised to be a whole lot more. "Actually," one reporter wrote, "the speeches were addressed to a jury constituting all the intelligence of the world."

The great attraction was Will Bryan, of course. When word got out that he would be breaking his silence on this day—finally!—the locals flocked to the courthouse. But as they mobbed the doorway, police were there to enforce Judge Raulston's new rule: there would be no more spectators than there were seats. And the seats were quickly taken. One reporter, determined to keep his place in the courtroom, brought a heavy chain and padlock to secure his chair. Disappointed spectators retreated to the courthouse square, where they could listen to the loudspeakers.

They didn't miss much at first.

There was the prayer, naturally. Short and sweet, but definitely with a point of view: "We pray Thy blessings upon the deliberations of this court, to the end that Thy Word may be vindicated."

There was William Jennings Bryan Jr. "He has none of the fire of his father," decided one reporter, a judgment shared by others. Arthur Hays and Sue Hicks followed. Not much of a show, either of them. Before the lunch break, prosecutor Ben McKenzie provided some entertainment.

"I want to say this," he started, "since the beginning of this lawsuit, and since I began to meet these distinguished gentlemen, I have begun to love them—everyone—and it is a very easy task, in fact, it was a case, when I met Colonel Darrow—a case of love at first sight. These other gentlemen come right on, but you know they wiggled around so rapidly that I could not get my lover turned loose on them until I got a chance, but I love the great men."

Unusual. But not one-sided. As Clarence later wrote, he found Ben McKenzie "most agreeable and even lovable," and they formed a strong bond. "After all," he added, "men in all lands and at all times have been found human and loving outside their religious attitudes."

When he was done showering his opponents with love, McKenzie showered the idea of evolution with ridicule. Evolutionists, he said, "want to put words into God's mouth, and have Him to say that He issued some sort of protoplasm, or soft dish rag, and put it in the ocean and said, 'Old boy, if you wait around about 6,000 years, I will make something out of you.'"

That got a good laugh from the audience.

Over the lunch adjournment, the sheriff installed ceiling fans in the courtroom. The room was still a steam bath. A very full steam bath. Half an hour before court was called back in session, crowds pressed into the room. Once again, the aisles were full. The judge's admonition against standing-room-only spectators was largely ignored. The Great Commoner was up next; to heck with the rules.

Looking at the multitudes in front of him, the judge again worried aloud. "I do not know how well it is supported, but sometimes buildings and floors give away when they are unduly burdened," he said, "so I suggest to you to be as quiet in the courtroom as you can; have no more emotion than you can avoid; especially have no applause, because it isn't proper in the courtroom."

Hundreds of people hushed themselves.

"Well," Judge Raulston said, "I believe Mr. Bryan then will speak next for the state."

Will took a long drink from the three-gallon jug of water on the table in front of him. He stood, his jaw set. He wore no jacket, submitting to the heat, but a collar was affixed to his shirt and he wore his usual black tie. In his left hand he held the palm-leaf fan.

He began quietly, calmly. The Butler Act was perfectly clear in outlawing the teaching of evolution. The state of Tennessee was within its rights to tell its teachers, paid for with taxes raised by its citizens, what they could teach. The people of Tennessee did not want their children learning about evolution. Experts should not now be permitted to undo the law because they thought it was a bad law.

Perspiration glistened on Will's head. So far he'd presented a fairly lawyerly and logical argument. Now he picked up the high school textbook—the "outlawed" book, he called it—Hunter's *A Civic Biology*. And he shifted gears, to tear apart evolution, which, he said, "commences with nothing and ends nowhere." In particular, Will was going to tear apart page 194 of the book that John had used in class.

"The Christian believes man came from above," he began, "but the evolutionist believes he must have come from below."

An appreciative chuckle bubbled up in the audience.

"On page 194, we have a diagram," Will continued. "We are told just how many animal species there are, 518,900."

Will pointed out that the diagram classified animals by different groups, from protozoa to mammals, with each group in the chart represented by a circle. The insect circle was the largest because, the text said, insects accounted for the largest number of species—360,000. The mammal circle was small, with 3,500 species, but not the smallest.

The Doctrine of Evolution. — We have now learned that animal forms may be arranged so as to begin with very simple one-celled forms and culminate with a group which contains man himself. This arrangement is called the *evolutionary series*. Evolution means

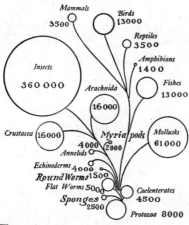

change, and these groups are believed by scientists to represent stages in complexity of development of life on the earth. Geology teaches that millions of years ago, life upon the earth was very simple, and that gradually more and more complex forms of life appeared, as the rocks formed latest in time show the most highly developed forms of animal life. The great English scientist, Charles Darwin, from this and other evidence, explained the theory of evolution. This is the

The evolutionary tree. Modified from Galloway. Copy this diagram in your notebook. Explain it as well as you can.

belief that simple forms of life on the earth slowly and gradually gave rise to those more complex and that thus ultimately the most complex forms came into existence.

The Number of Animal Species. — Over 500,000 species of animals are known to exist to-day, as the following table shows.

Protozoa	8,000	Arachnids	16,000
Sponges	2,500	Crustaceans	16,000
Cœlenterates	4,500	Mollusks	61,000
Echinoderms	4,000	Fishes	13,000
Flatworms	5,000	Amphibians	1,400
Roundworms	1,500	Reptiles	3,500
Annelids	4,000	Birds	13,000
Insects	360,000	Mammals	3,500
Myriapods	2,000	Total	518,900

The smallest circle was amphibians, to which was attributed 1,400 species.

"I see they are round numbers," Will said, "and I don't think all of these animals breed in round numbers, and so I think it must be a generalization of them."

Laughter in the courtroom, the trial transcript reads.

"Let us have order," the judge warned.

"Eight thousand protozoa, 3,500 sponges," Will read. "I am satisfied from some I have seen there must be more than 35,000 sponges."

More laughs.

"And then we run down to the insects, 360,000 insects. Two-thirds of all the species of all the animal world are insects. And sometimes, in the summer time we feel that we become intimately acquainted with them.... Now, we are getting up near our kinfolks, 13,000 fishes. Then there are the amphibia. I don't know whether they have not yet decided to come out, or have almost decided to go back."

Will continued to get laughs.

"And then we have the reptiles, 3,500; and then we have 13,000 birds. Strange that this should be exactly the same as the number of fishes, round numbers. And then we have mammals, 3,500," Will said, "and there is a little circle and man is in the circle, find him, find man."

The diagram did not actually place man in the "little circle" labeled "mammals." But it was true that on the next page the textbook confirmed that man is, indeed, a mammal.

And this was what got Will worked up.

"There is that book!" he cried. "There is the book they were teaching your children that man was a mammal and so indistinguishable among the mammals that they leave him there with thirty-four hundred and ninety-nine other mammals."

William Jennings Bryan making his big argument against evolution in court.

Now the audience was applauding, as well as laughing.

"Including elephants?" he added. Excellent comic timing.

"Talk about putting Daniel in the lion's den?" Will raised his arms in mock terror. "How dared those scientists put man in a little ring like that with lions and tigers and everything that is bad! Not only the evolution is possible, but the scientists possibly think of shutting man up in a little circle like that with all these animals, that have an odor, that extends beyond the circumference of this circle, my friends."

Extended laughter, reads the trial transcript. Evolutionists put man in the same little circle as stinky beasts!

"Tell me that the parents of this day have not any right to declare that children are not to be taught this doctrine?" Will declaimed. "Shall not be taken down from the high plane upon which God put man? Shall be detached from the throne of God and be compelled to link their ancestors with the jungle, tell that to these children? Why, my friends, if they believe it, they go back to scoff at the religion of their parents!"

Sweat dripped down Will's forehead. Next he held up Darwin's *The Descent of Man*. Darwinism proposed a "family tree," Will asserted (falsely), in which man descended from monkeys of the Old World. "Not even from American monkeys," he jokingly complained, "but from old world monkeys." The audience dutifully laughed. Perhaps they'd heard or read this joke before; it was one of Will's staples.

"Now, here we have our glorious pedigree," Will said, "and each child is expected to copy the family tree and take it home to his family to be submitted for the Bible family tree—that is what Darwin says."

Well, no. That was not what Darwin said.

There is no doubt that Will spoke from the heart:

> Because this principle of evolution disputes the miracle; there is no place for the miracle in this train of evolution, and the Old Testament and the New are filled with miracles, and if this doctrine is true, this logic eliminates every mystery in the Old Testament and the New, and eliminates everything supernatural.

He spoke like a man who truly believed that evolution was a dangerous idea:

> They do not explain the great riddle of the universe—they

do not deal with the problems of life—they do not teach the great science of how to live—and yet they would undermine the faith of these little children in that God who stands back of everything and whose promise we have that we shall live with Him forever bye and bye.

But he also spoke like a man who understood very little about evolution:

They say that evolution is a fact when they cannot prove that one species came from another, and if there is such a thing, all species must have come, commencing as they say, commencing in that one lonely cell down there in the bottom of the ocean that just evolved and evolved until it got to be a man.

If Will wanted to find ideas in Hunter's *A Civic Biology* that were truly dangerous and deserving of ridicule and scorn, he could have turned a few pages. He could have mentioned page 196, for example:

The Races of Man.—At the present time there exist upon the earth five races or varieties of man, each very different from the other in instincts, social customs, and, to an extent, in structure. These are the Ethiopian or negro type, originating in Africa; the Malay or brown race, from the islands of the Pacific; the American Indian; the Mongolian or yellow race, including the natives of China, Japan, and the Eskimos; and finally, the highest type of all, the Caucasians, represented by the civilized white inhabitants of Europe and America.

But this did not attract Will's attention. This didn't cause him to raise an eyebrow—maybe because this paragraph wasn't much different from the proud statement in his memoir about being a member of the Caucasian Race, which he dubbed "the greatest."

Or, if he was in search of an idea over which to express outrage, Will might have read a little further on in *A Civic Biology*, to the author's discussion of eugenics. Hunter cited studies (later discredited) that allegedly demonstrated that generations of "feeble-minded, alcoholic, immoral, or criminal persons" were descended from couples in which one or both of the original parents had "mental and moral defects."

The discussion continued:

> **Parasitism and its Cost to Society.**—Hundreds of families such as those described above exist to-day, spreading disease, immorality, and crime to all parts of this country. The cost to society of such families is very severe. Just as certain animals or plants become parasitic on other plants or animals, these families have become parasitic on society. They not only do harm to others by corrupting, stealing, or spreading disease, but they are actually protected and cared for by the state out of public money. Largely for them the poorhouse and the asylum exist. They take from society, but they give nothing in return. They are true parasites.

> **The Remedy.**—If such people were lower animals, we would probably kill them off to prevent them from spreading. Humanity will not allow this, but we do have the remedy of separating the sexes in asylums or other places and in various ways preventing intermarriage and the possibilities

of perpetuating such a low and degenerate race. Remedies
of this sort have been tried successfully in Europe and are
now meeting with success in this country.

But none of this rot—which was presented to teen readers as science—made its way into Will's screed against *A Civic Biology*. He was
agitated that children were learning that human beings are mammals.
But where was his outrage at the assertions, right there in the book
he was waving about, that "low and degenerate" people, that human
"parasites," should be snuffed out of the population? It was the hey-
day of eugenics in America—even the defense's expert, Dr. Metcalf,
supported it—and the Great Commoner failed to take a stand in court
against this pseudo-science when it was practically staring him in the
face. Instead, he took his stand against actual science.

After more than an hour, Will concluded his argument. Face
flushed, wiping his brow, he sat down to loud, approving applause.
The judge did not say a word about the possibility of the floor falling in.

When spectators heard that Dudley Malone, not Clarence Darrow, would be presenting the defense's final argument of the day, they
quietly grumbled in disappointment. No head-to-head between their
hero and the infidel?

Their disappointment did not last long.

Malone had endured five days in the roasting courtroom without
once removing his suit jacket. Everyone had noticed. Now, finally, he
took it off—and it was as if he'd called the room to attention. Everyone noticed. He methodically folded the coat and laid it on the table
where the defense lawyers sat.

"Whether Mr. Bryan knows it or not," he began, "he is a mammal,
he is an animal and he is a man."

But Malone wasn't there to ridicule Will. Will was "my old chief and friend," he explained. During Will's tenure as U.S. secretary of state a decade earlier, Malone had been undersecretary of state, reporting to him. So Malone was speaking from a personal place as he expressed disappointment toward his onetime boss.

Malone was disappointed that Will criticized religious beliefs because they did not completely align with his own.

Malone was disappointed that Will's arguments aimed barbs at teachers. "God knows," he boomed, "the poorest paid profession in America is the teaching profession, who devote themselves to science, forego the gifts of God, consecrate their brains to study, and eke out their lives as pioneers in the fields of duty, finally hoping that mankind will profit by his efforts, and to open the doors of truth."

And Malone was disappointed that Will spread misinformation—especially by focusing on what Darwin didn't know, and by refusing to acknowledge discoveries in biology, anthropology, and archaeology that were advancing the science of evolution. "Haven't we learned anything in seventy-five years? Are we to have our children know nothing about science except what the church says they shall know?"

With his roaring voice, his embrace of religious faith, his concise delivery, Malone had his listeners spellbound. Clarence got up from the counsel table and stood against the rail that separated it from the speaker's platform, nodding vigorously as his co-counsel nailed point after point.

"We say 'keep your Bible,'" Malone urged. "Keep it as your consolation, keep it as your guide, but keep it where it belongs, in the world of your own conscience"—not as a substitute for science class.

"I feel that the prosecution here is filled with a needless fear," Malone continued. If they would hear the defense experts, Malone said, they would see that scientists and teachers were not conspiring "to destroy the morals of the children." Preachers, he reminded his listeners, were not the only people who cared about young people. Churches were not the only sources of morality.

"And I would like to say something for the children of the country," Malone bellowed.

> We have no fears about the young people of America. They are a pretty smart generation. . . . I feel that the children of this generation are probably much wiser than many of their elders. . . . We have just had a war with twenty-million dead. Civilization is not so proud of the work of the adults. Civilization need not be so proud of what the grown ups have done. For God's sake let the children have their minds kept open—close no doors to their knowledge; shut no door from them.

When he finished, one observer wrote, "There was the fraction of a second of silence of the same sort that is felt at the Metropolitan Operahouse after the tenor has reached the high note." And then pandemonium broke out. The audience shrieked and cheered in admiration. Applause vibrated in the courtroom's still, stale air. Spectators—including Fundamentalists, including Will Bryan's fans—crowded into the aisles and climbed over the rail to try to reach the lawyer from New York to congratulate him. Malone had talked for twenty minutes. The demonstration went on for nearly as long—echoes of that evening in the Chicago Coliseum so many years ago when Will finished his "Cross of Gold" speech.

Once again, the jury had missed the show, having been excluded by the judge.

Finally, Judge Raulston gaveled down the hubbub. The judge,

who'd paid close attention all afternoon, was still trying to work things out in his mind. Under the defense's theory, he asked Clarence, might God have created man by a process of growth? Yes, Clarence responded. Or by development? Yes, Clarence said. So the defense was saying that God did not manufacture him like a carpenter would a table?

Yes, Clarence said. "That is what we claim." And, he added, that was consistent with the Bible story.

Attorney General Stewart gave the final argument of the day. He drew some applause from the audience. But as the afternoon came to a close, the air was still electric with the charge of Dudley Malone's speech. After the crowds cleared out, only Malone, John, and Will remained.

"Dudley," Will said to his former deputy, "that was the greatest speech I have ever heard."

"Thank you, Mr. Bryan," Malone said to his former boss. "I am sorry it was I who had to make it."

John Scopes standing between "greatest speech" maker Dudley Field Malone, left, and Clarence Darrow, right, July 1925.

CHAPTER 19
SOMETHING BRAND NEW

The next day's newspapers carried reports of the showdown between William Jennings Bryan and Dudley Field Malone. Even fans of the Great Commoner, reporters observed, were admiringly calling Malone "a northern Patrick Henry." They could not have known how close to the bone that comparison cut. Back when Will was a teenager at the Whipple Academy, his very first attempt at oration had been about Patrick Henry's famous "Give Me Liberty or Give Me Death" speech. It did not win him the declamation contest. Now, fifty years later, he again appeared not to have won the declamation contest.

It didn't matter. Dayton, and indeed the newspaper-reading, radio-listening country, may have been abuzz with Dudley Malone's stellar oration. But had it convinced Judge Raulston? He would have final say on whether the jury could hear from the defense experts on the meaning of evolution.

First, as always, was the prayer to open court. Thursday's had been brief. Not so Friday, July 17. In Jesus's name, the pastor thanked God for "the glorious land" and "civilization" of America. He prayed for Judge Raulston, the lawyers, and the press. He prayed for the jury, which had been excluded from Thursday's show. And from half of Wednesday's. And all of Tuesday's. And all of Monday's. And on this Friday morning, the jurors were in the pastor's prayers but still not in the courtroom.

After the prayer, Judge Raulston delivered his ruling: testimony from the defense's expert witnesses would not be allowed. The Butler Act, he said, only required the prosecutor to prove that John taught "the theory that man descended from a lower order of animals." The law did not depend on whether this theory denied the Bible's story of divine creation. And so, the judge concluded, the evidence of experts who would say that evolution was not in contradiction with the Bible "would shed no light on the issues."

The defense noted their intent to appeal Judge Raulston's ruling to a higher court, which then led to squabbling over how they could get their experts' testimony into the trial record. (They wanted the judges on appeal to know what the experts would have said, and since Judge Raulston had not allowed them to testify—only Professor Metcalf had taken the stand—some method for presenting the expert testimony to the higher court had to be devised.) The judge decided that the experts could submit affidavits—that is, sworn written state-ments—with what they would have said in court. More squabbling broke out over the schedule for submitting these affidavits. The judge and prosecutor wanted them immediately, but the defense lawyers explained that the written statements weren't ready. In the tussle that followed, Clarence kind of . . . lost it.

"If Your Honor takes a half a day to write an opinion"—Clarence was referring to the judge's ruling on the motion to quash earlier in

Judge Raulston reads his ruling on the admissibility of the defense's expert witnesses.

the week—"I do not understand why every request of the state and every suggestion of the prosecution would meet with an endless loss of time, and a bare suggestion of anything that is perfectly competent, on our part, should be immediately overruled."

"I hope you do not mean to reflect upon the court?" the judge said.

Clarence was aggravated. He turned his back to the judge. "Well," he said sarcastically, "your honor has the right to *hope*."

People in the courtroom laughed. Not the judge.

"I have a right to do something else, perhaps," Judge Raulston said.

What he meant was, in response to that disrespect, the judge had the right to hold Clarence in contempt of court. This could land Clarence in jail and would surely involve a substantial fine.

"All right, all right," Clarence grumbled.

The lawyers and judge moved on and agreed that the defense could have the weekend to get their expert witness statements together. At 10:30 a.m., court was adjourned.

The defense team's frustration lingered. Before leaving the courtroom, Judge Raulston wanted a photograph taken of him with Will and Clarence. Clarence made himself busy with letters at his counsel's table, snubbing the judge. Judge Raulston then asked Dudley Malone "to have your picture taken with Mr. Bryan and me." Malone rebuffed him, too. "We have had our pictures taken enough," he said. "Go have it taken with Mr. Bryan."

Not a very nice way to end a week. Or to end a trial—and the trial did seem to be over. There would be closing arguments from the prosecution and defense, probably on Tuesday—but, really, what more was there to be said?

Judge Raulston's request for a photo opportunity with the two great antagonists, William Jennings Bryan and Clarence Darrow, also suggested that he saw the case of *The State of Tennessee v. John Thomas*

Scopes as essentially finished. As did journalists, who started leaving Dayton right after adjournment. "Battle Now Over," announced H.L. Mencken's headline in the Baltimore *Evening Sun* as he left town. The New York Times, for one, was satisfied with Judge Raulston's decision to shut down the defense. It would save the public, the newspaper stated in an editorial, "from having its ears bethumped with millions more of irrelevant words."

Over the weekend, the defense team's experts prepared not millions, but tens of thousands, of words to be put into the court record on Monday. And so the clattering of typewriter keys echoed in "the Mansion"– the rambling, bat-ridden, plumbing-challenged house that served as the defense headquarters–where eight

The *Baltimore Sun*'s editorial cartoonist revealed his point of view on the anti-evolution movement, July 19, 1925.

scientists and four religion experts worked up their affidavits. Will put out a long statement on Saturday denouncing evolution. "The Tennessee case has uncovered the conspiracy against Biblical Christianity," it began. Clarence couldn't let Will's statement go unanswered. "Before the trial of this case I had no idea that there was only one interpretation of religion in the world," his reply began. From these openings, Will and Clarence went at it, bethumping the public with a whole lot of words.

Will let it be known that there were plenty more where those words came from. He was working on his closing argument, he told the reporters who remained in Dayton. He'd started writing it weeks earlier. This summation, he promised, would be "something brand new."

Clarence also had something brand new in mind.

Over the weekend, the Scopes trial made its way into Sunday church services. On July 20, 1925, the *Los Angeles Times* reported on the sermon President Calvin Coolidge heard when he attended church in Swampscott, Massachusetts, where he spent summers.

arguments begin.

COOLIDGES HEAR RECTOR'S DEFENSE OF DARWINISM

[EXCLUSIVE DISPATCH]

SWAMPSCOTT (Mass.) July 19. President and Mrs. Coolidge went to church this forenoon and heard the preacher, Rev. S. H. Beale, of Milwaukee, deplore the "pitiful exhibition" of religious dissension manifested in the Scopes evolution trial at Dayton, Tenn.

Dr. Beale unhesitatingly proclaimed his acceptance of all science as demonstrating the infinite grandeur of God. Evolution he accepts as a "Divine method of creation." But he confessed himself humiliated by the division of churchmen, which he pronounced no less pitiful than the divisions of nations and of statesmen.

Mr. and Mrs. Coolidge, accompanied only by Frank W. Stearns and followed, as always, by the secret service men and newspaper reporters, motored from White Court to the gray-stone Tabernacle Congregational Church in ancient Salem.

The President was dressed in a light gray suit. He wore a turn-down collar, a black and white figured tie and a sailor straw hat and carried a pair of dark-gray kid gloves.

Mrs. Coolidge was attired entirely in white, her frock a simple georgette crepe ensemble, her hat a wide-brimmed white straw trimmed with white flowers. She wore white silk gloves. The President's wife, radiating graciousness, was the most simply dressed woman in the congregation.

CHAPTER 20
ANY QUESTION THEY PLEASE

Monday morning, July 20. The pastor's brief prayer quickly got to the point: "Almighty God, our Father in Heaven . . . sometimes we have been stupid enough to match our human minds with revelations of the infinite and eternal."

"Mr. Sheriff," Judge Raulston said after the amens, "open court."

The courtroom was jammed—it was filled to capacity thirty minutes before the judge arrived. First things first: the judge made sure there were no jurors in the courtroom. Then he cited Clarence for contempt of court for the lawyer's insulting remarks last Friday. The spectators were buzzing.

"You people must keep quiet!" the court policeman called out. "This is not a circus."

The contempt citation wasn't a surprise, and Clarence didn't fight it. But he wasn't being hauled off to jail; he would remain free until the court prepared contempt papers against him. For now, he was still John's lead lawyer.

The crowd settled down.

Next, Arthur Hays read aloud summaries of the defense experts' statements about evolution. The jury was still excluded from the courtroom. It was not the most titillating of court sessions. Although a person could have learned plenty about science and theology by reading the 60,000 words in the affidavits, the recitation of summaries in an overheated courtroom was not a recipe for success. "The folks like it better when the sparks fly," one newspaper columnist wryly observed as seats emptied. At 11:40 a.m., the judge called for a lunch adjournment so everyone could escape the stifling room.

Two hours later, the judge called the court back in session. Clarence rose. He was sorry, he said to Judge Raulston. He apologized for his behavior the previous Friday. He was sweet as could be: "I have been treated better, kindlier and more hospitably than I fancied would have been the case in the north," Clarence purred, "and that is due largely to the ideas that southern people have and they are, perhaps, more hospitable than we are up north."

So nice, and yet—he wrapped all this sweetness around an apology in which he maintained that his behavior wasn't really so bad ("Personally, I don't think it constitutes a contempt"), and in which he emphasized his long career unblemished by any contempt citations from other judges. Still, this half-baked apology won applause from the audience and forgiveness from the judge. Maybe the people of Rhea County really were kindlier than people up north. Maybe Clarence really was a champion in the art of persuasion.

Judge Raulston leaned over his bench to shake Clarence's hand. But someone had told the judge that cracks were appearing in the first floor ceiling, just underfoot. He'd been worrying about the courtroom crashing down for days. "I am afraid of the building," he announced. "The court will convene down in the yard."

Audience members and lawyers scrambled to leave, carrying chairs, benches, and tables down the stairs with them.

"Go slowly! Go slowly!" cautioned Will.

They didn't go slowly. In just fifteen minutes, court was back in session outdoors. The judge sat on a platform raised on two-by-fours a few feet off the ground, backing up to the redbrick courthouse. The lawyers were close by, seated at tables. Spectators sat on the grass, perched on rough boards, or stood under the trees. Others hung out on the hoods or running boards of cars parked in the street. It was, one journalist wrote, "certainly the strangest session of court ever held." It was about to get stranger.

After the judge and court officer made sure that jurors were not in hearing distance, Arthur Hays finished reading the affidavit summaries into the record.

Arthur Garfield Hays reading the defense experts' statements into the trial record on July 20, 1925, after the proceedings moved outdoors.

"Send for the jury," Judge Raulston ordered as soon as Hays was done.

But no.

"Your honor," Clarence said, "before you send for the jury, I think it my duty to make this motion." He stood and put his hands in his pockets. "Off to the left of where the jury sits a little bit and about ten feet in front of them is a large sign about ten feet long reading, 'Read Your Bible,' and a hand pointing to it. The word 'Bible' is in large letters, perhaps a foot and a half long, and the printing—"

"Hardly that long I think, general," interrupted the judge. He seemed to have promoted Clarence from colonel.

Clarence didn't hear. "What is that?" he asked.

"Hardly that long," Judge Raulston repeated.

"Why, we will call it a foot," Clarence said.

"Compromise on a foot," the judge agreed.

"Fourteen inches," called out a spectator.

Whatever the size of the letters, Clarence wanted the sign removed.

Predictably, this produced debate. Clarence's point was that a read-your-Bible sign could prejudice the jury against the defense. One of the prosecutors suggested that the defense lawyers' stance against Bible-reading might mean they were "aligned with the devil and his satellites." The judge ordered such a slur expunged from the record. Back and forth, back and forth, laughter and applause, and then Will indicated that he had something to say. The crowd only got noisier.

"People, this is no circus," the court officer said. "There are no monkeys up here. This is a lawsuit, let us have order."

The judge invited "Colonel Bryan" to speak.

Will offered a generous response to Clarence's objection to the sign. "Paul said: 'If eating meat maketh my brother to offend,'" he quoted, "'I shall eat no meat while the world lasts.'"

That was enough for Judge Raulston. The sign came down.

Now, at last: "Let the jury be brought around," the judge said.

But, yet again—no.

"The defense desires to call Mr. Bryan as a witness," announced Arthur Hays.

The court officer did not have to call the spectators to order. Call Mr. Bryan as a witness? Hays's statement stunned them into silence.

Not so the prosecutors. They were on their feet. Talking. Shouting.

No one puts a prosecutor on the witness stand in the very case he's prosecuting! This simply isn't done! It would turn the trial into even more of a circus than it already was. What would be the point? What evidence could William Jennings Bryan possibly give in the criminal trial of John Scopes? What a terrible idea!

Except—William Jennings Bryan was all in.

No, I don't object to going on the stand, he told Judge Raulston. "Not at all."

Will's response was exactly what Clarence had counted on.

On Saturday Clarence had called Rabbi Louis Ginzberg, an eminent scholar at the Jewish Theological Seminary in New York. He had a question for the rabbi: where did Cain (one of the sons of Adam and Eve, the first man and woman God created, according to the Bible) get his wife? After all, the Bible didn't mention any other people in any other families being created. But it did mention Cain having a wife. Where did she come from?

Well, maybe the creation story didn't mean that Adam and Eve were the only human beings in existence. Maybe, even if you were a religious person, you could say that biblical stories were not intended as exact and literal accounts of things that happened—and therefore teaching evolution didn't contradict the creation story or anything else in the Bible.

On Friday the judge had rejected this very argument when he rejected the defense's scientific and theological experts. All that mattered, he ruled, was whether John Scopes taught evolution.

Apparently, that wasn't going to stop Clarence from trying again.

The devout Rabbi Ginzberg was observing the Jewish Sabbath on Saturday and didn't take his friend's call. Clarence wasn't deterred. He'd been thinking about the problem (and, to him, the absurdity) of biblical literalism for a while—at least since 1923, when the *Chicago Daily Tribune* printed his fifty-five questions addressed to William Jennings Bryan. Questions like, "Did God curse the serpent for tempting Eve and decree that thereafter he should go on his belly? How did he travel before that time?" Then, such questions seemed designed to ridicule biblical literalists. Now Clarence was treading a more delicate path. He'd repeatedly assured his audiences during the trial that he understood the Bible offered them comfort and teaching; he didn't come to Dayton to insult them or their Scripture.

But now, here, on the courthouse lawn, in his final effort to win his case—or at least to win over the millions of Americans who were paying attention—he wouldn't mind insulting William Jennings Bryan.

On Sunday Clarence had conferred with fellow defense lawyer Arthur Hays and with Kirtley Mather, a Harvard University scholar who'd come to Dayton as one of the defense experts. Mather knew a lot about science and a lot about religion. They'd secretly staged a mock trial, with Mather playing William Jennings Bryan and the two lawyers asking him questions about the Bible. It was a rehearsal for what the defense team was springing on the court—and especially on Will—now, on Monday.

The defense stated that the purpose of questioning Will in front of Dayton and the world (but not the jury—they were still under the judge's exclusion order) was to add his testimony to the written record that would go up to an appeals court. Will was an authority on the Bible. The Great Commoner's testimony, preserved in the trial transcript, would help a higher court review the case on appeal.

The unstated purpose was something else entirely.

"You have given considerable study to the Bible, haven't you, Mr. Bryan?" Clarence asked.

"Yes, sir," Will responded. "I have tried to."

"Well, we all know you have," soothed Clarence. "We are not going to dispute that at all."

Will confirmed that he'd studied the Bible for about fifty years, maybe more.

"Do you claim that everything in the Bible should be literally interpreted?" Clarence asked.

"I believe everything in the Bible should be accepted as it is given

Clarence Darrow questioning William Jennings Bryan in the open-air courtroom on July 20, 1925.

there; some of the Bible is given illustratively. For instance: 'Ye are the salt of the earth.' I would not insist that man was actually salt, or that he had flesh of salt, but it is used in the sense of salt as saving God's people."

Clarence asked Will whether he believed the biblical story of Jonah being swallowed by a whale was true. Will was cautious in his answer: the Bible said a fish, not a whale. They jousted around that for a while. The bottom line, though, was that Will believed that the events did in fact happen—Jonah was swallowed and lived to tell the tale—and it was a miracle wrought by God.

Clarence moved on to the story of Joshua: did Will believe that Joshua made the sun stand still, as the Bible says?

"I accept the Bible absolutely," Will said.

Did that mean, then, that Will believed that the sun rotates around the earth?

No, Will understood, just as everyone did, that the earth moves around the sun.

So, then, Clarence continued, "If the day was lengthened by stopping either the earth or the sun, it must have been the earth?"

"Well, I should say so."

For Clarence, this was a "gotcha!" moment. After all, Will was saying that the earth must have stood still in the Joshua story—even though the biblical text said it was the sun that stood still. So Clarence pressed Will to admit that even *he* was interpreting the Bible, rather than taking its literal meaning. But Will would not give Clarence the satisfaction of an answer. He saw where Clarence was going: if Will had no objection to interpreting this biblical story to bring it in line with the science of astronomy, then how could he object to interpreting the biblical accounts of creation to be consistent with the science of evolution?

No. Will would not agree that he was "interpreting" the Bible. Clarence moved on.

"Now, Mr. Bryan, have you ever pondered what would have happened to the earth if it had stood still?"

"No."

"You have not?"

"No; the God I believe in could have taken care of that, Mr. Darrow."

Clarence persisted. "Don't you know it would have been converted into a molten mass of matter?"

"I would want to hear expert testimony on that."

"You have never investigated that subject?"

"I don't think I have ever had the question asked."

"Or ever thought of it?"

"I have been too busy on things that I thought were of more importance than that."

On to the biblical story of the flood. Yes, Will believed that story literally. No, he did not know when it took place. Yes, there was a famous bishop of the seventeenth century, James Ussher, who fixed the time of creation at 4004 B.C., and the flood took place after that. No, Will could not say if this date was accurate. No, he could not say how it was calculated.

Well, Clarence asked, was it calculated by toting up the generations of man recounted in the Bible? (This was, in fact, part of Bishop Ussher's methodology.)

"I would not want to say that," Will said.

"What do you think?" Clarence pressed.

"I do not think about things I don't think about."

"Do you think about things you do think about?" Clarence was becoming harsh.

"Well, sometimes."

People in the courtyard—there were between 2,000 and 3,000 spectators—laughed.

The policeman called for order. He got it, but only momentarily. The trial had become a joust. Clarence, the agnostic attacker, in his trademark suspenders. Will, wearing a dark suit for the first time since the trial began—as if he dressed for his star turn in defending the faith. Men and women craned their necks to see and hear, waiting for the next opportunity to laugh or howl. Their young children played in the back of the audience on seesaws made from pine boards. Boys snaked through the crowd selling soda pop.

The other prosecutors stood to object to Clarence's questioning. But Will did not want their help. "These gentlemen . . . they did not come here to try this case," he cried, referring to Clarence and the other defense lawyers. "They came here to try revealed religion. I am here to defend it, and they can ask me any question they please."

The audience roared its approval.

"All right," said Judge Raulston.

"Great applause from the bleachers," Clarence noted.

"From those whom you call 'yokels,'" snapped Will.

"I have never called them yokels," Clarence replied.

"Those are the people whom you insult," Will said.

"You insult every man of science and learning in the world because he does not believe in your fool religion!" shouted Clarence.

Tom Stewart, the lead prosecutor, tried to stop the show again.

No, said Will.

No, said the judge.

"Then your honor rules, and I accept," said Clarence.

As if this wasn't exactly what he wanted. He dug in.

CHAPTER 21
"I AM NOT AFRAID"

C larence got back to the age of the earth and the Bible's story of
Noah and the flood. Bishop Ussher had said the flood occurred
in 2348 B.C. Clarence pressed Will to either confirm or deny this
date. Will, still cautious, would do neither. "I don't pretend to say that is
exact," he parried. Clarence asked him to consider the possibility of life
before 4004 B.C.—that is, before the bishop's calculation of creation.

"You are not satisfied there is any civilization that can be traced
back 5,000 years?" Clarence asked.

"I would not want to say there is," Will responded, "because I have
no evidence of it that is satisfactory."

Clarence was relentless: "Do you say that you do not believe that
there were any civilizations on this earth that reach back beyond
5,000 years?"

"I am not satisfied by any evidence that I have seen."

"I didn't ask you what you are satisfied with. I asked you if you
believe it?"

"I am satisfied by no evidence, that I have found," Will said, "that would justify me in accepting the opinions of these men against what I believe to be the inspired Word of God."

Still Clarence wouldn't let go. Over and over he asked Will to specify when he thought creation occurred. Didn't Will know that ancient civilizations were known to exist at least 6,000 or 7,000 years ago? No, Will did not. Did Will know that religions that are not based on the Bible also describe a flood? No.

"Have you ever read anything about the origins of religions?" Clarence asked.

"Not a great deal."

"And you don't know whether any other religion ever gave a similar account of the destruction of the earth by the flood?"

"The Christian religion has satisfied me," Will replied, "and I have never felt it necessary to look up some competing religions."

In fact, other religions and cultures do have flood stories. The unspoken purpose of Clarence's strategy was clear: to spin a web around Will from which he would not be able to escape without exposing his ignorance of—and lack of curiosity about—science, archaeology, anthropology, history, and even comparative religion. Clarence was well beyond trying to show that religion and evolution could coexist. He was there to take down Will.

For two hours, it was thrust and parry, thrust and parry. Will pushed back repeatedly against Clarence's efforts to paint him into corners on questions of the earth's age, the emergence of life on the planet, and the accuracy of Bible stories ranging from the Garden of Eden to the Tower of Babel. Sometimes he showed good humor in turning questions around on Clarence:

Clarence: Don't you know that the ancient civilizations of

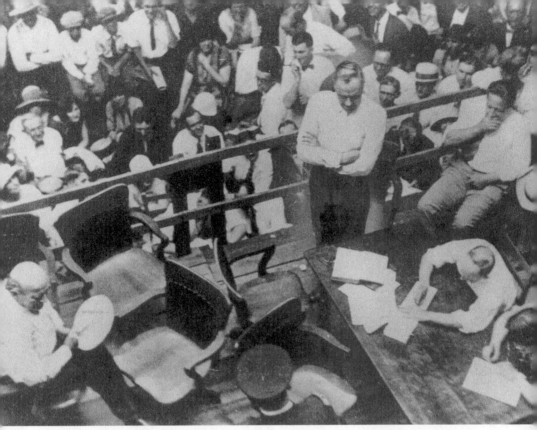

An aerial view of Clarence Darrow and William Jennings Bryan during their extraordinary exchange under the trees outside the courthouse.

China are 6,000 or 7,000 years old, at the very least?

Will: No; but they would not run back beyond the creation, according to the Bible, 6,000 years.

Clarence: You don't know how old they are, is that right?

Will: I don't know how old they are, but probably you do.

(Laughter in the courtyard.)

Clarence: What about the religion of Confucious [*sic*] or Buddha? . . . .

Will: Buddhism is an agnostic religion.

Clarence: To what?—what do you mean by agnostic?

Will: I don't know.

Clarence: You don't know what you mean?

Will: That is what "agnosticism" is—I don't know. When I was in Rangoon, Burma, one of the Buddhists told me that they were going to send a delegation to an agnostic congress that was to be held soon at Rome and I read in an official document—

Clarence: Do you remember his name?

Will: No, sir, I don't.

Clarence: What did he look like, how tall was he?

Will: I think he was about as tall as you but not so crooked.

But as the questioning continued, the good humor—on both sides—evaporated.

"Do you think the earth was made in six days?" Clarence asked.

"Not six days of twenty-four hours," Will replied.

Among the spectators there was movement. For the Fundamentalists in the audience, six days meant six days. That's what the Bible said.

Tom Stewart again rose to strenuously object. "What is the purpose of this examination?" he asked. Anyone would have seen that, once again, Clarence was leading Will down the path of interpreting the Bible to mean something other than what its literal words said. Leading Will down the path of revealing his inconsistency.

"The purpose," Will exclaimed, "is to cast ridicule on everybody who believes in the Bible, and I am perfectly willing that the world shall know that these gentlemen have no other purpose than ridiculing every Christian who believes in the Bible."

"We have the purpose of preventing bigots and ignoramuses from controlling the education of the United States," shouted Clarence, "and you know it, and that is all."

"I am simply trying to protect the word of God against the greatest atheist or agnostic in the United States," Will cried. "I want the papers to know I am not afraid to get on the stand in front of him and let him do his worst. I want the world to know."

The audience exploded in applause.

Clarence carried on.

"Mr. Bryan," he said, "do you believe that the first woman was Eve?"

"Yes."

"Do you believe she was literally made out of Adam's rib?"

"I do."

"Did you ever discover where Cain got his wife?"

"No, sir; I leave the agnostics to hunt for her."

"The Bible says he got one, doesn't it?" Clarence continued. "Were there other people on the earth at that time?"

"I cannot say."

"You cannot say. Did that ever enter your consideration?"

"Never bothered me."

"There were no others recorded, but Cain got a wife."

"That is what the Bible says."

This move in Clarence's game of "gotcha" didn't stir the audience. Presumably the puzzle of Cain's wife didn't bother them.

"All right," Clarence said. "Does the statement, 'The morning and the evening were the first day,' and 'The morning and the evening were the second day,' mean anything to you?"

"I do not think it necessarily means a twenty-four-hour day," Will responded.

So his earlier answer hadn't been a slip. Perhaps realizing that he risked disappointing his Fundamentalist supporters, Will tried again: "I think it would be just as easy for the kind of God we believe in to make the earth in six days as in six years or in 6,000,000 years or in

600,000,000 years," he said. "I do not think it important whether we believe one or the other."

As if to put a point on it, Clarence asked the question again, in a different form: "The creation might have been going on for a very long time?"

"It might have continued for millions of years," said Will.

There went Will's commitment to taking the words of the Bible literally. Another strand in the web Clarence was weaving to trap Will in his own inconsistency and unawareness.

By the time Clarence got to the story of the serpent in the Garden of Eden, he was openly scornful of Will—and of the Bible. "Faces grew strained and lips tightened among the spectators at the apparent irreverence of some of the questions," one news article observed. Will, another reporter wrote, had anguish on his face and a tremor in his voice.

"Do you believe the story of the temptation of Eve by the serpent?" Clarence asked.

"I do."

"Do you believe that after Eve ate the apple, or gave it to Adam, whichever way it was, that God cursed Eve, and that time decreed that all womankind thenceforth and forever should suffer the pains of childbirth in the reproduction of the earth?"

"I believe what it says," Will responded.

"And you believe that is the reason that God made the serpent to go on his belly after he tempted Eve?" Clarence asked.

"I believe the Bible as it is, and I do not permit you to put your language in the place of the language of the Almighty," Will retorted. "I will not answer your questions in your language." He insisted that Clarence read the passage from the Bible.

Clarence didn't mind. "I will read it to you from the Bible," he agreed. "'And the Lord God said unto the serpent, because thou hast done this, thou art cursed above all cattle, and above every beast of the field; upon thy belly shalt thou go and dust shalt thou eat all the days of thy life.' Do you think that is why the serpent is compelled to crawl upon its belly?"

"I believe that," Will avowed.

"Have you any idea how the snake went before that time?" The disdain was obvious.

"No, sir."

"Do you know whether he walked on his tail or not?"

"No, sir," Will said. "I have no way to know."

The audience burst into laughter.

That, it turned out, was the last laugh.

"Your honor, I think I can shorten this testimony," Will said. (Although, in truth, it was too late to shorten the testimony.) "The only purpose Mr. Darrow has is to slur at the Bible, but I will answer his question. I will answer it all at once, and I have no objection in the world." By now Will was red-faced and shouting. "I want the world to know that this man, who does not believe in a God, is trying to use a court in Tennessee—"

"I object to that," Clarence interjected.

"—to slur at it, and while it will require time, I am willing to take it."

"I object to your statement," Clarence shouted. "I am examining you on your fool ideas that no intelligent Christian on earth believes."

Both men were on their feet, glowering, furious.

The audience was entranced. What next? Fisticuffs?

"Court is adjourned," Judge Raulston announced abruptly.

He rapped his gavel.

And so, reported the London *Daily Telegraph's* correspondent,

Editorial cartoon from the *Commercial Appeal* (Memphis), published after Clarence Darrow and William Jennings Bryan's face-off in the outdoor courtroom.

"Judge Raulston . . . put an end to a situation unprecedented in the court annals of this, and probably of any other, country."

"Unprecedented," agreed the *Boston Daily Globe*.

"Unique," said the *Philadelphia Inquirer*.

"Probably the most amazing judicial performance ever witnessed in America," concluded the *Baltimore Sun*'s man on the scene.

There was never before, and has never been, another day in court like it.

CHAPTER 22
VERDICTS

In Tuesday's newspapers, the verdict was mixed.

Bryan Holds His Own In Meet With Darrow, the *Knoxville Journal*'s headline announced. The article below the headline asserted, "At no time was the one time boy orator of the Platte in distress." Another reporter stated that Clarence asked Will "trick questions"

CRUSADER BRANDS FOE AS AGNOSTIC DURING CLASH

Commoner Admits Days Mentioned in Genesis May be Construed to Mean Ages in Length

The *Los Angeles Times* highlighted William Jennings Bryan's admission that he might not take every aspect of the Bible's creation story literally.

and appeared to be "seeking an excuse to discredit the Bible and the Christian religion."

Science vs. Fundamentalism, began the *St. Louis Post-Dispatch*, followed by **Commoner Becomes Almost Hysterical Under Lawyer's Pitiless Fire of Questions**. The *New York Times* correspondent concluded that the audience had "no pity" for Will's "admissions of ignorance of things boys and girls learn in high school." But it was the reporter for the *Chattanooga Daily Times* who probably came closest to reading the crowd: "Mr. Bryan made a monkey out of Mr. Darrow, said the fundamentalists who were present. Mr. Darrow made a monkey out of Mr. Bryan, say the evolutionists who were present."

The judge who was present was done monkeying around. While across the nation readers drank their morning coffee with dispatches from the case of *Darrow v. Bryan*, on Tuesday morning Judge Raulston, presiding once again in his second-floor courtroom, decided to get back to the case of *The State of Tennessee v. John Thomas Scopes*.

First, as always, prayer: a quick four sentences.

The judge was quick to get to his point, too: he'd been wrong, he said, in letting Will testify. "The lawsuit . . . is whether or not Mr. Scopes taught that man descended from a lower order of animals," he said. That was the only question. And so, "I am pleased to expunge this testimony, given by Mr. Bryan on yesterday, from the records of this court and it will not be further considered."

All that drama—expunged?

"I want to say a word, if you please," Clarence said.

No. The judge was through with him, and with this. He had allowed the case to spiral about as far away from a typical trial as imaginable. Now he was lassoing it back in. He was done being unprecedented, unique, and amazing. Not only Will's testimony from the day before, but all the defense's expert statements about evolution and religion would be excluded from the court record as well.

There was no clamoring from the lawyers. They, too, were through. As usual, Clarence thought quickly. He asked the judge to bring in the jury.

"We claim that the defendant is not guilty," Clarence said, "but as the court has excluded any testimony, except as to the one issue as to whether he taught that man descended from a lower order of animals, and we cannot contradict that testimony, therefore, there is no logical thing to come except that the jury find a verdict that we may carry to the higher court, purely as a matter of proper procedure."

The judge agreed. The jurors filed into the courtroom. They had missed everything the rest of the country was buzzing about. They'd missed Clarence's opening statement. They'd missed Will's heartfelt argument and Dudley Malone's thundering response. They'd missed the judge's stumbling over himself when he thought some unscrupulous journalist had stolen his ruling. They'd missed Professor Metcalf's tutorial on evolution. They'd missed the extraordinary performances under the trees yesterday. But at least they would get to hear Will's carefully, beautifully crafted closing argument—

Wait, what about Will's closing argument? Clarence, cunning trial lawyer that he was, had outmaneuvered Will in a final ploy. By telling the judge that the defense would not fight a guilty verdict, Clarence was giving up a closing argument for the defense. Under Tennessee's rules of procedure, that meant no closing argument for the prosecutor, either. The "something brand new" that Will had been working on so hard, the oration to out-orate not only Clarence Darrow but even himself, would not be heard.

Judge Raulston gave the jurors their simple charge—

But not before he posed for the cameras, pretending to read the piece of paper on which he'd written his instructions to the jurors—

Now Judge Raulston could give the jurors their charge: if they found, beyond a reasonable doubt, that the evidence proved that John Thomas Scopes had taught that man had descended from a lower order of animals, then they needed to return a guilty verdict. That was the only question. They should not concern themselves with whether this teaching also contradicted the Bible's story of divine creation.

After having been barred from all but two hours of the eight-day trial, what evidence did the jurors have to consider? Only the testimony of John's two students and that of the two members of the drugstore group—all of which corroborated the fact that John had taught that man had descended from a lower order of animals.

The jurors left the courtroom.

Nine minutes later, they returned.

"Mr. Foreman, will you tell us whether you have agreed on a verdict?" asked the judge.

"Yes, sir. We have, your honor."

"What do you find?"

"We have found for the state," the foreman said, "found the defendant guilty."

No gasps, laughter, clapping, roaring, stomping, or hissing in the courtroom.

"Mr. Scopes," the judge said, "will you come around here, please, sir."

After eight days of drawn-out, leisurely proceedings, it was all moving so quickly now. John stood in front of Judge Raulston. He was wearing a tie. He'd tried to brush his hair off his forehead. A policeman stood beside him.

"The jury have found you guilty," the judge said. "The statute

John Scopes standing while Judge Raulston pronounces his sentence.

makes this an offense punishable by fine of not less than $100 nor more than $500. The court now fixes your fine at $100, and imposes that fine upon you—"

It was moving too quickly.

"May it please your honor, we want to be heard a moment," interjected John Neal.

Normally a criminal defendant is given the opportunity to speak before his sentence is handed down. Judge Raulston seemed to have forgotten that now that he was barreling toward a conclusion.

"Oh—Have you anything to say, Mr. Scopes, as to why the court should not impose punishment upon you?" the judge asked.

It was the only time John had the chance to utter a word in his own defense.

"Your honor," he began, folding his arms as he spoke, "I feel that I have been convicted of violating an unjust statute. I will continue in the future, as I have in the past, to oppose this law in any way I can." He seemed nervous; his voice trembled a little. "Any other action would be in violation of my ideal of academic freedom—that is, to teach the truth as guaranteed in our constitution, of personal and religious freedom. I think the fine is unjust."

The judge didn't say, *Yeah, whatever*, but he also didn't miss a beat.

"So then the court now imposes on you a fine of $100 and costs," he continued, "which you will arrange with the clerk."

And then began, as one newspaper put it, "an all-around love fest."

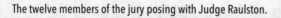
The twelve members of the jury posing with Judge Raulston.

Dudley Malone started it. He thanked the people of the state of Tennessee.

A newspaper reporter spoke for all the press in thanking the court for "the courtesies and kindnesses."

A reporter from Canada one-upped the American reporter by saying that he'd been shown "extreme courtesy" from the locals.

Applause, applause, applause.

"Has any other press man anything to say?" Judge Raulston called out. He seemed in no hurry to leave. "Let me hear you, Mr. Bell—did you say anything?"

"No, sir," said Mr. Bell. It was like being called on in class when you hadn't raised your hand.

A voice from the audience piped up: "As one of the public, who has come a number of miles to hear this trial, I desire to express my appreciation of the hospitality and reasonable expenses that have been incurred while here."

Applause!

Finally, after a few more thank-yous, Will and Clarence each spoke briefly. Theirs were not the words of a love fest. Will said the trial was "a little case of little consequence as a case." Clarence thanked the people of Dayton for their hospitality and the judge for not throwing him in jail—which drew a laugh from the audience.

And in his characteristic sweet-and-sour way, Clarence paired his gratitude with sharp criticism. The case would be remembered, he bellowed, "because it is the first case of this sort since we stopped trying people in America for witchcraft."

"We will adjourn," Judge Raulston said after he gave an emotional little speech of his own. But first— "Brother Jones will pronounce the benediction."

One last prayer, a single sentence long.

Will and Clarence may have been finished in the Rhea County Courthouse, but they kept up their battle in the newspapers that afternoon and the next day. Will issued a statement calling Clarence "the finished product of evolution," personifying "all that is cruel, heartless and destructive in evolution." Clarence expressed his pity for Will's public display of "gross ignorance." And Will promised that his closing argument would be ready for the next Sunday's newspapers. It would be, he vowed, "the mountain peak of my life's effort."

Newspapers gave the outcome of the trial front-page headlines and big coverage.

So, the American Civil Liberties Union had its guilty verdict to appeal to a higher court. The state of Tennessee had its anti-evolution law intact. John had his wallet intact, because the *Baltimore Sun* newspaper paid his fine. Was it unusual for a newspaper to involve itself in this way? Yes, indeed. But so much about the trial had been unusual; why should it stop now? It was also unusual for a man convicted of a crime to help the journalists who had covered his trial write their final stories to send out to their newspapers—but that was what John did. And then he saw them off at the railroad station, where they boarded a train that displayed a large banner: "PROTOPLASM SPECIAL."

Clarence and Will also left town at the end of the week. Clarence gave a lecture in Knoxville and then headed to the Smoky Mountains to unwind. Will traveled around Tennessee giving speeches and returned to Dayton in time to attend church on Sunday morning. He led the congregation in prayer and after services enjoyed his midday meal with Mary, his wife, at his guesthouse. Later that afternoon, Will went to his bedroom for his usual nap.

He never woke up.

CHAPTER 23
AFTERLIVES AND LEGENDS

The sudden death of William Jennings Bryan shocked the nation. He had appeared to be in fine health. A story made the rounds that, before he went to take that final afternoon nap, he'd told his wife he'd never felt better in his life and was eager to continue his fight for the primacy of the Bible.

But his fight was over. Doctors in Dayton who examined Will concluded that he had died of "apoplexy"—that is, a stroke. Others, without the benefit of examining Will's body, came to a different conclusion: "Clarence Darrow was, unquestionably, an immediate instrument in the early passing of the great 'Commoner,'" wrote an Alabama journalist. It was a judgment shared by many, angry at Clarence for his harsh and irreverent treatment of Will on the witness stand.

The Great Commoner received a great statesman's honors. Flags in the nation's capital were lowered to half-staff. Flags in state capitals, too. President Calvin Coolidge sent a letter of condolence to Mary Bryan, praising her husband as "a leader in the advocacy of many

Darrow An Instrument In Sudden Death Of Bryan, Says Writer Who Saw Clash

Commoner's Rage Over Grilling He Received On Witness Stand At Dayton Probably Was Beginning Of The End

Many people blamed Clarence Darrow for William Jennings Bryan's death, as this front-page headline from the *Birmingham News* (Alabama) of July 27, 1925, suggests.

moral reforms." Before setting off on a winding journey through the countryside between Dayton and Washington, DC, where he would be buried, Will's body lay in a bronze coffin in the front room of the cottage where he died. Among the many local people who came to pay respects was John Scopes. "The young professor" bowed his head, a reporter noted, and "gazed for a long time upon the grimly set features of the veteran crusader of fundamentalism."

As the special funeral train made its way through Tennessee and Virginia, throngs of people came to the tracks to see off their hero. At every station and along the route, wrote a journalist who rode the train, "men in shirt sleeves and overalls, women in gingham, and barefoot children have come to see the train pass and to gaze with bared heads and sorrowful faces at the last car on the train," where Bryan's casket rested. As the train rolled into Washington's Union Station rail yard, hundreds of railroad workers removed their hats in respect. People stood in line outside the church where Will's body lay in state for the chance to file past the open casket inside; 20,000 people got a final glimpse of his face. The U.S. Department of State closed down for a day to mark its former leader's death.

Official death certificate of William Jennings Bryan.

Nellie Kenyon rode the funeral train to Washington, attended the church service, and described a scene that took place in Mary Bryan's hotel room after her husband had been laid to rest. The "little gray-haired widow," as Nellie described her, gave a gift to a policeman from Chattanooga who had been an honor guard at the funeral. "It is a sterling silver pen," Nellie wrote, "the one the great commoner used . . . to sign all important documents, and is the pen that placed his signature at the close of all communications written by him in connection with the Scopes evolution trial at Dayton." The policeman, choked up with emotion, said he would keep it always.

Not everyone grieved. H.L. Mencken vilified Will: "Hour by hour he grew more bitter," wrote the so-called Sage of Baltimore. "The hatred in the old man's eyes was not for the enemies of God; it was for the enemies of Bryan. . . . The Bryan I shall remember is . . . broken, furious, and infinitely pathetic . . . ridiculous . . . disgusting . . . deluded."

Other critics made their points with less vitriol. "I believe that God expects more of his children than to simply defend this great but much misunderstood Book, the Bible," began the editorial writer for the *California Eagle*:

> And too, the question naturally arises, where has brother Bryan been when the 14th and 15th Amendments of the U.S. Constitution were being grossly violated in every southern state in America and especially his own adopted home state, Florida? Is it not contrary to the teaching of the Bible to discriminate against, disfranchise and lynch American Negroes in the State of Florida and Tennessee?

In contrast, the editorial continued, "Clarence Darrow . . . believes in the brotherhood of man first; not that a man's face must be white in order to be entitled to that brotherhood but because of his knowledge of Evolution and the origin of man makes it plain to him that of one blood all men were created equal. This part of the Bible was too much for Mr. Bryan."

The *Eagle* was a leading African American–owned newspaper.

The *Pittsburgh Courier*, one of the most widely read Black newspapers, editorialized in a similar vein:

> The life of Bryan was sincere, we think, from his point of view. His point of view, however, suffered a shocking change after he left Nebraska and went to Florida. He was the Commoner in Nebraska. He became a militant disciple of color-phobia, race discrimination, and religious bigotry after he settled in Florida. Negroes have nothing to treasure out of the life of Bryan.

On Friday, July 31, 1925, a funeral service for Will was held in a church just a few blocks from the building that he had three times tried to make his home: the White House. The event was by invitation only. But before the service started, two special microphones were installed inside. These microphones belonged to radio companies that would broadcast the service, with its praise of God and of Will, to people as far west as Minneapolis and north to parts of Canada. Three years earlier, Will had enthusiastically embraced the newfangled technology of radio "as the most wonderful of all the mysteries that man has unraveled." He spoke of the thrill of reaching what he called "an invisible audience." At that time—it was late 1922—the *New York Times* estimated that about sixty million people had already heard Will's voice. Now that voice was stilled. But thanks to that "most wonderful of all the mysteries," an invisible audience numbering in the hundreds of thousands would be remembering William Jennings Bryan's voice and life in the hour before his body was lowered into the ground.

And Will wasn't done with his audience.

BRYAN STRIKES FROM GRAVE AT EVOLUTION, announced the page-one headline in the *Austin American-Statesman*.

VOICE FROM DEAD BACKS TENN. LAW, intoned the front page of the *El Paso Herald*.

BRYAN'S "SUPREME EFFORT" IS GIVEN TO THE WORLD; SPEAKS AGAIN, THOUGH LIPS ARE MUTE, declared North Carolina's *Charlotte Observer*.

With such melodramatic headlines—and others more sober ("Full Text of Bryan's Defense of Bible," offered the Memphis *Commercial Appeal*)—newspapers around the country brought Will's final big speech to millions. On the witness stand, Will had been reduced to focusing on the supernatural aspects of Bible stories and on whether the earth was very, very old or fairly new. These were not the issues that, over the years, had won him so many followers.

On the witness stand, Will hadn't emphasized the message of kindness and love through Christianity that had always been such a big part of his appeal. Lost in his responses to Clarence's interrogations was Will's concern for the moral and spiritual lives of ordinary people. Lost, too, was the banner he'd been waving ever since his 1896 run for the presidency—that the country's undemocratic elites (bankers and business magnates in 1896, scientists and intellectuals in 1925) should not be allowed to impose their views and rules on the general populace. Here, in his final message, Will came back to the ideals that people most admired.

The speech was long, spilling over page after page of newsprint. Will would have needed a couple of hours to give it. Whether people read it in one sitting, or over the course of days and evenings, they found in it all the familiar and stirring notes that had been muted in the Rhea County Courthouse. "Science is a magnificent material force," he wrote, "but it is not a teacher of morals. It can perfect machinery, but it adds no moral restraints to protect society from the misuse of the machine." Evolution, he asserted, "would eliminate love and carry man back to a struggle of tooth and claw." It was a "bloody, brutal doctrine" that demanded, "as the rabble did 19 hundred years ago that He be crucified."

This was vintage Will. This was a far more fitting last word—a more fitting last 12,000 words, to be precise—than his performance on the witness stand.

He did not mention the name John Thomas Scopes.

Will did have quite a bit to say about Clarence Darrow in this final speech, particularly about Clarence's defense of the "evolution-ist" and "atheist" Leopold and Loeb. For his part, Clarence kept his comments respectful in the wake of Will's death. "Mr. Bryan was a man of very extraordinary powers as a speaker or campaigner in any cause in which he believed," he said the day after Will died. "I always considered him fairly honest." A few years later, in his autobiography, Clarence was less restrained. "Mr. Bryan had made himself ridicu-lous" during the trial, Clarence wrote, "and had contradicted his own faith. I was truly sorry for Mr. Bryan." But not too sorry: "I consoled myself," Clarence continued, "by thinking of the years through which he had busied himself tormenting intelligent professors with impu-dent questions about their faith, and seeking to arouse the ignora-muses and bigots to drive them out of their positions."

Three months after Dayton, Clarence was once again in a court-room defending a controversial cause. This time, his clients were Dr. Ossian Sweet and his wife, Gladys. The Sweets, who were Black, had bought a house in a nice neighborhood in Detroit—a nice *white* neigh-borhood. A hostile white mob welcomed them to the neighborhood by attacking their home. The Sweets, who were inside with some of their friends, fought back with guns—and a white neighbor was killed. Prosecutors charged the Sweets and their companions with murder.

Clarence's great challenge was to convince a jury that the ancient precept that "a man's home is his castle"—which excuses a person fighting back in self-defense against those who threaten his home—applied not only to white people but to Black people as well. This was far from a sure thing. But he worked his magic on two different all-white juries. None of the defendants was convicted. The defense, said the *Pittsburgh Courier*, succeeded with "matchless and brilliant oratory."

The Sweet trial was Clarence's last great courtroom drama. He defended more accused murderers and saved some from execution. He wrote his autobiography and had speaking engagements. But a decade after Dayton, Clarence was unwell, plagued by heart disease. The once giant of a man shrunk to ninety pounds. On March 13, 1938, Clarence Darrow died at home in Chicago. He had almost lived to see his eighty-first birthday.

Newspapers put Clarence's death on their front pages, as they had Will's death, but the headlines for Clarence were not the double-decker extravaganzas that marked the Great Commoner's demise. By 1938, Clarence had been out of the public eye for a few years. Also, his death was eclipsed by a more earth-shattering event on that same day.

"Clarence Darrow died yesterday afternoon," his hometown newspaper reported under a modest headline.

"Once proud Austria died as a nation tonight," announced that same paper under a giant headline that took over the front page: **VIENNA HAILS HITLER TODAY.**

Nazi Germany's takeover of Austria ushered in a new era, a war of unprecedented destruction, and the Holocaust. Clarence had lived long enough to witness and denounce Hitler's rise. No doubt he would have seen these developments, in part, as grotesque products of bigotry and intolerance. No doubt William Jennings Bryan would have blamed the Nazis' genocidal obsession with "racial purity" on Darwinism gone wild.

———◆•◆———

After his trial, John received requests to appear on vaudeville stages talking about evolution—essentially to be a Monkey Trial sideshow. He wasn't interested. The expert witnesses at his trial had put together a scholarship fund for him to pursue graduate studies in any field he chose. He considered attending law school at his alma mater, the University of Kentucky. But when the dean, hoping to convince John to enroll, told him that he could become the next Clarence Darrow—that was the end of that idea. John's admiration for Clarence was boundless. But he didn't want to spend his life in a profession where he would always be compared to the Great Defender.

So John turned to science—in particular, to geology. During his two years studying at the University of Chicago, he and Clarence Darrow got together nearly every week. After he left school, John took a job with an oil company. A big draw of the job: it was in Venezuela, with forays into the jungles east of Lake Maracaibo. Here was one pocket of the world where he could hope that no one had heard of him.

Later, John returned to the United States and continued working as a geologist. He married and had two children. Once back in the States, John could not remain hidden. Students writing school papers tracked him down; news reporters, especially on the anniversaries of the July trial; preachers wanting to show him the way to God. For the most part, John ignored them all.

But they did not ignore him, and the trial did not fade from memory. Memory, though—like genes—has a way of mutating. Memory can morph into myth.

The myth-making started immediately at the trial's end. Mostly it was to the glory of William Jennings Bryan. A genre of music emerged: "Scopes songs." Will was barely buried when Columbia Records released one by a popular country music singer, Vernon Dalhart, called "William Jennings Bryan's Last Fight." In a quavering tenor, Dalhart sang:

A record of one of the "Scopes songs" that became popular after William Jennings Bryan's death.

When the good folks had their troubles
down in Dayton far away
Mr. Bryan went to help them
and he worked both night and day.
There he fought for what was righteous
and the battle it was won
Then the Lord called him to heaven
for his work on earth was done.

Another song made John out to be a sort of ineffectual villain:

Oh the folks in Tennessee
Are as faithful as can be,
And they know the Bible teaches what is right.
They believe in God above

And His great undying love
And they know they are protected by His might.

Then to Dayton came a man
With his ideas new and grand
And he said we came from monkeys long ago.
But in teaching his belief
Mr. Scopes found only grief
For they would not let their old religion go.

Then the folks throughout the land
Saw his house was built on sand
And they said, "We will not listen anymore."
So they told him he was wrong
And it wasn't very long
Till he found that he was turned from every door.

Not everyone agreed that the occasion called for myths and music. A month after the trial's end, *The Crisis* magazine, edited by the scholar and civil rights pioneer W.E.B. DuBois, offered a sober reflection:

> The truth is and we know it: Dayton, Tennessee, is America: a great, ignorant, simple-minded land, curiously compounded of brutality, bigotry, religious faith and demagoguery, and capable not simply of mistakes but of persecution, lynching, murder and idiotic blundering, as well as charity, missions, love and hope. . . .
>
> Dayton, Tennessee, is no laughing matter. It is menace and warning. It is a challenge to Religion, Science and Democracy.

On the ten-year anniversary of the trial, Nellie Kenyon, who was still working as a journalist in Tennessee, went back to Dayton and asked a waitress at a local restaurant, "What was this Scopes evolution trial about?"

"Oh, it happened over there at the drugstore," the young woman replied. "Bryan, Darrow and a fellow named Scopes tried to claim we came from monkeys. They got into a big argument. Bryan got mad and got right up there in the drugstore and made a big speech. It was too much for him so he went home that night and died."

The "trial which rocked the world," Nellie wrote, had become "a warped legend."

Legend had it that Clarence killed Will with his words. "What was it," a letter writer asked John, "that Darrow said to Bryan that killed him?"

Legend had it that Will utterly vanquished the evolutionists. "He not only won his case in the judgment of the Judge, in the judgment of the Jurors, in the judgment of the Tennessee populace attending," wrote William Bell Riley, the Fundamentalist leader who had recruited the Great Commoner to Dayton, "he won it in the judgment of an intelligent world."

Legend had it that Clarence conquered the Fundamentalists. "Theoretically, Fundamentalism had won, for the law stood," wrote Frederick Lewis Allen in a bestselling book published in 1931. "Yet really Fundamentalism had lost. Legislators might go on passing anti-evolution laws . . . but civilized opinion everywhere had regarded the Dayton trial with amazement and amusement, and the slow drift away from Fundamentalism certainly continued."

The legend of Clarence's moral victory over Will and Fundamentalism became entrenched in American lore when the play *Inherit the Wind* took the New York theater world by storm in 1955 and was made into a movie five years later. Funny, poignant, absorbing, and frightening, *Inherit the Wind* told a story based on the Scopes trial—but it wasn't quite the story of the Scopes trial.

The dramatic movie poster for *Inherit the Wind*.

In the story, the character based on John Scopes is nabbed in his classroom smack-dab in the middle of a lesson on evolution and thrown in jail. The writers took many liberties with the facts, but their most significant inventions were what they made of the people of Dayton and the character based on William Jennings Bryan. The Dayton (fictionalized as "Hillsboro") locals are strident, even dangerous, religious fanatics. Will—his character is named Matthew Harrison Brady—is a bumbling fool, practically a clown. He calls evolution "evil-ution." His pathetic performance on the witness stand, in this fictional version, turns even his supporters against him. In the end, the jury returns a guilty verdict against John, and the judge fines him $100—which is what happened in real life—and releases him from jail, where he never was in real life. Matthew Harrison Brady is deprived of his chance to deliver his closing argument, again, as in real life. But as the crowd is hurrying away from him—he is no longer their idol—he starts to make his speech anyway. Mid-sentence, he collapses and dies. The Clarence Darrow character soberly walks off into the future, carrying a Bible and Darwin's *Origin of Species*. Science, reasonableness, and tolerance, the ending suggests, have prevailed.

The play, which ran from 1955 to 1957, became one of the longest-running dramas on Broadway. The 1960 film featured three major stars—Spencer Tracy, Fredric March, and Gene Kelly—and received four Academy Award nominations. There's no way to count up the number of people who have seen *Inherit the Wind* on stage or on screen. But for many audiences, it *is* the story of the Scopes trial.

The film finally brought John Scopes out of the shadows. He hadn't gone to New York to see the play when it was on Broadway. But at the request of the movie's producer, John and his wife, Mildred, traveled back to Dayton for the premiere of *Inherit the Wind* on the thirty-fifth anniversary of the trial.

Dayton dressed itself up for the movie screening. Banners, flags, and bunting decorated Main Street. Vintage cars and clothing styles from 1925 were on display. A parade, a concert, a reception for John—it was quite the event. The mayor gave John the key to the city. Employees at Robinson's Drug Store dressed in '20s clothing and served "Bryan Ale" and "Scopes Soda." The cost of a root beer was rolled back to the 1925 price of five cents.

The drugstore cabal's dream of bringing new life and industry to their town through the publicity of the trial didn't work out exactly as they'd hoped—but it wasn't a total bust, either. In 1930, William Jennings Bryan University opened its doors a short walk from the Rhea County Courthouse. The school, which still exists, was established by Will's admirers for the purpose of offering higher education infused with Christianity and committed, as its organizers announced, to the "infallibility of the Bible." So by the time John returned to Dayton in 1960, it had become a college town. Later, other industries made their homes in Dayton, such as the furniture manufacturer La-Z-Boy.

All in all, the premiere of *Inherit the Wind* was a convivial gathering. John gave interviews. At the drugstore, he sipped a Bryan Ale—one-and-one-half teaspoons of extract of ginger, two drops of tincture of pepper, and seven grains of saccharine mixed with water, said to be William Jennings Bryan's own recipe. And yet—if the townspeople wanted a carnival, John seemed interested in making a more serious point. "Freedom of teachers and educators to say what is to be taught was the great principle involved in the case," he said at a press conference.

Was it? Was that the "great principle" at issue in John's trial? Historians and other scholars continue to disagree not only about who really won, but also what was really at stake. Some say the case was entirely and only about the conflict between the two wings of

Christianity: Fundamentalism and modernism. Others view the trial more broadly, as a mirror of the rift between city people and country people in the 1920s, between North and South, between white supremacy and anti-bigotry.

But to John Scopes, the fight was about the freedom of teachers to teach. And he harbored no second thoughts. "My thinking now is the same as it was then," he said at the press conference. "I would do the whole thing over again if necessary, but I don't want to start an argument."

CHAPTER 24
A VICTORY

"Mr. Chief Justice, may it please the Court," the lawyer began, as lawyers do when they open their arguments before the Supreme Court of the United States.

The courtroom fell silent. The nine Supreme Court justices sat up on their bench, eyes on the lawyer at the lectern in front of them.

"This case involves the constitutionality of . . . the so-called monkey bill, or the anti-evolution law," the lawyer continued in a pronounced Southern twang.

The lawyer's client, the twenty-something teacher at the center of the case, sat quietly behind him. The argument didn't last long—eleven minutes, hardly enough time for someone like Clarence Darrow, master of the eight-hour argument, to clear his throat. But the Supreme Court had strict limits on how long attorneys were permitted to argue before them.

The state's lawyer, too, spoke briefly. He began in an unusual way, telling the justices that the case began under the administration of a previous state attorney general.

"What was the significance of that?" asked Justice William Brennan.

The lawyer stumbled. "I was just giving you background, Your Honor," he replied.

"I thought you were telling us your administration doesn't like the statute," countered Justice Brennan.

Laughter in the courtroom.

"No," the state's lawyer said, "I am not here prepared to say that."

"It might not be too late, you know," quipped Justice Abe Fortas.

The laughter got louder.

Things didn't get much better for the state's attorney. By the end of his allotted time, he admitted to Justice Fortas that, under the challenged law, teachers could instruct students in the Bible's story of creation—but not in the theory of evolution.

Justice Fortas wanted to make sure he got this statement right. "In other words," he said, "out of that whole area of the origin of man," the state had only prohibited "a segment, that segment being the Darwin Theory; is that correct?"

"That is correct."

So ended the argument. The Supreme Court issued its decision less than a month later—a very quick turnaround. The anti-evolution law, it ruled, was in clear violation of the U.S. Constitution.

"The law's effort," wrote Justice Fortas for the court, "was confined to an attempt to blot out a particular theory because of its supposed conflict with the Biblical account, literally read." But, he explained, "There is and can be no doubt that the First Amendment does not permit the State to require that teaching . . . must be tailored to . . . any religious sect or dogma." The law could not stand because it violated the First Amendment's prohibition of laws "respecting an establishment of religion or prohibiting the free exercise thereof."

Victory for the teacher! Victory for the evolutionists! For the first time ever, the U.S. Supreme Court struck down a law that barred the teaching of Darwin's theory.

Susan Epperson, the Arkansas high school teacher who successfully challenged the state's anti-evolution law in the U.S. Supreme Court.

The young high school teacher at the center of the case was named Susan Epperson, not John Scopes. The anti-evolution law in question was on the statute books in Arkansas, not Tennessee. The winning lawyer who spoke so briefly before the Supreme Court was named

Eugene, not Clarence. And the year was 1968, three decades after Clarence Darrow's death.

John's own case never made it to the U.S. Supreme Court. His lawyers did appeal to the Tennessee Supreme Court, in Nashville. John declined to attend. He was done with the whole affair. The court's decision on the appeal showed that it was even more done with the Monkey Trial than John was. In 1927, the court upheld Tennessee's anti-evolution law. But it also reversed John's sentence. The reason, the state justices said, was that Judge Raulston had ruled on the amount of the fine, but Tennessee law gave that job to the jury. The jury: those twelve men who had been barred from witnessing a single dramatic episode in the trial and also, the high court now ruled, from doing the job that Tennessee law specifically reserved for them.

So John did not have to pay the $100 penalty.

Also, the court said, with a touch of weariness, enough already. "We see nothing to be gained by prolonging the life of this bizarre case," the justices wrote. Make it go away, they told the state of Tennessee. The next day the state's attorney general did just that. He issued a legal notice that said, basically, this prosecution never happened.

The state of Tennessee took back its charges against John. He heard about it when a reporter called him at home.

John went on to live his life, dipping his toe in the evolution/anti-evolution pond when *Inherit the Wind* was released in theaters—and then again in January 1969. Susan Epperson had just won her case in the U.S. Supreme Court. She traveled to Shreveport, Louisiana, where John was living in retirement. They had lunch together at a Holiday Inn: two high school teachers from two generations who thought that teenagers could handle learning about evolution.

John Thomas Scopes died a year later. He was seventy years old.

CHAPTER 25
THE EVOLUTION OF EVERYTHING

During the forty years between John's carnival of a trial and Susan's journey to the Supreme Court of the United States, much had evolved. Law evolved. Textbooks evolved. Science evolved. The nation and its politics evolved. They are all evolving still.

First, law: at the state and local level, the outcome of John's trial emboldened legislators and other officials to continue the fight against evolution in schools. Between 1925 and 1930, fifteen state legislatures considered anti-evolution bills. While only two states— Arkansas and Mississippi—passed the proposals into law, anti-evolutionists had other, more effective, ways by which they furthered their cause. In many places, they didn't need new laws on the books because local school boards simply went ahead and nixed evolution-ary teaching. State textbook authorities rejected school science books that included sections on evolution.

As these anti-evolution policies took hold, mostly in the South, a funny thing happened to high school science books. They evolved, too, everywhere, not only in the South. Publishers wanted to sell biology textbooks, not deal with controversy. So, starting after John's trial, most publishers changed their books by deleting chapters on evolution and Darwin. Without discussions of evolution in biology textbooks, discussions of evolution in biology classes disappeared. By 1940, most high school science classes—across the country, not just in Arkansas, Mississippi, and Tennessee—had evolved into evolution-free zones.

At the same time, American constitutional law was evolving. The First Amendment to the U.S. Constitution says that "Congress shall make no law respecting an establishment of religion, or pro-hibiting the free exercise thereof." As Thomas Jefferson wrote back in 1802, these clauses put up a "wall between church and State." They stand for the principle of separation of church and state. It's not a wild argument to say that a law that bans the teaching of evo-lution because it contradicts Fundamentalist Christian thinking is a law that supports and establishes religion—in violation of the First Amendment's so-called Establishment Clause. And yet in all their hours of argument, John Scopes's lawyers didn't forcefully press this challenge. They mostly focused on various provisions of the Tennes-see Constitution. The ACLU and John himself fixed on academic freedom of thought.

The reason for this omission was simple: at the time, the First Amendment applied to Congress, not to the states. *Congress* shall make no law establishing religion. The legislature of Tennessee could. But the law is always evolving, and in 1947, the Supreme Court ruled (in a case having nothing to do with evolution) that the First Amend-ment's Establishment Clause does in fact apply to the states, as well as to the national government. In 1962 and 1963, the Supreme Court applied its interpretation to classrooms, ruling that the First

Amendment did not allow public schools to sponsor or lead prayer or Bible readings with their students.

For John Scopes, this change came too late to be of use in his case. For Susan Epperson, it made all the difference. The Supreme Court found that the Arkansas anti-evolution law violated the Establishment Clause.

But—it took two whole decades for Susan's case to arise after the Supreme Court opened up the possibility of challenging anti-evolution laws on First Amendment grounds. Where was a Scopes or Epperson during those twenty years? Answer: wherever they were, they probably were not teaching evolution in their classrooms. Without evolutionary textbooks, prosecutors had no one to prosecute and school authorities had hardly anyone to discipline for violating rules against teaching the prohibited science. So, the debate lay dormant.

Science, though, was not dormant. In Darwin's day, the fossil record of humans' ancestors was practically nonexistent. By the time of the Scopes trial, the record had filled out, but still was sparse. In the years following the trial, paleontologists found hundreds of fossils of human ancestors and cousins, dating back six to seven million years. Scientists discovered fossils of our most direct ancestors in Africa, dating from hundreds of thousands of years ago. They learned how to analyze the genetic material of living people and extinct human ancestors to understand their relationships.

Scientists also learned how to calculate the age of the earth more accurately. Darwin's theory of descent with modification—of random mutations gradually leading to new species—only made sense if the earth was very, *very* old. Six thousand years? A blink of an eye in evolutionary time. A hundred million? Still not enough time for the type of gradual evolution Darwin proposed. By the 1930s, however, geologists determined that the earth is billions of years old—plenty of time for the diversity of its life-forms to have developed by descent with modification.

And about that super-slow Darwinian evolution—as the twentieth century progressed, so did scientists' understanding of the mechanics of evolution. Yes, still, to Darwin's random mutation and natural selection of the organisms that inherit beneficial mutations. But scientists unearthed information about other ways evolution occurs. In some cases, researchers found that it can happen much more quickly than Darwin assumed. Change occurs not only when genes mutate, but also when they recombine as part of the reproductive process—in other words, sex is part of the engine of evolution.

Evolution is also pushed along by other important processes. There's gene flow, which refers to the migration of genetic material—such as in prehistoric humans—from one population to another. There's genetic drift, which is about the totally random survival of individuals, not because they contain a mutation that better adapts them to survival than others, but just because they are lucky. (Like a bug that doesn't get squashed under a person's foot and lives on to populate the world.)

Not everything in the science of evolution got resolved during the decades after John Scopes's trial—far from it. Not everything is resolved today, even as newer scientific tools such as genetic sequencing provide powerful evidence of evolution by revealing striking similarities in the genomes of different species. Scientists still debate the *mechanisms* of evolution, but evolution itself is widely settled. "Facts do not go away when scientists debate rival theories to explain them," wrote Stephen Jay Gould, one of the most famous paleontologists and evolutionary biologists of the twentieth century. "Einstein's theory of gravitation replaced Newton's, but apples did not suspend themselves in mid-air, pending the outcome."

All these changes in law and textbooks and scientific theory might have been interesting only to lawyers and book publishers and scientists, but in 1957 another change came along that got Americans worried. This time they were worried about whether their kids were being well educated in science. That year, the Soviet Union became the first country to send a satellite into space. The launch of Sputnik I by America's main rival after World War II was a shock to the public. How could the Soviets have outperformed the United States in the technological race to space? What else would their superior scientific minds achieve—and at what cost to peace and prosperity?

"One Hundred Years Without Darwinism Are Enough," implored Hermann Joseph Muller, a Nobel Prize-winning geneticist, in a much-quoted speech in 1959. It was the hundredth anniversary of *On the Origin of Species*. By the early 1960s, evolution was back in biology books. That was what prompted Susan Epperson's case: the new textbook she was told to teach from included evolution. The old Arkansas law told her she couldn't teach evolution. She went to court, and the rest is . . . the rest really is history. And even before the Supreme Court's decision in Susan's case, in 1967 Tennessee repealed the Butler Act, the law under which John Scopes was prosecuted.

So evolution was back in public schools—in some places. (Thankfully, it was shorn of the eugenics nonsense of Hunter's old *A Civic Biology*.) The Supreme Court had said that states couldn't outlaw evolutionary teaching. If Clarence Darrow could come back from the dead, would he have declared victory?

Probably not. The battle between evolutionists and anti-evolutionists was not over. Americans now cared about science? Creationists pivoted to science, too. They published scientific journals and founded colleges. They wrote law review articles. They built museums. Instead of the science of evolution, however, they put forward "creation science," or "scientific creationism," and said that it belonged in schools as part of science classes. Creation science was the same as creationism, but with evidence from the natural world presented in support of biblical stories such as divine creation and the Genesis flood.

This new approach found some success. Creationists were no longer seeking to outlaw evolutionary teaching. Rather, they argued, there should be balanced treatment, in science classes, of evolutionary science and creation science. Some states and school boards, North and South, were convinced—it seemed only fair. No, countered evolutionary scientists; this wasn't a matter of fair or unfair. Still, "creation science" found its way into classrooms.

It also found its way into national politics. Campaigning for the presidency in 1980, Ronald Reagan said that evolution "is a scientific theory only. And in recent years it has been challenged in the world of science and is not believed in the scientific community to be as infallible as it once was." (In fact, evolution was challenged only in the creation-science community, not in the larger scientific community.) The biblical story of creation, Reagan said, should be taught in schools as a counterpoint to evolution.

Reagan was a Republican; half a century after the death of the Great Commoner, it was now Republican Party politicians, not Democrats, who were more likely to embrace creationism. Reagan won the election and served two terms as president. He also got his wish: "equal time" laws and policies took off. But in 1987, toward the end of President Reagan's second term, the Supreme Court shot them down. Creationists responded with another theory in support of creationism in schools: intelligent design. Intelligent design holds that life is so complex and amazing that it could not have merely evolved from simple to more complex life-forms. Under this theory, the best explanation for life is that it has been put together intentionally by an intelligent designer and maker—and that would be, for most adherents of this idea, God.

In 2005, a federal judge struck down a Pennsylvania school district's efforts to introduce ninth-grade biology students to intelligent design as an alternative to Darwinian evolution. Judge John E. Jones III explained that his ruling was required by the First Amendment and by U.S. Supreme Court decisions, including Susan Epperson's case.

"This is why I believe in intelligent design. There's no way I'm related to that!"

A cartoon poking fun at the creationist idea of "intelligent design" as an explanation of life on Earth.

Judge Jones received so many death threats that the U.S. Marshals Service gave him and his family special protection.

On the other hand, the school board members who had voted for the intelligent design policy were booted out of office by voters.

The Pennsylvania ruling didn't apply to the entire country; a similar case in another court or the U.S. Supreme Court could lead to a different result. And anti-evolutionists have developed additional positions to convince school officials and judges to permit the teaching of creationism. There is the "teach the controversy" argument: science classes should, at the very least, instruct high school students in the debate between evolutionary scientists and creation scientists. (Evolutionary scientists counter that creation science isn't science, so while there may be debate, it isn't a scientific one and doesn't belong in a science curriculum.) There is the "religion of secularism" argument: when the government elevates evolution over all other possible theories of life and promotes hostility to religion, it is establishing a type of religion—an atheistic, anti-Christian creed. This, the argument goes, violates the First Amendment's Establishment Clause.

Millions of people believe that the Bible offers the most important bulwark against societal and moral breakdown. Like William Jennings Bryan, they express concerns about the ethical life of young people. They worry about young people turning away from religion.

If children are taught that they are descended from animals, these creationists fear the worst for civilization. They see Darwinism, as Will did, as the source of man's inhumanity to man.

But evolution doesn't want people to be religious or irreligious, to be cruel or kind. The theory of evolution describes; it doesn't pre-

"Do you honestly believe we evolved from a single snow flake?"

An evolution joke that doesn't take sides.

scribe. It has no shoulds. It doesn't say that people should struggle against one another to survive. It doesn't say the strong should vanquish the weak. Evolution—descent with modification—just is.

And many deeply religious people today fully embrace evolution, as did the faith leaders and biblical scholars who backed John Scopes in his stand against the Butler Act in 1925. Thought leaders like

A creation joke that doesn't take sides.

Dr. Francis Collins, who used to head the National Institutes of Health and the Human Genome Project, have made it their mission to show that religious belief and the theory of evolution are not in conflict. "They were two ways of knowing, but knowing different things and asking different questions," Dr. Collins said in 2019. "Science asking how, faith answering why."

Charles Darwin asked *how* the natural world came to be as he, and we, have found it. He came up with powerful answers that have convinced legions of ordinary people and brilliant thinkers alike and have stood the test of time, modern evidence, and research. He didn't pretend to answer *why* human beings are here on Earth, or why life exists at all. He left that to each person, alone or in community with others, believing, or not believing, in a Supreme Being.

EPILOGUE

Legislators pass laws. School officials adopt policies. Courts issue rulings. But neither laws, nor policies, nor rulings show up in school every day and stand in front of a biology class. The 100,000 public schools in the United States don't all follow the same playbook. A large percentage of the American public rejects the theory of evolution (and may not understand it). And what goes on in any given science classroom depends on the particular community in which it's situated—on teachers, principals, students, parents, and politicians.

So whether your biology textbook includes a sticker disclaiming evolution as "only" a theory depends on where you live. Whether science teachers promote creationism may depend on the attitudes in their communities. Whether teachers dive deep into Darwinism or avoid the subject may depend on whether they think such instruction will bring them grief from parents or school board members or a governor.

And parents and politicians will not hesitate to heap grief on teachers. They will agitate over what they view as unwholesome subjects in school. It's been going on for more than a hundred years. History books that were insufficiently patriotic; or too negative about the South in the Civil War, or too negative about slavery; classes in sex education—all provoked heated controversies, and when? Before 1930. The journalist Nellie Kenyon, writing a couple of weeks in advance of the Scopes trial in 1925, tried to give her readers a map of the landscape. "Freedom of teaching," she wrote, "has been more interfered with by law in the past six months than at any time in American history." There were laws requiring Bible readings, laws forbidding hiring teachers who were "radical," laws disqualifying teachers who were "pacifist," and laws prohibiting teaching "that ours is an inferior form of government." Not to mention the anti-evolution law.

Today, complaints about science in the classroom go well beyond evolution. Some parents and lawmakers don't want schools to teach about climate change. They don't want laws and policies to address climate change, either, because they think it's a hoax or not caused by human activity. This is contrary to scientific evidence. Climate-change deniers found a friend in the White House in President Donald Trump. "I don't believe it," he said in 2018. "One of the problems that a lot of people like myself, we have very high levels of intelligence but we're not necessarily such believers" in climate change.

The COVID-19 pandemic, starting in 2020, also spurred epic resistance to science among large swaths of the American public and their leaders. When leading scientists—the preeminent experts on infectious and viral diseases—tried to guide the public on how to protect themselves from the novel coronavirus, President Trump called them "idiots."

And so, here are two persistent threads lifted from the pattern woven a century ago. First: ridicule. Anti-evolutionists at the time of the Scopes trial made fun of scientists because, as Will Bryan scoffed, "They cannot agree with each other." Will's mockery was a cheap shot—just as it was a cheap shot, a century later, to mock scientists for altering their advice, in response to new and evolving discoveries, on how to protect against getting sick or dying from the coronavirus. That is what happens in science as a result of ongoing observation, experimentation, and, yes, disagreement among scientists: knowledge evolves.

And second: lumping together science and belief, by couching science as something you "believe" in, or not. Forcing, or even strongly urging, people to "believe" in a creed (science) that doesn't appeal to them—that's a bad thing to do, isn't it? It's un-American, isn't it? But science isn't a religious creed. And religion isn't science.

What accounts for the persistence of resistance to science among Americans? Is it because scientific theories aren't well understood? ("People come from monkeys.") Is it because they make people uncomfortable? (*People come from monkeys?!*") Is it because, in the case of the coronavirus or climate change, for example, they point to the need to change our behaviors?

The same questions arise when confronting the persistence of resistance to historical facts. Is it because history isn't understood? ("The Civil War was about the South preserving 'states' rights,' not slavery.") Is it because it makes people uncomfortable? ("Students shouldn't feel distress for the racism of people in the past.") Is it because it points to the need to change our thinking?

As in the Scopes case, none of this is just about history. It isn't just about science. It's also cultural. That is, these conflicts reflect divisions in attitudes, values, and even life goals. *Us v. Those People. Right-Thinking Folks v. Morons.* Sometimes the cultural rift breaks along geographic lines: North/South, coastal/non-coastal. Sometimes it breaks along religious lines. Or political party lines.

And much as people say they crave peace, many also seem drawn to conflict—the louder the better. So the cultural divides give rise to boisterous cheering sections and booing sections. People come to watch the show. The ridicule, misrepresentations, and heat are turned up. Accusations of "conspiracy" are flung about. Opinions are firm and final. "Liberals, radicals and conservatives are alike in this respect," the *Boston Globe* observed. "Few of them act upon Shakespeare's admonition: 'Take heed lest by your heat you burn yourselves.'"

The *Globe* editorialist was commenting in July 1925 on the just-concluded trial in Dayton, Tennessee. But William Jennings Bryan wasn't the last leader to whip up his audiences' feelings of being disrespected by pointy-headed elites. Clarence Darrow wasn't the last skeptic whose tolerance turned to shouted insults. H.L. Mencken wasn't the last journalist to smirk at people he didn't really understand and exaggerate their behaviors and beliefs as a means of gaining an audience. Look around and you'll know: the beat goes on, and so does the heat.

But also—Nellie Kenyon wasn't the last journalist to try to hew to facts and avoid sensationalism. John Thomas Scopes wasn't the last teacher to stand up for a principle without trashing those who thought otherwise. Neither was Susan Epperson.

Their beats go on, too.

ACKNOWLEDGMENTS

Thank you to Professor Edward J. Larson, historian and legal scholar at Pepperdine University, and author of multiple books and articles on evolution, creationism, the Scopes trial, and other fascinating topics. His book *Summer for the Gods* won the 1998 Pulitzer Prize for History and was the first book I read about *The State of Tennessee v. John Thomas Scopes*. I was hooked. Professor Larson generously made time to meet with me when visiting Washington, DC, and our discussions aided me immeasurably—as did his books and other writings—as I found my way through this complicated story.

A similar note of gratitude goes to Professor Randy Moore of the University of Minnesota, whose research, books, and publications on how evolution is taught, learned, accepted, and rejected are so important, and whose devotion to the story of John T. Scopes is remarkable—and so necessary for the rest of us. Professor Moore obliged me with a wide-ranging Zoom conversation that was invaluable, as were his books and articles.

I am also thankful to Dr. Briana Pobiner, research scientist and museum educator in the Human Origins Program at the Smithsonian Institution, for guidance on my treatment of the evolutionary science in this book. Any errors, of course, remain my own.

I am indebted to Ben Hoffman, who helped get me started on the original manuscript, and whose fingerprints are all over these pages, especially in the opening chapters. I don't have a better editor who also has another day job.

But if I'm speaking of editors who do this work as their day jobs, I would be hard-pressed to find a better one than Megan Abbate at Bloomsbury Children's Books. Thank you, Megan, for your thoughtfulness, sensitivity, eye for detail, and for being a pleasure to work with. The rest of the team at Bloomsbury—Diane Aronson, Jeffrey Curry, Lara Kennedy, John Candell, Donna Mark, Henry Sene Yee, Nicholas Church, Laura Phillips, Mary Kate Castellani, Sarah Shumway, Beth Eller, Kathleen Morandini, Erica Barmash, and Lex Higbee—also do not disappoint and I am grateful to them all.

My literary agent Caryn Wiseman has been on my team for two decades and continues to be that rare combination of wise counselor and enthusiastic cheerleader, for which I am grateful.

And the greatest thank-you goes to my husband, Rick Hoffman. He supports all my book projects, but he does have his favorites and this is one of those. We were classmates at the University of Michigan Law School, and it's the lawyer in each of us, I think, that draws us to stories like this one. Thank you, Rick, for talking through so many sections of the book, for reading the manuscript as it evolved, and for sharing my passion for the ideas, events, and history that make up this narrative and the characters who populate these pages.

TIMELINE

=================== **1831–36** ===================

Charles Darwin takes his globe-spanning voyage on the HMS *Beagle*.

=================== **1857** ===================

Clarence Seward Darrow is born near Kinsman, Ohio.

=================== **1859** ===================

Darwin presents his theory of descent with modification—also known as evolution—in his book *On the Origin of Species*.

=================== **1860** ===================

William Jennings Bryan is born in Salem, Illinois.

=================== **1871** ===================

Darwin publishes *The Descent of Man*, in which he extends his theory of evolution to human beings.

=================== **1878** ===================

Darrow launches his career as a lawyer near his hometown of Kinsman.

=================== **1882** ===================

Darwin dies at his home near London, England.

=================== **1883** ===================

Bryan begins working as a lawyer in Jacksonville, Illinois.

=================== **1887** ===================

Darrow moves to Chicago, Illinois, with his wife and little boy. Bryan moves to Lincoln, Nebraska, and is soon joined by his wife and baby daughter. The Bryans will go on to have another daughter and a son.

=================== **1890** ===================

Bryan wins election to the U.S. House of Representatives, representing a Nebraska congressional district.

=========================== **1894** ===========================

Bryan gives up his congressional seat to run for the U.S. Senate. He loses the election.

Darrow represents Patrick Prendergast in a trial to review Prendergast's death sentence for murdering the mayor of Chicago. It is the first of Darrow's 102 cases against the death penalty. He loses the case, and Prendergast is executed.

=========================== **1896** ===========================

In July, Bryan gives his famous "Cross of Gold" speech at the Democratic National Convention in Chicago. Democrats then nominate him as their candidate for president of the United States, with the general election to take place in November. Darrow also attends the convention and hears Bryan's speech. He runs for the U.S. House of Representatives from the third congressional district of Illinois. Neither Bryan nor Darrow wins election.

Libraries in New York City report that Darwin's *The Descent of Man* is one of their most popular titles among library patrons.

=========================== **1900** ===========================

John Thomas Scopes is born in Paducah, Kentucky. Bryan makes his second run for the U.S. presidency as the Democrats' candidate; he loses again.

=========================== **1901** ===========================

Bryan founds his newspaper, *The Commoner*.

=========================== **1903** ===========================

Darrow represents anthracite coal mine workers in hearings to settle a dispute over wages, exploitative working conditions, and other labor issues. He wins better wages and shorter hours for the workers. The case is considered a milestone in the history of U.S. labor relations.

=========================== **1908** ===========================

Bryan runs for president for a third time and loses.

═══════════════════ **1913** ═══════════════════

Bryan becomes secretary of state in the administration of President Woodrow Wilson. He also draws large audiences as a speaker on the Chautauqua circuit, giving his "Prince of Peace" lecture, in which he takes aim at Darwin's theory of evolution.

═══════════════════ **1914** ═══════════════════

George William Hunter's high school textbook *A Civic Biology* is published.

═══════════════════ **1915** ═══════════════════

Bryan resigns as secretary of state in protest over the Wilson administration's sympathy toward the Allied powers in World War I. Bryan wished for the U.S. to remain neutral in the conflict.

═══════════════════ **1918** ═══════════════════

All forty-eight states in the United States have laws on their statute books requiring parents to send their children to school.

═══════════════════ **1919** ═══════════════════

Bryan embarks on a campaign against teaching evolution with a speech he calls "Back to God." He also speaks at the graduation ceremony at Salem High School in his hometown of Salem, Illinois. John Scopes is in the audience as one of the graduating seniors.

Tennessee adopts Hunter's *A Civic Biology* for use in the state's high schools. The book includes brief sections on Darwin and evolution.

═══════════════════ **1921** ═══════════════════

Bryan intensifies his attacks on teaching evolution in a series of new speeches with titles such as "The Menace of Darwinism" and "The Bible and Its Enemies."

═══════════════════ **1923** ═══════════════════

The *Chicago Daily Tribune* publishes Darrow's list of fifty-five questions for Bryan on the front page. The questions aim to draw out Bryan's views on the Bible and his knowledge, and lack of knowledge, about theology and science. Bryan does not respond.

========================= **1924** =========================

Bryan gives a major speech titled "Is the Bible True?" in Nashville, Tennessee. Copies of the address are circulated among Tennessee lawmakers. Darrow represents confessed teenage murderers Nathan Leopold and Richard Loeb and defeats prosecutors' request for the death penalty for his clients.

John Scopes graduates from the University of Kentucky. He accepts a job to teach at Rhea Central High School in Dayton, Tennessee, and moves to Dayton to begin his new job.

========================= **1925** =========================

JANUARY 21: John Washington Butler, a member of the Tennessee House of Representatives, introduces a bill to make the teaching of evolution in the state's schools a crime.

MARCH 21: Having been adopted by the Tennessee House and Senate, the Butler Act is signed into law by Tennessee Governor Austin Peay.

MAY 4: The New York–based American Civil Liberties Union runs a notice in a Chattanooga newspaper seeking a Tennessee teacher who is willing to be charged under the Butler Act with the crime of teaching evolution. The ACLU promises to represent the teacher, for free, with "distinguished counsel" in a case that would challenge the statute as an unlawful exercise of state power.

MAY 5: Meeting around a table in Robinson's Drug Store in downtown Dayton, town leaders formulate a plan to take the ACLU up on its offer by bringing a prosecution under the Butler Act against their high school's biology teacher. They understand that the case will attract widespread national attention, and hope that this will shine a spotlight on their town and help its economy. Scopes has been teaching biology at Rhea Central High School in the semester just ended. They ask him if he would agree to be charged. He does.

JULY 7: Bryan arrives in Dayton to join in the prosecution of Scopes.

JULY 9: Darrow arrives in Dayton, leading Scopes's team of defense lawyers.

JULY 10 (FRIDAY): Proceedings in the case of *State of Tennessee v. John Thomas Scopes* begin, Judge John Raulston presiding. Much of this first day of the trial is devoted to jury selection.

JULY 13 (MONDAY): The defense moves to quash the indictment against Scopes. The judge excludes the jury from the courtroom. Darrow presents arguments for more than two hours before court is adjourned.

JULY 14 (TUESDAY): Clarence objects to the judge's practice of opening court with prayer, but the objection is not sustained. Later, Judge Raulston says that he has written his ruling on the defense motion to quash the indictment, but he will not issue it because he has learned that the ruling has been leaked to the press. The jury is again not allowed in the courtroom.

JULY 15 (WEDNESDAY): Judge Raulston learns that he, not a reporter or anybody else, accidentally leaked the contents of his ruling, which he then proceeds to read. He rules against the defense motion to quash. The prosecution will proceed. Scopes's lawyers enter his plea of not guilty. The jury is brought into court to hear the evidence. The prosecutors put on their witnesses: two of Scopes's students, who say that he taught them evolution, and two of the town's leaders, who say that Scopes had admitted to them that he'd taught evolution. After the prosecution rests its case, Darrow tells the court that Scopes will not be testifying in his own defense, because everything the prosecution witnesses said is true. Instead, Darrow puts on the witness stand the first of several experts that he wishes to question, experts in science and theology who will explain evolution and how it is consistent with religious belief and not in conflict with a nonliteral reading of the Bible's creation story. Judge Raulston orders the jury to leave the courtroom, as he hasn't yet decided if he'll allow the expert testimony in as evidence.

JULY 16 (THURSDAY): The jury is still barred from the courtroom. Lawyers for both sides present arguments on whether the defense should be allowed to present the testimony of its expert witnesses to the jury. Bryan makes his first speech of the trial.

JULY 17 (FRIDAY): Judge Raulston decides that testimony from the defense team's expert witnesses will not be allowed because the only issue that matters in the trial is whether Scopes taught that humans descended from a lower order of animals. He does allow the defense to put together written statements from their experts, which will be part of the record of the case when it is appealed to a higher court. The statements are due the following Monday, and most observers of the trial conclude that the trial is now essentially over. The jury has missed this day in court, too.

JULY 20 (MONDAY): The expert statements are read or otherwise submitted into the record. The judge moves the proceedings outside to the courthouse lawn. The defense announces that it wishes to call Bryan as a witness. All the other members of the prosecutorial team strenuously object to this extremely unorthodox request, but Bryan insists that he wants to testify, and so he takes the witness stand. Darrow questions him extensively, and contentiously, on his beliefs in the literal truth of the Bible and on his understanding (or lack of understanding) of science and other fields. It is high drama, unprecedented in a courtroom. The jury has been excluded from these proceedings as well.

JULY 21 (TUESDAY): Judge Raulston says he was wrong to allow Bryan to testify and strikes all of the previous day's testimony from the record. The jury is brought in and, based on the four witnesses they heard, they find Scopes guilty. Before the judge sentences him, Scopes utters four sentences in his own defense, his only statement during his trial. The judge sentences him to a fine of $100. The Butler Act stays on the statute books in Tennessee.

JULY 26 (SUNDAY): Bryan dies in his sleep. His death sends shock waves around the nation, and he receives a hero's honors and funeral.

JULY 28 (TUESDAY): The 12,000-word closing statement that Bryan never got to deliver at the trial is published in newspapers everywhere.

SEPTEMBER: Having given up teaching, Scopes attends the University of Chicago graduate school to study geology. He will go on to work in that field for petroleum companies.

=========================== 1927 ===========================

On the appeal of Scopes's conviction, the Tennessee Supreme Court upholds the Butler Act but overturns the punishment that Judge Raulston imposed.

=========================== 1930 ===========================

Admirers of Bryan open William Jennings Bryan Memorial University in Dayton, Tennessee. A Christian college, today it is known as Bryan College.

=========================== 1938 ===========================

Darrow dies at his home in Chicago.

=========================== 1955 ===========================

Inherit the Wind opens on Broadway and is a hit.

=========================== 1960 ===========================

A film adaptation of *Inherit the Wind* has its world premiere in Dayton. Scopes attends the premiere and is celebrated by the town leaders and residents, thirty-five years after his conviction. The movie receives four Academy Award nominations.

=========================== 1967 ===========================

Tennessee repeals the Butler Act. Scopes publishes *Center of the Storm*, an account of his life and the trial.

246 | **A DANGEROUS IDEA**

===================================== **1968** =====================================

For the first time, the U.S. Supreme Court considers the validity of an anti-evolution law. In *Epperson v. Arkansas*, the court invalidates an Arkansas law that bans the teaching of evolution.

===================================== **1970** =====================================

Scopes dies in Shreveport, Louisiana, where he has been living with his wife, Mildred. They had two children.

===================================== **1987** =====================================

In *Edwards v. Aguillard*, the U.S. Supreme Court invalidates a Louisiana law requiring public schools to teach creationism if they teach evolution.

===================================== **2005** =====================================

A federal district court judge in Pennsylvania rules unconstitutional a school board's policy requiring that teachers introduce students to "intelligent design" alongside evolution.

SOURCE NOTES

Chapter 1: The Drugstore Plan

p. 1 "Mr. Robinson says": John T. Scopes and James Presley, *Center of the Storm: Memoirs of John T. Scopes* (New York: Holt, Rinehart and Winston, 1967), 57.

pp. 2-4 "John, we've . . . violating the law": *Center of the Storm*, 58-59.

p. 4 "Any theory . . . order of animals": "The Butler Act" reproduced in University of Tennessee, Knoxville, *Of Monkeys and Men: Public and Private Views from the Scopes Trial*, H.B. 185, https://digital.lib.utk.edu/collections/islandora/object /scopes%3A364#page/1/mode/1up. (Text of House Bill 185, the Butler Act.)

p. 5 "Distinguished counsel": "Plan Assault On State Law On Evolution," *Chattanooga Daily Times*, May 4, 1925, 5.

p. 6 "Mr. Robinson . . . morning paper": Warren Allem, "Backgrounds of the Scopes Trial at Dayton, Tennessee" (Master's thesis, University of Tennessee, 1959), 58, https://trace.tennessee.edu/utk_gradthes/941, quoting interview with Frank E. Robinson.

p. 8 "Our teachers": Knoxville school official statement in Edward J. Larson, *Summer for the Gods: The Scopes Trial and America's Continuing Debate Over Science and Religion* (New York: Basic Books, 1996), 84.

p. 8 "John, would you": *Center of the Storm*, 59.

p. 9 "This is F.E. Robinson": *Center of the Storm*, 60.

Chapter 2: The Real Target

p. 12 "I am almost convinced": University of Cambridge, Darwin Correspondence Project, "Letter no. 729," To J.D. Hooker, January 11, 1844, https://www .darwinproject.ac.uk/letter/?docId=letters/DCP-LETT-729.xml.

p. 12 "The marks of *design*": William Paley, *Natural Theology* (Boston: Lincoln & Edmands, 1829), 249, https://tile.loc.gov/storage-services/public /gdcmassbookdig/naturaltheologyo03pale/naturaltheologyo03pale.pdf.

p. 13 "Seeing this gradation": Charles Darwin, *Journal of Researches* (London: John Murray, 1845), 380, http://darwin-online.org.uk/converted/pdf/1845_Beagle _F14.pdf.

p. 14 "My dear Sir": Darwin Correspondence Project, "Letter no. 1675," To Asa Gray, April 25, 1855, https://www.darwinproject.ac.uk/letter/?docId=letters/DCP -LETT-1674.xml.

p. 14 "I rejoice": Darwin Correspondence Project, "Letter no. 1707," From Asa Gray, June 30, 1855, https://www.darwinproject.ac.uk/letter/?docId=letters/DCP -LETT-1707.xml.

p. 15 "But as an honest man": Darwin Correspondence Project, "Letter no. 2125," To Asa Gray, July 20, 1857, https://www.darwinproject.ac.uk/letter/?docId=letters /DCP-LETT-2125.xml.

p. 15 "The Creator established": Asa Gray, *First Lessons in Botany and Vegetable Physiology* (New York: Ivison & Finney, 1857), 173.

p. 15 "No one can": Darwin Correspondence Project, "Letter no. 2129," From Asa Gray, August 1857, https://www.darwinproject.ac.uk/letter/?docId=letters/DCP -LETT-2129.xml.

p. 16 "Mr. Wallace, who is": Charles Darwin, *The Essential Darwin: On the Origin of*

Species and The Descent of Man (New York: Halcyon Press, 2009), Introduction to *On the Origin of Species.*

p. 16 "Well put . . . Yes . . . !!!": Asa Gray's notations in David B. Williams, "A Wrangle Over Darwin," *Harvard Magazine*, September 1998. https://www.harvardmagazine.com/sites/default/files/html/1998/09/darwin.html.

p. 16 "The conception of One Mind": Asa Gray, *Lessons in Botany and Vegetable Physiology* (New York: Ivison, Blakeman, Taylor & Co., 1870), 175.

p. 17 "This is truly . . . mislead": Louis Agassiz's notations in "A Wrangle Over Darwinism."

p. 18 "I think I shall avoid": Darwin Correspondence Project, "Letter no. 2192," To A.R. Wallace, December 22, 1857, https://www.darwinproject.ac.uk/letter/?docId=letters/DCP-LETT-2192.xml.

p. 18 "Our ancestor": Darwin Correspondence Project, "Letter no. 2647," To Charles Lyell, January 10, 1860, https://www.darwinproject.ac.uk/letter/?docId=letters/DCP-LETT-2647.xml.

p. 19 "Man" . . . "still bears": Charles Darwin, *The Essential Darwin: The Descent of Man*, chapter 21.

p. 20 "Almost unprecedented . . . masterminds of the age": Journals quoted in Kimberly A. Hamlin, "Darwin's Bawdy: The Popular, Gendered and Radical Reception of the *Descent of Man* in the US, 1871-1910," *BJHS Themes*, volume 6, 2021, https://www.cambridge.org/core/journals/bjhs-themes/article/darwins-bawdy-the-popular-gendered-and-radical-reception-of-the-descent-of-man-in-the-us-18711910/53E66A9732DABB55D94DF5AB6A339855.

Chapter 3: Clarence and Will

p. 24 "How does the bird": *McGuffey's First Eclectic Reader* (New York: John Wiley & Sons, 1879-1920), 79-80, https://www.gutenberg.org/files/14640/14640-pdf.pdf.

Chapter 4: Boy Orator of the Platte

p. 27 "Don't go . . . the asylum": Mary Baird Bryan and William Jennings Bryan, *The Memoirs of William Jennings Bryan* (Chicago: John C. Winston Company, 1925), 88-89.

p. 28 "The judges": *The Memoirs of William Jennings Bryan*, 85.

pp. 28-29 "My classmates . . . good enough": *The Memoirs of William Jennings Bryan*, 451.

p. 29 "Diversions . . . church social": *The Memoirs of William Jennings Bryan*, 450.

p. 29 "Make men mad": *The Memoirs of William Jennings Bryan*, 64.

pp. 30-31 "Mary . . . use it wisely": *The Memoirs of William Jennings Bryan*, 248-49.

p. 31 "Where is the Nebraskan": Nebraska newspaper quoted in Michael Kazin, *A Godly Hero: The Life of William Jennings Bryan* (New York: Anchor Books, 2007), 34.

p. 33 "That was one": Missouri newspaper quoted in *A Godly Hero*, 40.

pp. 33-34 "I am Bill . . . exclamation points": "The Boy Orator Introduces Himself," *Buffalo News*, August 14, 1896, 2.

p. 34 "I was born": *The Memoirs of William Jennings Bryan*, 10.

pp. 36-37 "Producing masses . . . cross of gold": William Jennings Bryan, "A Cross of Gold," July 9, 1896, reprinted in *The First Battle: A Story of the Campaign of 1896* (Chicago: 1897), 199-206, and https://billofrightsinstitute.org/activities/william-jennings-bryan-cross-of-gold-speech-1896.

p. 37 "The whole convention . . . maniacs": "Flow of Oratory," *Indianapolis News*, July 10, 1896, 2, 5.

p. 37 "I have enjoyed": Clarence Darrow, *The Story of My Life* (New York: Charles Scribner's Sons, 1932), chapter 11.

Chapter 5: "Whatever Degrades Another Degrades Me"

p. 38 "Never has life": *The Story of My Life*, chapter 2.

p. 39 "My instinct": *The Story of My Life*, chapter 4.

p. 39 "I enjoyed": *The Story of My Life*, chapter 3.

p. 41 "Each of us . . . degrades me": From Walt Whitman, discussed by Darrow in Clarence Darrow, *A Persian Pearl and Other Essays* (Chicago: C.L. Ricketts, 1899), 56.

p. 41 "It is a sad mistake": *A Persian Pearl*, 56.

p. 42 "The religion": Speech at Secular Union quoted in John A. Farrell, *Clarence Darrow: Attorney for the Damned* (New York: Doubleday, 2011), 38.

p. 42 "Now and then": Clarence Darrow, "The Problem of the Negro," May 19, 1901, reprinted in Douglas O. Linder, "Darrow Speaks Out About Race," Famous Trials website, https://www.famous-trials.com/sweet/122-darrowessay.

p. 43 "The people who heard": "Darrow To Be Here Again," *The Daily Review* (Decatur, IL), October 27, 1892, 2.

p. 44 "Here is Prendergast . . . handiwork of the infinite God": *Clarence Darrow: Attorney for the Damned*, 61, and transcript of *In Re Prendergast*, http://moses.law .umn.edu/darrow/documents/Prendergast_Transcript.pdf.

p. 45 "It takes more . . . say, anyhow": *The Story of My Life*, chapter 11.

p. 47 "You'd better . . . believing in God": Darrow and Bryan exchange quoted in *Clarence Darrow: Attorney for the Damned*, 80.

Chapter 6: Two Tall Men, Talking

p. 50 "Bryan Speaks . . . applauding the speaker": *The Elmcreek Beacon* (Nebraska), June 26, 1908, 1.

p. 51 "Mr. Bryan's . . . white comes first": "Mr. Bryan on the South," *The Commoner* (Lincoln, NE), October 30, 1903, 11.

p. 51 "One of the most stupendous": "The Reformer," *The Appeal* (St. Paul, MN), September 29, 1906, 2.

pp. 53-54 "I am not yet . . . it is not water": William Jennings Bryan, *The Prince of Peace* (New York: Fleming H. Revell Company, 1909).

p. 54 "This Is the Address": *New York Times*, September 7, 1913, 10.

pp 56-57 "The poor devil . . . his soup bowl": *Clarence Darrow: Attorney for the Damned*, 101.

p. 58 "They have come": Darrow, quoted in *Clarence Darrow: Attorney for the Damned*, 114; see also "Blame For Coal Famine: Darrow Says The Operators Are Autocratic and Stupid," *Baltimore Sun*, February 14, 1903, 8.

p. 58 "The man who owns": Clarence Darrow, "Crime and Criminals: Address to the Prisoners in the Chicago Jail" (1902), reprinted in *Socialist Viewpoint* (November /December 2009), https://www.marxists.org/history/etol/newspape/socialist -viewpoint-us/novdec_09/novdec_09_30.html.

p. 59 "Great Attraction . . . Unsurpassed": *The Ottawa Herald*, May 18, 1905, 1.

p. 59 "A close observer": *The Story of My Life*, chapter 29.

Chapter 7: Proofs and Perversions

p. 60 "Well-known": "Great Books of the Century," *The Nashville American*, December 8, 1900, 4.

p. 63 "This survival of the fittest": Spencer, quoted in Dan Falk, "The Complicated Legacy of Herbert Spencer, the Man Who Coined 'Survival of the Fittest,'" *Smithsonian Magazine*, April 29, 2020, https://www.smithsonianmag.com/science -nature/herbert-spencer-survival-of-the-fittest-180974756/.

p. 64 "Eugenics": Francis Galton, *Inquiries into Human Fertility and Its Development* (1883), quoted in National Human Genome Research Institute, "Eugenics: Its Origin and Development (1883–Present)," https://www.genome.gov/about -genomics/educational-resources/timelines/eugenics.

pp. 64–65 "Religious dogma": Galton, quoted in Facing History and Ourselves, "The Origins of Eugenics," August 4, 2015, https://www.facinghistory.org/resource -library/origins-eugenics.

p. 65 "Idiots . . . promiscuous": Legislation quoted in National Human Genome Research Institute, "Eugenics: Its Origin and Development (1883–Present)."

p. 66 "The several so-called": *The Essential Darwin: The Descent of Man*, chapter 7.

p. 67 "Exaggerated . . . creations": *The Essential Darwin: The Descent of Man*, chapter 2.

Chapter 8: Darwinism Goes to School

p. 68 "I cannot avoid": *The Story of My Life*, chapter 3.

p. 69 "Schools probably became": *The Story of My Life*, chapter 3.

p. 69 From 2,500 public high schools: *Trial and Error*, and Paul Beston, "When High Schools Shaped American Destiny," *City Journal: The Shape of Work to Come* (2017), https://www.city-journal.org/html/when-high-schools-shaped-americas -destiny-15254.html.

p. 69 a new school opened: Jill Lepore, "Why the School Wars Still Rage," *The New Yorker*, March 14, 2022.

p. 69 By 1918, all forty-eight states: Michael S. Katz, *A History of Compulsory Education Laws* (Bloomington, IN: Phi Delta Kappa Educational Foundation, 1976), 5.

p. 70 "Strange how anxious": *The Story of My Life*, chapter 29.

p. 70 "40 to 45 percent": James H. Leuba, *The Belief in God and Immortality* (Boston: Sherman, French and Company, 1916), 280.

p. 72 "The greatest need . . . challenge the unbeliever." "Many Hear Bryan on 'Back To God,'" *Wausau Daily Herald* (Wisconsin), May 13, 1919, 1.

p. 73 "Will soon be turned": "12 Boys, 10 Girls In Class of 1919," *Marion County Democrat* (Salem, IL), May 8, 1919, 1.

pp. 73–74 "He was one . . . whistling effect": *Center of the Storm*, 26.

Chapter 9: Better to Destroy

p. 75 "William Jennings Bryan thrilled": "Bryan Flays Atheists," *Baltimore Sun*, January 6, 1919, 12.

p. 75 "William Jennings Bryan was given": "Bryan Comes Home To Cast His Vote," *The Nebraska State Journal*, November 3, 1920, 3.

pp. 75-76 "'THE MENACE OF DARWINISM'": *Miami Herald*, March 28, 1921, 3.

p. 76 "William Jennings Bryan, speaking": "Bible Critics Assailed By Bryan As Great Menace to World Peace," *The Courier-Journal* (Louisville, KY), September 20, 1921, 2.

p. 76 "How can teachers tell": Bryan, quoted in *Summer for the Gods*, 116.

p. 76 "All the ills": Bryan, quoted in Maynard Shipley, *The War on Modern Science: A Short History of the Fundamentalist Attacks on Evolution and Modernism* (New York: A.A. Knopf, 1927), 254-55.

pp. 76-77 "There is not a single fact": William Jennings Bryan, *The Menace of Darwinism* (New York: Fleming H. Revell Company, 1921), 20.

p. 77 "The word hypothesis": *The Menace of Darwinism*, 21.

p. 77 "It is better": *The Menace of Darwinism*, 22.

p. 78 "The parents who pay": William Jennings Bryan, *In His Image* (New York: Fleming H. Revell Company, 1922), 122.

p. 78 "Why don't you": "Heckler Harasses Bryan at Lecture," *New York Times*, April 3, 1922, B19.

pp. 78-79 "He seemed . . . say anything": "Dartmouth Charts Mr. Bryan's Argument," *New York Times*, January 13, 1924, X8.

pp. 80-81 "Darrow Asks . . . that time": "Darrow Asks W.J. Bryan To Answer These," *Chicago Daily Tribune*, July 3, 1923, 1.

Chapter 10: "What Are Mothers to Do"

p. 82 "Don't even allow": "Bryan Flays Modernists," *Nashville Banner*, January 25, 1924, 6.

p. 82 "I didn't know anything": "Butler Disappointed," *Chattanooga Daily Times*, July 18, 1925, 1.

pp. 82-84 "An Act . . . each offense": "Butler Act," March 21, 1925, Tennessee Virtual Archive, https://teva.contentdm.oclc.org/digital/collection/scopes/id/168.

p. 85 "What are mothers to do": Mrs. E.P. Blair, "Communications," *The Tennessean*, March 16, 1925, 4.

p. 87 "I can find nothing": Peay, quoted in Peter Neal Herndon, "The Constitution, Censorship and the Schools: Tennessee v. John Thomas Scopes," Yale-New Haven Teachers Institute, 1998, https://teachersinstitute.yale.edu/curriculum /units/1988/1/88.01.02/17 and in "In Signing Anti-Evolution Bill, Governor Pleads for the Bible," *Buffalo News*, March 24, 1925, 3.

Chapter 11: The Road to Dayton

p. 89 "The Rhea High team": "Rockwood Player Severely Injured," *Chattanooga Daily Times*, October 25, 1924, 12.

p. 89 "Rhea High . . . path of defeat": "Rhea High's Raw Material Squad Developed Into Winner As Season Progressed To Turkey Day," *Chattanooga Daily Times*, November 30, 1924, 17.

p. 91 "My father had read": *Center of the Storm*, 53.

p. 92 "I've come a long way": "Brown Students Jeer Bryan on Evolution," *Peninsula Times Tribune* (Palo Alto, CA), May 15, 1925, 1.

p. 92 "Boy, . . . I'm interested": *Center of the Storm*, 63.

p. 92 "Neal rarely impressed": *Center of the Storm*, 63-64.

p. 93 "Obviously a towering": "Make It Bryan v. Darrow," *St. Louis Post-Dispatch*, May 14, 1925, 20.

p. 93 "At once I wanted": *The Story of My Life*, chapter 29.

p. 96 "The arguments . . . I want Darrow": *Center of the Storm*, 72.

Chapter 12: The Circus Comes to Town

p. 97 "Well, . . . I'm here": William Losh, "Crowds Meet His Train," *Knoxville News-Sentinel*, July 7, 1925, 1.

p. 97 "Long have I looked": John P. Fort, "Dayton Greets Bryan With Cheers," *Chattanooga News*, July 7, 1925, 1.

p. 98 Inherited it from his father: "Bryan in Dayton, Calls Scopes Trial Duel to the Death," *New York Times*, Wednesday, July 8, 1925, 1.

p. 98 "Practically every home": Untitled article by Nellie Kenyon, *Chattanooga News*, July 7, 1925, 1.

p. 99 "Where It Started": Douglas O. Linder, "State v. John Scopes ('The Monkey Trial'): An Account," Famous Trials website, https://famous-trials.com/scopesmonkey /2127-home. See also Marquis James, "Around Town At The Scopes Trial," *New Yorker*, July 4, 1925.

p. 99 "Darwin Is Right—Inside": Nellie Kenyon, "Darwin, Dayton Merchant, Holds to Uncle's Theory," *Chattanooga News*, June 20, 1925. See also *Center of the Storm*, 84.

p. 100 "An acre": "Around Town At The Scopes Trial."

p. 100 "Your old man's": *Center of the Storm*, 84.

p. 101 "Monkey Trial": *Center of the Storm*, 66.

p. 101 "All out": "Around Town At The Scopes Trial."

p. 101 "It has aroused": "Curios [sic] Ones Give Monkey the Once Over," *Nashville Banner*, June 13, 1925, 1.

p. 102 "I will probably": "Darwin, Dayton Merchant, Holds To Uncle's Theory."

p. 102 "Read Your Bible . . . Your Business": "Around Town At The Scopes Trial," and *Center of the Storm*, 100.

p. 103 "Are These Your Ancestors": "Crowds Meet His Train."

p. 103 "The social event": *Center of the Storm*, 85.

pp. 103-04 "John[,] I know . . . No, Mr. Bryan": *Center of the Storm*, 85-86, and John Thomas Scopes, "Reflections—Forty Years After," Famous Trials website, https:// famous-trials.com/scopesmonkey/2139-reflections.

p. 104 "The contest . . . United States": "Evolution As Bryan Sees It," *Nashville Banner*, July 8, 1925, 1, and "Bryan in Dayton, Calls Scopes Trial Duel to the Death."

p. 104 "Warns That if Defeated": "Bryan Threatens National Campaign To Bar Evolution," *New York Times*, July 9, 1925, 1.

p. 104 "He has worked for two months": "Bryan Threatens National Campaign To Bar Evolution."

p. 105 "I was born": *Center of the Storm*, 88.

p. 105 "The old master": "Around Town At The Scopes Trial."

p. 105 "Newspaper Stars": Ralph Perry, "Newspaper Stars Reaching Dayton," *Nashville Banner*, July 8, 1925, 2.

p. 107 "One of the greatest": William Pickens, "Bryan and Evolution," *California Eagle*, June 5, 1925, 1.

p. 107 "If Monkeys Could . . . in the South": "If Monkeys Could Speak," *Chicago Defender*, May 23, 1925, reprinted in Historical Thinking Matters website, https://historicalthinkingmatters.org/scopestrial/0/inquiry/main/resources/43/index.html.

p. 107 "Thomas A. Edison": "Thomas A. Edison Coming To Dayton," *Chattanooga News*, June 16, 1925, 1.

p. 107 "Mrs. Thomas A. Edison": "Edison Not to Attend," *Nashville Banner*, June 17, 1925, 1.

p. 108 "Last summer . . . radio": "Dayton School Official Tells Evolution Views," *Columbia Record* (South Carolina), June 23, 1925, 2.

pp. 108–09 "Editor's Note . . . one viewpoint": "Trial Really Begins When Scopes Is Convicted, Mencken Says," *Chattanooga News*, July 10, 1925, 1.

p. 109 "Morons . . . preachers": H.L. Mencken, "Scopes At Least in No Danger of Lynching, Says Mencken," *Chattanooga News*, July 16, 1925, 2.

p. 109 "Here is the 'inside story'": Nellie Kenyon, "How Scopes Case Really Started Is Told First Time," *Chattanooga News*, June 29, 1925, 1.

p. 110 "William Jennings Bryan . . . there somewhere": John P. Fort, "Bryan vs. Darrow Battle of Giants," *Chattanooga News*, July 10, 1925, 1.

p. 110 "John T. Scopes, United States of America": Nellie Kenyon, "Plans For Scopes Trial Are Many," *Chattanooga News*, June 2, 1925, 1.

p. 110 "Contemptible cur . . . stake": Nellie Kenyon, "Scopes Jury Is Picked, Meets Next Monday," *Chattanooga News*, May 23, 1925, 1. (The jury referred to in this May 1925 article is the grand jury that indicted Scopes, not the jury that would ultimately judge his case.)

p. 110 "I don't plan": "Scopes Jury Is Picked, Meets Next Monday."

Chapter 13: In the Beginning

p. 111 "Coats off": "'Coats Off,' Judge Rules," *Chattanooga Daily Times*, July 9, 1925, 1.

p. 112 "Beaming . . . this trial": "Farmers Will Try Teacher," *New York Times*, July 11, 1925, 1.

p. 112 "Has been provided": Nellie Kenyon, "Dayton Greets Bryan With Cheers," *Chattanooga News*, July 7, 1925, 1.

p. 113 "Young man who": W.O. McGeehan, "Bryan, In Belt, Blushes As Darrow Snaps Galluses," *Los Angeles Times*, July 11, 1925, 1.

p. 114 "Here comes . . . Key West": PBS, *American Experience*, "Monkey Trial: An All Out Duel Between Science and Religion," February 17, 2022 [transcript], https://www.pbs.org/wgbh/americanexperience/films/monkeytrial/#transcript. See also PBS, *American Experience*, "WGN Radio Broadcasts the Trial," https://www.pbs.org/wgbh/americanexperience/features/monkeytrial-wgn-radio-broadcasts-trial/

p. 114 "The court will come to order": *The World's Most Famous Court Trial* (Cincinnati: National Book Co., 1925), 3.

p. 114 "Interminably": *Center of the Storm*, 105.

p. 114 "Amens": *Center of the Storm*, 105.

p. 114 "In the beginning": *The World's Most Famous Court Trial*, 5–6.

p. 115 "I regard a violation": *The World's Most Famous Court Trial*, 7.

pp. 116–17 "W.F. Roberson . . . take him": *The World's Most Famous Court Trial*, 10–11.

pp. 117–18 "Do you know . . . you are fortunate": *The World's Most Famous Court Trial*, 12–13.

pp. 118–19 "Ever preach . . . of course": *The World's Most Famous Court Trial*, 14–15.

p. 119 "There are eight": Nellie Kenyon, "Jury Composed of Churchmen," *Chattanooga News*, July 11, 1925.

p. 120 "The grade": Jack Lait, "Collarless, Coatless, Rawboned," *San Francisco Examiner*, July 12, 1925, 2.

p. 120 "Scopes is a convicted man": Philip Kinsley, "Conviction Of Scopes Seems Certain As Eager Men Quickly Fill Jury Box," *Pittsburgh Post*, July 11, 1925, 4.

p. 121 "There is no doubt": Bugs Baer, "Dayton Afraid to Eat Peanuts as Monkeys Do," *St. Louis Star and Times*, July 13, 1925, 1.

Chapter 14: To Strangle Puppies

p. 122 "Beyond a cough": Jack Lait, "Chautauqua Shekels Clinking For Bigwigs in Scopes Trial," *St. Louis Star and Times*, July 13, 1925, 2.

p. 122 "Messenger boys": "Sabbath Brings Messages of Praise to Evolution Teacher," *Birmingham News*, July 13, 1925, 1.

p. 123 "Dear Judge": "Hard Hitting In The Evolution Case," *Daily Telegraph* (London), July 15, 1925, 11.

pp. 123–24 "Oh, God, . . . ends of the earth": *The World's Most Famous Court Trial*, 45.

p. 124 "What is your plea . . . quash the indictment": *The World's Most Famous Court Trial*, 47.

p. 125 "Mr. Officer . . . less at ease": *The World's Most Famous Court Trial*, 53.

pp. 126–27 "I will hear you . . . with you, Colonel": *The World's Most Famous Court Trial*, 74.

pp. 127–30 "Is responsible . . . with them at all": *The World's Most Famous Court Trial*, 74–79.

p. 130 "Along comes somebody": *The World's Most Famous Court Trial*, 84.

pp. 131–32 "To strangle puppies . . . the human mind": *The World's Most Famous Court Trial*, 87.

p. 132 "Wonderful speech": "Darrow, In Outstanding Speech Of His Career, Hits Opponents Of Evolution," *Santa Ana Register*, July 14, 1925, 1.

p. 133 "The damned infidel!": "Darrow, In Outstanding Speech Of His Career, Hits Opponents Of Evolution."

p. 133 "The net effect": H.L. Mencken, "The Scopes Trial: Darrow's Eloquent Appeal Wasted on Ears That Heed Only Bryan," *Evening Sun* (Baltimore), July 14, 1925, 1.

p. 133 "I ain't agoin' to say": W.O. McGeehan, "Dayton Cringes At 'Jedgments,'" *Los Angeles Times*, July 15, 1925, 2.

Chapter 15: Prayers and Chairs

pp. 134–35 "I object to prayer . . . from which I came": *The World's Most Famous Court Trial*, 90.

p. 135 "Reverence to the Great Creator": *The World's Most Famous Court Trial*, 91.

p. 135 "If you want to make": *The World's Most Famous Court Trial*, 91.

pp. 135 "I will deal with them": *The World's Most Famous Court Trial*, 92.

pp. 136-37 "I submit . . . the vehemence": *The World's Most Famous Court Trial*, 92.

p. 137 "I am now informed . . . absolutely exhausted": *The World's Most Famous Court Trial*, 93-94.

p. 138 "This constant heckling . . . divine guidance": *The World's Most Famous Court Trial*, 96.

p. 138 "It has been ascertained . . . Well": *The World's Most Famous Court Trial*, 97-98.

p. 139 "Is that your decision . . . Yes": *Center of the Storm*, 118.

p. 139 "If you gentlemen": John Herrick, "Evolution Law Valid, Says Judge Raulston," *Commercial Appeal* (Memphis), July 16, 1925, 1, and *The World's Most Famous Court Trial*, 99.

p. 140 "This has required": *The World's Most Famous Court Trial*, 109.

p. 140 "Can we have chairs . . . or the press": *The World's Most Famous Court Trial*, 111.

p. 140 "I would like to make the request": *The World's Most Famous Court Trial*, 111.

p. 141 "What is your plea": *The World's Most Famous Court Trial*, 112.

Chapter 16: Four Witnesses and a Textbook

p. 142 "Not guilty": *The World's Most Famous Court Trial*, 112.

p. 142 "The prosecution has twice": *The World's Most Famous Court Trial*, 115.

p. 143 "There might be a conflict . . . involved in this case": *The World's Most Famous Court Trial*, 117.

p. 143 "I ask no protection": *The World's Most Famous Court Trial*, 117.

p. 143 "I cannot tolerate": *The World's Most Famous Court Trial*, 117.

pp. 143-47 "Just state in your own words . . . That's all": *The World's Most Famous Court Trial*, 126-28.

pp. 147-48 "Did anybody ever tell you . . . That is all": *The World's Most Famous Court Trial*, 129.

p. 148 "If the boys": *Center of the Storm*, 134.

p. 149 "That was all right": *Center of the Storm*, 161.

p. 149 "Geology teaches": *The World's Most Famous Court Trial*, 131.

p. 150 "In nature": George William Hunter, *A Civic Biology: Presented in Problems* (New York: American Book Company, 1914). 253.

Chapter 17: Speechless

p. 151 "Your honor . . . What is the use?": *The World's Most Famous Court Trial*, 133.

p. 153 "So I sat speechless": *Center of the Storm*, 136.

p. 153 "A sort of Scopes-goat": Robert T. Small, "Trial or Debate Is Question as Trial Begins," *Tampa Times*, July 13, 1925, 2.

p. 154 "Will you state what . . . divine creation and evolution": *The World's Most Famous Court Trial*, 138.

pp. 154-55 "The whole series . . . a very modest guess": *The World's Most Famous Court Trial*, 140-41.

p. 155 "He is about as authoritative": "Indictment Is Sustained," *New York Times*, July 16, 1925, 1.

p. 155 "Colonel Darrow": *The World's Most Famous Court Trial*, 143.

p. 155 "A friend of mine": "Bryan and Darrow Exchange Gifts of Carved Monkey," *New York Times*, July 16, 1925, 1.

Chapter 18: The Greatest Speech

p. 157 "Manifestations": *The World's Most Famous Court Trial*, 153.

p. 158 "Actually": Charles Michelson, "William Jennings Bryan Scores Scopes Defense," *Miami News*, July 17, 1925, 2.

p. 158 "We pray Thy blessings": *The World's Most Famous Court Trial*, 145.

p. 158 "He has none": "William Jennings Bryan Scores Scopes Defense."

p. 158 "I want to say this": *The World's Most Famous Court Trial*, 165.

p. 159 "Most agreeable": *The Story of My Life*, chapter 29.

p. 159 "Want to put words": *The World's Most Famous Court Trial*, 167.

pp. 159-60 "I do not know how well . . . next for the state": *The World's Most Famous Court Trial*, 170.

p. 160 "Outlawed": *The World's Most Famous Court Trial*, 172.

p. 160 "Commences with nothing": *The World's Most Famous Court Trial*, 177.

p. 160 "The Christian believes": *The World's Most Famous Court Trial*, 174.

pp. 160-64 "On page 194 . . . that is what Darwin says": *The World's Most Famous Court Trial*, 174-76.

p. 164 "Because this principle of evolution": *The World's Most Famous Court Trial*, 178.

pp. 164-65 "They do not explain": *The World's Most Famous Court Trial*, 178.

p. 165 "They say that evolution is a fact": *The World's Most Famous Court Trial*, 177.

p. 166 "the greatest": *The Memoirs of William Jennings Bryan*, 10.

pp. 166-67 "Feeble-minded, alcoholic . . . success in this country": *A Civic Biology*, 262-63.

p. 167 "Whether Mr. Bryan knows it": *The World's Most Famous Court Trial*, 183.

p. 168 "My old chief": *The World's Most Famous Court Trial*, 183.

p. 168 "God knows": *The World's Most Famous Court Trial*, 183.

p. 168 "Haven't we learned": *The World's Most Famous Court Trial*, 183-84.

p. 168 "We say 'keep your Bible'": *The World's Most Famous Court Trial*, 185.

pp. 168-69 "I feel that . . . shut no door from them": *The World's Most Famous Court Trial*, 187.

p. 169 "There was the fraction": W.O. McGeehan, "Bryan Speech Grieves Dayton," *Los Angeles Times*, July 17, 1925, 2.

p. 170 "That is what we claim": *The World's Most Famous Court Trial*, 187.

p. 170 "Dudley . . . make it": *Center of the Storm*, 155.

Chapter 19: Something Brand New

p. 171 "A northern Patrick Henry": "Malone Demands Freedom of Mind," *New York Times*, July 17, 1925, 3.

p. 172 "The glorious land": *The World's Most Famous Court Trial*, 201.

p. 172 "The theory . . . on the issues": *The World's Most Famous Court Trial*, 203.

pp. 172-74 "If Your Honor . . . all right": *The World's Most Famous Court Trial*, 207.

p. 174 "To have your picture": "Malone Declines Judge's Request to Pose With Him," *St. Louis Star and Times*, July 17, 1925, 1.

p. 175 "Battle Now Over": H.L. Mencken, "Battle Now Over, Mencken Sees; Genesis Triumphant And Ready For New Jousts," *Evening Sun* (Baltimore), July 18, 1925, 1.

p. 175 "From having its ears": "The End In Sight At Dayton," *New York Times*, July 18, 1925, 12.

p. 175 "The Tennessee case": "Bryan And Darrow Wage War Of Words In Trial Interlude," *New York Times,* July 19, 1925, 1, 2.

p. 175 "Before the trial": "Bryan And Darrow Wage War Of Words In Trial Interlude."

p. 176 "Something brand new": John Herrick, "Bryan Stirs Up Animus Among Tennessee Folk," *Chicago Tribune,* July 20, 1925, 4.

Chapter 20: Any Question They Please

p. 177 "Almighty God . . . open court": *The World's Most Famous Court Trial,* 211.

p. 177 "You people": *The World's Most Famous Court Trial,* 211.

p. 178 "The folks like it better": Verne Prater, "The Mammal Hunt," *Chattanooga Daily Times,* July 21, 1925, 3.

p. 178 "I have been treated": *The World's Most Famous Court Trial,* 226.

p. 178 "I am afraid": *The World's Most Famous Court Trial,* 227.

p. 179 "Go slowly . . . ever held!": Henry M. Hyde, "Bryan On Stand, Upholds Bible Statements As True; Questioned By Darrow," *Baltimore Sun,* July 21, 1925, 1.

p. 180 "Send for the jury": *The World's Most Famous Court Trial,* 280.

pp. 180-81 "Your honor . . . while the world lasts": *The World's Most Famous Court Trial,* 280-82.

p. 181 "Let the jury be brought . . . Not at all": *The World's Most Famous Court Trial,* 283-84.

p. 183-86 "You have given . . . and I accept": *The World's Most Famous Court Trial,* 284-88.

Chapter 21: "I Am Not Afraid"

pp. 187-93 "I don't pretend to say . . . Court is adjourned": *The World's Most Famous Court Trial,* 289-304.

p. 194 "Judge Raulston . . . put an end": "Mr. Bryan's Evidence," *Daily Telegraph* (London), July 22, 1925, 11.

p. 194 "Unprecedented": "Hot-Heads," *Boston Globe,* July 22, 1925, 16.

p. 194 "Unique": "Scopes Guilty, Jury Decides in Nine Minutes," *Philadelphia Inquirer,* July 22, 1925, 1, 4.

p. 194 "Probably the most amazing": "Bryan On Stand, Upholds Bible Statements As True; Questioned By Darrow."

Chapter 22: Verdicts

p. 195 "Bryan Holds His Own": W.S. Goodson, "Bryan Holds His Own In Meet With Darrow," *Knoxville Journal,* July 21, 1925, 1.

pp. 195-96 "Trick questions . . . Christian religion": "Darrow And Bryan Debate The Bible," *Evening World-Herald* (Omaha, NE), July 21, 1925, 4.

p. 196 "Science vs. Fundamentalism": Paul Y. Anderson, "Science vs. Fundamentalism," *St. Louis Post-Dispatch,* July 21, 1925, 1.

p. 196 "No pity": "Big Crowd Watches Trial Under Trees," *New York Times,* July 21, 1925, 1.

p. 196 "Mr. Bryan made a monkey": "Bryan Called As A Witness For Scopes," *Chattanooga Daily Times,* July 21, 1925, 1.

p. 196 "The lawsuit": *The World's Most Famous Court Trial*, 305.

p. 196 "I want": *The World's Most Famous Court Trial*, 306.

p. 197 "We claim": *The World's Most Famous Court Trial*, 308.

pp. 198–200 "Mr. Foreman . . . arrange with the clerk": *The World's Most Famous Court Trial*, 313.

p. 200 "An all-around love fest": "Tennessee Men and Women Stage Near-Riot To Shake Darrow's Hand as Case Ends," *Ottawa Journal*, July 22, 1925, 1.

p. 201 "The courtesies . . . while here": *The World's Most Famous Court Trial*, 315.

p. 201 "A little case": *The World's Most Famous Court Trial*, 316.

p. 201 "Because it is the first": *The World's Most Famous Court Trial*, 317.

p. 201 "We will adjourn": *The World's Most Famous Court Trial*, 319.

p. 202 "The finished product . . . gross ignorance": "Evolution Battle Rages Out Of Court," *New York Times*, July 22, 1925, 2.

p. 202 "The mountain peak": Bryan, quoted in Lawrence W. Levine, *Defender of the Faith: William Jennings Bryan, the Last Decade, 1915–1925* (Cambridge, MA: Harvard University Press, 1987), 347.

p. 203 "Protoplasm Special": William K. Hutchinson, "Appeal of Scopes Due," *Washington Times*, July 22, 1925, 1.

Chapter 23: Afterlives and Legends

p. 204 "apoplexy": "Apoplexy Causes His Death," *New York Times*, July 27, 1925, 1.

p. 204 "Clarence Darrow was": D.B.F. Stovall, "Darrow An Instrument In Sudden Death of Bryan, Says Writer Who Saw Clash," *Birmingham News*, July 27, 1925, 1.

pp. 204–05 "A leader in the advocacy": "Coolidge Praises Bryan as Sincere Leader In Message of Condolence Sent to Widow," *New York Times*, July 28, 1925, 1.

p. 205 "The young professor": "Scopes Stands With Mourners At Bryan Bier," *Los Angeles Evening Express*, July 28, 1925, 9.

p. 205 "Men in shirt sleeves": "Caravan of Death Goes East," *Chicago Daily Tribune*, July 30, 1925, 1.

pp. 206–07 "Little gray-haired widow": Nellie Kenyon, "Heart of Mrs. Bryan Won By Kelso Rice," *Chattanooga News*, August 1, 1925, 1.

p. 207 "Hour by hour": H.L. Mencken, "Bryan," *Evening Sun* (Baltimore), July 27, 1925, 5.

p. 207 "I believe that God": "Heaven, Evolution, Fundamentalism, What?" *California Eagle*, July 31, 1925, 8.

p. 208 "The life of Bryan": "Bryan and the American Press," *Pittsburgh Courier*, August 1, 1925, 16.

p. 208 "As the most wonderful": "Bryan Hails Radio As Aid To His Party" *New York Times*, September 4, 1922, 10.

p. 209 "Bryan Strikes": "Bryan Strikes From Grave At Evolution," *Austin American-Statesman*, July 28, 1925, 1.

p. 209 "Voice from Dead": "Voice From Dead Backs Tenn. Law," *El Paso Herald*, July 28, 1925, 1.

p. 209 "Bryan's 'Supreme Effort'": "Bryan's 'Supreme Effort' Is Given To the World; Speaks Again, Though Lips Are Mute," *Charlotte Observer*, July 29, 1925, 1.

p. 209 "Full Text of Bryan's": "Full Text of Bryan's Defense of Bible," *Commercial Appeal* (Memphis, TN), July 29, 1925, 10.

pp. 209–10 "Science is a . . . atheist": "Full Text of Bryan's Defense of Bible."

p. 210 "Mr. Bryan was a man": "Darrow and Scopes Comment on Death," *Chattanooga Daily Times*, July 28, 1925, 11.

p. 210 "Mr. Bryan had made himself": *The Story of My Life*, chapter 31.

p. 211 "Matchless and brilliant oratory": Benj. S. Scruggs, "Acquittal Expected in Case," *Pittsburgh Courier*, November 28, 1925, 1.

p. 211 "Clarence Darrow died": "Darrow Dies at 80; Famed Trial Lawyer," and Edmond Taylor, "Vienna Hails Hitler Today," *Chicago Daily Tribune*, March 14, 1938, 1.

p. 213 "William Jennings Bryan's Last Fight": Mike Palumbo, "The Scopes Trial," 20th Century History Song Book, https://20thcenturyhistorysongbook.com/song-book /the-roaring-twenties/the-scopes-trial. See also Vernon Dalhart, "William Jennings Bryan's Last Fight," New York, Columbia Records, recorded August 10, 1925, https://www.youtube.com/watch?v=-ns8L4d9CwA.

pp. 213-14 "Oh the folks in Tennessee": Vernon Dalhart and Company, "Edison matrix 10555: The John T. Scopes Trial (The old religion's better after all)," Discography of American Historical Recordings, https://adp.library.ucsb.edu /index.php/matrix/detail/2000157412/10555-The_John_T._Scopes_trial_The _old_religions_better_after_all (with recording). See also PBS, *American Experience*, "The Trial as Folk Event," https://www.pbs.org/wgbh/americanexperience /features/monkeytrial-trial-folk-event. Recording here: https://maxhunter .missouristate.edu/songinformation.aspx?ID=418.

p. 214 "The truth is": "Scopes," *The Crisis*, September 1, 1925, 218.

p. 215 "What was this Scopes": Nellie Kenyon, "Town Changed But Slightly During Debate," *Chattanooga News*, July 10, 1035, 9.

p. 215 "What was it": *Center of the Storm*, 204.

p. 215 "He not only won": Riley, quoted in Ronald L. Numbers, *Darwinism Comes to America* (Cambridge, MA: Harvard University Press, 1998), 83-84.

p. 215 "Theoretically, Fundamentalism": Allen, quoted in *Darwinism Comes to America*, 85.

p. 218 "Infallibility of the Bible": "Bryan University," *Time*, August 18, 1930.

p. 218 "Freedom of teachers": Nellie Kenyon, "Dayton, Scopes Relive Monkey Trial," *Tennessean*, July 22, 1960, 1, 3.

p. 219 "My thinking now": "Dayton, Scopes Relive Monkey Trial."

Chapter 24: A Victory

pp. 220-21 "Mr. Chief Justice . . . That is correct": *Epperson v. Arkansas*, Official transcript, Supreme Court of the United States, *In the Matter of Susan Epperson and H. H. Blanchard, Appellants, v. State of Arkansas, Appellee*, Docket No. 7, October 16, 1968, https://www.supremecourt.gov/pdfs/transcripts/1968/68-7_10-16-1968. pdf.

p. 221 "The law's effort": *Epperson v. Arkansas*, 393 U.S. 97 (1968).

p. 223 "We see nothing": *Scopes v. State*, 154 Tenn. 105, 289 S.W. 363 (1927).

Chapter 25: The Evolution of Everything

p. 225 "Wall between church and State": Jefferson, quoted in John S. Baker Jr., "Wall of Separation," *First Amendment Encyclopedia*, Middle Tennessee State University, https://mtsu.edu/first-amendment/article/886/wall-of-separation.

pp. 225–26 Supreme Court rulings on prayer and Bible reading in public schools: *Engel v. Vitale*, 370 U.S. 421 (1962); *School District of Abington Township v. Schempp*, 374 U.S. 203 (1963).

p. 227 "Facts do not go away": Stephen Jay Gould, "Evolution as Fact and Theory," *Discover*, May 1981, excerpted at https://wise.fau.edu/~tunick/courses/knowing /gould_fact-and-theory.html.

p. 228 "One Hundred Years Without Darwinism": H.J. Muller, "One Hundred Years Without Darwinism Are Enough," *School Science and Mathematics*, April 1959, 304, https://onlinelibrary.wiley.com/doi/10.1111/j.1949-8594.1959.tb08235.x.

p. 229 "Is a scientific theory only": Richard Bergholz, "Reagan Tries To Cement His Ties With TV Evangelicals," *Los Angeles Times*, August 23, 1980, 1, 28.

p. 230 Federal ruling on teaching "intelligent design": *Kitzmiller v. Dover Area School District*, 400 F. Supp. 2d 707 (M.D. Pennsylvania 2005).

p. 232 "They were two ways": Francis Collins, "Is there a God and does he care about me?" BioLogos.com, December 16, 2019, https://biologos.org/personal-stories /is-there-a-god-and-does-he-care-about-me-the-testimony-of-biologos-founder -francis-collins.

Epilogue

p. 234 "Freedom . . . form of government": Nellie Kenyon, "How Scopes Case Really Started Is Told First Time."

p. 234 "I don't believe it": Sabin Center for Climate Change Law, "Accuracy of National Climate Assessment Questioned by Trump Administration," https://climate.law.columbia.edu/content/accuracy-national-climate-assessment -questioned-trump-administration-0.

p. 234 "Idiots": NPR, "Trump Rails Against 'Fauci And These Idiots' In Campaign Call," October 19, 2020, https://www.npr.org/2020/10/19/925435610/trump -rails-against-fauci-and-these-idiots-in-campaign-call.

p. 235 "They cannot agree": *Prince of Peace*, 14.

p. 236 "Liberals, radicals and conservatives": "Hot-Heads," *Boston Daily Globe*, July 22, 1925, 14.

SELECTED BIBLIOGRAPHY

Books

Bryan, Mary Baird, and William Jennings Bryan. *The Memoirs of William Jennings Bryan*. Chicago: John C. Winston Company, 1925.

Bryan, William Jennings. *In His Image*. New York: Fleming H. Revell Company, 1922.

_____. *The Menace of Darwinism*. New York: Fleming H. Revell Company, 1921.

_____. *The Prince of Peace*. New York: Fleming H. Revell Company, 1909.

Darrow, Clarence. *A Persian Pearl and Other Essays*. Chicago: C.L. Ricketts, 1899.

_____. *The Story of My Life*. New York: Charles Scribner's Sons, 1932.

Darwin, Charles. *The Essential Darwin: On the Origin of Species and The Descent of Man*. New York: Halcyon Press, 2009.

DeSilva, Jeremy M., ed. *A Most Interesting Problem: What Darwin's Descent of Man Got Right and Wrong About Human Evolution*. Princeton, NJ: Princeton University Press, 2021.

Farrell, John A. *Clarence Darrow: Attorney for the Damned*. New York: Doubleday, 2011.

Hunter, George William. *A Civic Biology: Presented in Problems*. New York: American Book Company, 1914.

Kazin, Michael. *A Godly Hero: The Life of William Jennings Bryan*. New York: Anchor Books, 2007.

Kersten, Andrew E. *Clarence Darrow: American Iconoclast*. New York: Hill and Wang, 2011.

Laats, Adam. *Creationism USA: Bridging the Impasse on Teaching Evolution*. New York: Oxford University Press, 2020.

Larson, Edward J. *Evolution: The Remarkable History of a Scientific Theory*. New York: Modern Library, 2006.

_____. *Summer for the Gods: The Scopes Trial and America's Continuing Debate Over Science and Religion*. New York: Basic Books, 1996.

_____. *Trial and Error: The American Controversy Over Creation and Evolution*. New York: Oxford University Press, 2003.

Moore, Randy, and Susan E. Brooks. *The Scopes Trial: An Encyclopedic History*. Jefferson, NC: McFarland & Company, 2023.

Moran, Jeffrey P. *The Scopes Trial: A Brief History with Documents*. Boston: Bedford/St. Martin's, 2021.

Numbers, Ronald L. *Darwinism Comes to America*. Cambridge, MA: Harvard University Press, 1998.

Scopes, John T., and James Presley. *Center of the Storm: Memoirs of John T. Scopes*. New York: Holt, Rinehart and Winston, 1967.

The World's Most Famous Court Trial. Cincinnati: National Book Co., 1925. (This is the trial transcript of *The State of Tennessee v. John Thomas Scopes*.)

Articles, Papers, and Reports

Allem, Warren. "Backgrounds of the Scopes Trial at Dayton, Tennessee." Master's thesis, University of Tennessee, 1959. https://trace.tennessee.edu/utk_gradthes/941.

Anti-Defamation League. "Religious Doctrine in the Science Classroom." March 3,

2017, https://www.adl.org/resources/tools-and-strategies/religious-doctrine
-science-classroom.

Arnold-Forster, Tom. "Rethinking the Scopes Trial: Cultural Conflict, Media Spectacle, and Circus Politics." *Journal of American Studies* 56 (2022).

Arold, Benjamin. "The Costs of Canceling Darwin." *Education Next*, Summer 2022, https://www.educationnext.org/costs-of-canceling-darwin-fewer-scientists-more
-skepticism-science-states-limit-evolution-instruction.

Bakalar, Nicholas. "On Evolution, Biology Teachers Stray From Lesson Plan." *New York Times*, February 7, 2021.

Beston, Paul. "When High Schools Shaped American Destiny." *City Journal: The Shape of Work to Come* (2017), https://www.city-journal.org/html/when-high-schools
-shaped-americas-destiny-15254.html.

Boot, Max. "Foes of science faced ridicule at the Scopes trial. We're paying the price 95 years later." *Washington Post*, July 8, 2020.

Branch, Glenn. "What Ever Happened to John Scopes?" National Center for Science Education, October 30, 2013, https://ncse.ngo/whatever-happened-scopes.

Branch, Glenn, and Ann Reid. "Evolution Education in the U.S. Is Getting Better." *Scientific American,* September 12, 2020.

Cather, Willa. "The Personal Side of William Jennings Bryan." *Prairie Schooner*, Winter 1949, https://www.jstor.org/stable/40624159.

Christensen, Jon. "Teachers Fight for Darwin's Place in U.S. Classrooms." *New York Times*, November 24, 1998.

Conn, Steven. "Charles Darwin's American Adventure: A Melodrama in Three Acts." *Origins: Current Events in Historical Perspective*, February 2020, https://origins.osu
.edu/article/charles-darwin-s-american-adventure-melodrama-three
-acts?language_content_entity=en.

Dean, Cornelia. "Opting Out in the Debate on Evolution." *New York Times*, June 21, 2005.

Edwards, Karin Lynn. "Six Days of Twenty-Four Hours: The Scopes Trial, Antievolutionism, and the Last Crusade of William Jennings Bryan." Master's thesis, University of Mississippi, 2012, https://egrove.olemiss.edu/etd/96.

Eshchar, Yonat. "Evolution: A Matter of Chance?" Weizmann Institute of Science, Davidson Institute, February 15, 2023, https://davidson.weizmann.ac.il/en
/online/sciencepanorama/evolution-matter-chance.

Falk, Dan. "How Darwin's 'Descent of Man' Holds Up 150 Years After Publication," *Smithsonian Magazine*, February 24, 2021, https://www.smithsonianmag.com
/science-nature/how-darwins-descent-man-holds-150-years-after-publication
-180977091.

Ferguson, Daniel G., et al. "Popular media and the bombardment of evolution misconceptions." *Evolution: Education and Outreach*, December 16, 2022, https://evolution-outreach.biomedcentral.com/articles/10.1186/s12052-022
-00179-x.

Frail, T.A. "Everything You Didn't Know About Clarence Darrow." *Smithsonian Magazine*, June 10, 2011, https://www.smithsonianmag.com/history/everything
-you-didnt-know-about-clarence-darrow-14990899.

Fuentes, Agustin. "'The Descent of Man,' 150 Years on." *Science*, May 21, 2021.

Hamlin, Kimberly A. "Darwin's Bawdy: The Popular, Gendered and Radical Reception of the *Descent of Man* in the US, 1871–1910." *BJHS Themes*, volume 6, 2021,

https://www.cambridge.org/core/journals/bjhs-themes/article/darwins-bawdy
-the-popular-gendered-and-radical-reception-of-the-descent-of-man-in-the-us
-18711910/53E66A9732DABB55D94DF5AB6A339855.

Harris, Malcolm. "The Dark History of Liberal Reform." *New Republic*, January 21,
2016.

Hayden, Thomas. "What Darwin Didn't Know." *Smithsonian Magazine*, February 2009,
https://www.smithsonianmag.com/science-nature/what-darwin-didnt-know
-45637001.

James, Marquis. "Around Town at the Scopes Trial." *New Yorker*, July 4, 1925, https://
www.newyorker.com/magazine/1925/07/11/dayton-tennessee.

Kenyon, Nellie. "How Scopes Case Really Started Is Told First Time." *Chattanooga
News*, June 29, 1925.

Khazan, Olga. "I Was Never Taught Where Humans Came From." *Atlantic*, September
19, 2019.

Laats, Adam. "An eternal monkey trial? Evolution and creationism in U.S. schools." *Phi
Delta Kappan*, January 25, 2021, https://kappanonline.org/eternal-monkey-trial
-evolution-creationism-u-s-schools-laats.

Larson, Edward J., David Depew, and Ronald Isetti. "Inheriting *Inherit the Wind*:
Debating the Play as a Teaching Tool." *Evolution: Education and Outreach*, February
15, 2008, https://evolution-outreach.biomedcentral.com/articles/10.1007
/s12052-008-0039-6.

Lepore, Jill. "Blatherskites." *New Yorker*, May 16, 2011.

_____. "Why The School Wars Still Rage," *New Yorker*, March 14, 2022.

Mayr, Ernst. "Darwin's Influence on Modern Thought." *Scientific American*, November
25, 2009, https://www.scientificamerican.com/article/darwins-influence-on
-modern-thought1/#:~:text=By%20rejecting%20the%20constancy%20of,any%20
invocation%20of%20teleology%20unnecessary.

_____. "The Modern Evolutionary Theory." *Journal of Mammalogy*. February 1996,
https://doi.org/10.2307/1382704.

Moore, Randy. "The Lingering Impact of the Scopes Trial on High School Biology
Textbooks." *BioScience*, September 2001, https://academic.oup.com/bioscience
/article/51/9/790/288261.

_____. "The Long & Lingering Shadow of the Scopes Trial." *The American Biology
Teacher*, 2020.

_____. "Racism and the Public's Perception of Evolution." Reports of the National
Center for Science Education, May–June 2002.

Murphy, Troy A. "William Jennings Bryan: Boy Orator, Broken Man, and the
'Evolution' of America's Public Philosophy." *Great Plains Quarterly*, 2002, https://
digitalcommons.unl.edu/greatplainsquarterly/40.

National Science Teachers Association. "NSTA Position Statement: The Teaching of
Evolution," 2013.

PBS. *American Experience*. "Monkey Trial: An All Out Duel Between Science and
Religion" (Transcript), February 17, 2022, https://www.pbs.org/wgbh
/americanexperience/films/monkeytrial/#transcript.

Pew Research Center. "The Biology Wars: The Religion, Science and Education
Controversy" (Transcript), December 5, 2005, https://www.pewresearch.org
/religion/2005/12/05/the-biology-wars-the-religion-science-and-education-
controversy.

____. "Fact Sheet: The Social and Legal Dimensions of the Evolution Debate in the U.S.," February 3, 2014, https://www.pewresearch.org/religion/2009/02/04/the-social -and-legal-dimensions-of-the-evolution-debate-in-the-us.

Pobiner, Briana, and Rick Potts. "These are the Decade's Biggest Discoveries in Human Evolution." *Smithsonian Magazine,* April 28, 2020, https://www.smithsonianmag .com/blogs/national-museum-of-natural-history/2020/04/28/these-decades -biggest-discoveries-human-evolution.

Reid, Ann. "Good news: US classrooms are warming to evolution, thanks in part to scientist outreach." *Nature,* June 11, 2020, https://www.nature.com/articles /d41586-020-01454-x.

Robinson, Shantá R. "A Crusader and an Advocate: The Black Press, the Scopes Trial, and Educational Progress." *The Journal of Negro Education,* Winter 2018, 5, https:// www.jstor.org/stable/10.7709/jnegroeducation.87.1.0005#metadata_info_tab _contents.

Strauss, Valerie. "What the latest assaults on science education look like." *Washington Post,* April 22, 2017.

Taylor, John E. "30 years after Edwards v. Aguillard: Why creationism lingers in public schools." *The Conversation,* June 23, 2017, https://theconversation.com/30 -years-after-edwards-v-aguillard-why-creationism-lingers-in-public-schools -79603.

Williams, David B. "A Wrangle Over Darwin." *Harvard Magazine,* September 1998, https://www.harvardmagazine.com/sites/default/files/html/1998/09/darwin.html.

Wright, Robert. "The 'New' Creationism." *Slate,* April 16, 2001.

Many more newspaper articles from the Scopes era and years leading up to it also informed the writing of this book. See Source Notes, starting on page 247, for the articles that provided direct quotations.

Video

PBS. NOVA. "Judgment Day: Intelligent Design on Trial." November 13, 2007, https:// www.youtube.com/watch?v=x2xyrel-2vI (video) and https://www.pbs.org/wgbh /nova/video/judgment-day-intelligent-design-on-trial (transcript).

WKMS Documentary. "I Am John Scopes," July 20, 2015. https://www.wkms.org /society/2015-07-20/audio-wkms-documentary-i-am-john-scopes#stream/0.

Audio

Bryan, William Jennings. "Immortality (from Mr. Bryan's lecture 'The Prince of Peace')." Camden, NJ: Victor Talking Machine Co., recorded June 15, 1908, https://www.historyonthenet.com/authentichistory/1898-1913/2 -progressivism/4-TR-Taft/19080615_Immortality-William_Jennings_Bryan.html. The WGN radio broadcast of the Scopes trial was not recorded. But you can hear William Jennings Bryan on this vintage recording, available online.

Dalhart, Vernon. "William Jennings Bryan's Last Fight." New York: Columbia Records, recorded August 10, 1925, https://www.youtube.com/watch?v=-ns8L4d9CwA. This is an example of a "Scopes song."

Websites

Answers in Genesis. Creation Museum. https://creationmuseum.org. Answers in Genesis is an organization that promotes a literal interpretation of the Bible and rejects the theory of evolution. Its 75,000-square-foot Creation Museum in Petersburg, Kentucky, presents the Bible's creation story as fact, and includes exhibits that assert that Earth is only around 6,000 years old, and that dinosaurs and humans coexisted. Hundreds of thousands of people visit the Creation Museum each year.

Arizona State University, Institute of Human Origins. "Becoming Human." http://www.becominghuman.org. Dedicated to the science of how human beings evolved over seven million years, this website includes an interactive timeline, a video, learning materials, and classroom activities.

Linder, Douglas O. "Famous Trials: Scopes 'Monkey' Trial (1925)." https://famous-trials.com/scopesmonkey. Hosted by the University of Missouri–Kansas City Law School, this is a rich resource on the Scopes trial, with articles, biographical essays, photos, and more.

Tennessee State Library and Archives, Tennessee Virtual Archive. "The Scopes 'Monkey' Trial." https://teva.contentdm.oclc.org/customizations/global/pages/collections/scopes/scopes.html. This state website contains historical documents and photographs related to the Scopes case.

University of Cambridge. "Darwin Correspondence Project." https://www.darwinproject.ac.uk. Historians, archivists, and other experts created this searchable, annotated collection of letters by and to Charles Darwin.

University of Tennessee, Knoxville. "Of Monkeys and Men: Public and Private Views from the Scopes Trial." https://digital.lib.utk.edu/collections/scopescollection. The University of Tennessee, Knoxville has digitized selected documents and photographs concerning the Scopes trial.

Interviews

Larson, Edward J. University Professor of History and Hugh and Hazel Darling Chair in Law, Pepperdine University, March 21, 2023, in Washington, DC.

Moore, Randy. Professor of Biology, University of Minnesota, May 1, 2023, via Zoom.

Further Reading

Smithsonian National Museum of Natural History. "What Does It Mean To Be Human?" https://humanorigins.si.edu.

Teach Democracy. "Bill of Rights in Action: The Scopes Trial: Who Decides What Gets Taught in the Classroom?" Spring 2006, https://teachdemocracy.org/online-lessons/bill-of-rights-in-action/bria-22-2-a-4.

Turner, Pamela S. *How to Build a Human: In Seven Evolutionary Steps.* Watertown, MA: Charlesbridge Publishing, 2022.

University of California, Berkeley. "Understanding Evolution," https://evolution.berkeley.edu.

PHOTOGRAPH CREDITS

2: Courtesy of Tennessee State Library and Archives; **3:** retrieved from Amazon.com; **5:** *Chattanooga Daily Times* via Newspapers.com; **7:** Photo by George Rinhart/Corbis via Getty Images; **9:** Courtesy of Smithsonian Institution Archives, SIA2008-1122; **11:** Courtesy of Smithsonian Institution Archives, SIA2008-0865; **13:** Photo by Ann Ronan Pictures/Print Collector/Getty Images; **19 top:** Photo by Universal History Archive/Universal Images Group via Getty Images; **19 bottom left:** Photo by Oxford Science Archive/Print Collector/Getty Images; **19 bottom right:** *Punch*; **23:** retrieved from DarwinOnline.org; **25:** The Picture Art Collection/Alamy Stock Photo; **32:** Perry-Castaneda Library, University of Texas at Austin; **35:** Library of Congress/Corbis/VCG via Getty Images; **36:** original copyright by Geo. H. Van Norman, retrieved from Library of Congress; **43:** Reading Room 2020/Alamy Stock Photo; **46:** The Frent Collection/Corbis/Getty Images; **49:** Photo by © CORBIS/Corbis via Getty Images; **52:** Photo by PhotoQuest/Getty Images; **55:** *New York Times* Article Archive; **59:** Courtesy of the Risenfeld Rare Books Research Center, University of Minnesota Law Library; **61:** retrieved from InternetArchive.org, from a copy of the original publication held by the National Library of Canada; **73:** *Marion County Democrat* via Newspapers.com; **76-77:** original copyright by W. A. Fishbaugh, retrieved from Library of Congress; **79:** *Washington Post* ProQuest; **80:** *Chicago Tribune* via Newspapers.com; **83:** *Baltimore Sun* via Newspapers.com; **85:** *Atlanta Constitution* via Newspapers.com; **86:** *Pittsburgh Courier* via Newspapers.com; **90:** Bettmann/Getty; **94:** Photo by *NY Daily News* via Getty Images; **95 top:** *Commercial Appeal* via Newspapers.com; **95 bottom:** *New Yorker*; **98:** Courtesy of Tennessee State Library and Archives; **99:** *Literary Digest*; **100:** Photo by George Rinhart/Corbis via Getty Images; **101:** Courtesy of Tennessee State Library and Archives; **102:** Bettmann/Getty; **106:** Courtesy of Tennessee State Library and Archives; **112:** Photo by George Rinhart/Corbis via Getty Images; **113:** Courtesy of Tennessee State Library and Archives; **118:** Photo by George Rinhart/Corbis via Getty Images; **120 top:** Created by Clifford Kennedy Berryman, retrieved from Cartoon Drawings collection at the Library of Congress; **120 middle:** *Birmingham News* via Newspapers.com; **120 bottom:** *Pasadena Evening Post* via Newspapers.com; **121 top left:** *Pittsburgh Post* via Newspapers.com; **121 top right:** *New York Times* Article Archive; **121 bottom:** *Philadelphia Inquirer* via Newspapers.com; **123:** *Birmingham News* via Newspapers.com; **126:** Bettmann/Getty; **127:** Bettmann/Getty; **136:** *Atlanta Constitution* via Newspapers.com; **137:** *Johnson City Staff-News* via Newspapers.com; **144:** retrieved from FamousTrials.com; **146:** Courtesy of Tennessee State Library and Archives; **152:** Courtesy of Smithsonian Institution Archives, SIA2015-006841; **156:** Photo by Hulton Archive/Getty Images; **161:** Courtesy of Tennessee State Library and Archives; **163:** Photo by © Bettmann/CORBIS/Bettmann Archive via Getty; **170:** Courtesy of Tennessee State Library and Archives; **173:** Bettmann/Getty; **175:** *Baltimore Sun* via Newspapers.com; **176:** *Los Angeles Times* via Newspapers.com; **179:** Courtesy of Smithsonian Institution Archives, 2009-21079; **183:** Courtesy of Smithsonian Institution Archives, SIA2007-0124; **189:** Photo by Hulton Archive/Getty Images; **194:** *Commercial Appeal* via Newspapers.com; **195:** *Los Angeles Times* via Newspapers.com; **199:** Bettmann/Getty; **200:** Photo by *New York Times* Co./Getty Images; **202, from top to bottom:** *Montreal Daily Star, Boston Evening Globe, Miami Daily News, St. Louis Star*, all via Newspapers.com; **205:** *Birmingham News* via

Newspapers.com; **206:** Courtesy of Tennessee State Library and Archives; **213:** University of California Santa Barbara Library, retrieved from Archive.org; **216:** United Artists/Album/Alamy Stock Photo; **222:** Everett Collection Historical/Alamy Stock Photo; **230:** Cartoonstock; **231:** Cartoonstock; **232:** Cartoonstock.

INDEX

Note: *Italic* page numbers indicate
illustrations.

Academic freedom
    current status of, 233-234
    in Scopes trial, 153, 200, 218-219,
        225
ACLU
    on academic freedom, 153, 225
    goal for trial, 4, 95, 153
    search for client, 4-6, *5*, 9
    selection of Darrow by, 92-96
Adam (biblical figure), 181, 191-193
Affidavits, from expert witnesses,
    172-175, 178-179, 197
African Americans. *See* Black people
Agassiz, Louis, 17-18
Agnosticism
    of Darrow, 41, 44, 186, 191
Aldrich, Thomas Bailey, 38
Allegheny College, 38
Allen, Frederick Lewis, 215
Altgeld, John, 45, 46
American Civil Liberties Union.
    See ACLU
American Library Association, 60, *61*
The American Mercury (magazine), 108
Anti-evolution laws
    in Arkansas, 222-224, 226, 228
    Bryan's support for, 78, 79
    failed attempts at passing, 81, 91, 224
    in Mississippi, 224
    Supreme Court on, 220-223, 226,
        228, 230, 246
    in Tennessee (*See* Butler Act)
Anti-Evolution League, 102, *102*
Anti-evolutionism
    changes after Scopes trial to, 224-232
    in Dayton for Scopes trial, 102-103
Anti-evolutionism, of Bryan
    as campaign against scientific
        knowledge, 54, 59, 76-77
    on Chautauqua circuit, 54-56
    Darrow's fifty-five questions about, *80*,
        80-81, 182
    on evolution as dangerous idea, 71, 78
    last statement on, 209-210
    monkeys in, 53, 72, 76, 82, 164
    in "The Prince of Peace" speech, 54,
        55, 71
    rise in focus on, 70-72, 75-79

start of, 53-54, 59, 67
straw man arguments in, 53-54
students' opposition to, 78-79
timeline of, 241-245
The Appeal (newspaper), 51
Arkansas, anti-evolution law in, 222-224,
    226, 228
Atlanta Constitution (newspaper), *85*,
    136
Austin American-Statesman (newspaper),
    209

"Back to God" speech (Bryan), 72, 75
Baltimore Sun (newspaper), 75, 83, 108,
    175, *175*, 194, 203
Baseball, 38-40
Beagle, HMS, 10-11, 13
Beamish, Richard, 138-139
Belief, in science, 235. *See also* Religious
    belief
Bell, Alexander Graham, 54-56
Berryman, Clifford K., *120*
Bible. *See also* Biblical literalism; Creation
    story
    Bryan on superiority of, 76
    Darrow on nature of, 129-131
"The Bible and Its Enemies" speech
    (Bryan), 76
Bible study, 25, 72, 76-77
Biblical Alliance, 72
Biblical literalism
    Bryan's beliefs about, 71, 95
    Bryan's testimony at trial on, 182-196
    creation of all species at once in,
        12-15
    Darrow's views on, 181-182
    six days of creation in, 5-6, 190
    Supreme Court on, 221
    translations of Bible and, 152-153
Bill collections, 29, 40, 41
Biology education. *See also* A Civic Biology;
    Public schools, evolution in
    current status of, 233-234
    after Scopes trial, 224-226, 228
Birds, 11, 13-14
Birmingham News (newspaper), 122, *123*,
    205
Black newspapers. *See also* specific publi-
    cations
    on Bryan's death, 207-208
    coverage of trial by, 106-107

Black people
  Bryan's views on, 34, 51
  Darrow's views on, 42
  Darwin's views on, 66
  discrimination against (*See* Racism)
  enslavement of, 17, 21–22
  racial equality for, 17, 42
  in Social Darwinism, 64, 65–66
  voting rights for, 51
Boston Daily Globe (newspaper), 194, 236
Brennan, William, 221
Brown University, 92
Bryan, Mariah, 24
Bryan, Mary Baird, 28–31, 114, 203–206
Bryan, Silas, 24
Bryan, William Jennings
  childhood of, 24–26
  The Commoner under, 48, 49, 51
  Darrow's quarrel with, start of, 46–47
  death of, 203–208, 205, 206, 215
  education of, 24–29, 68–69
  against evolution (*See* Anti-
    evolutionism)
  as Great Commoner, 48
  health problems of, 91
  legacy of, 213–218
  legal career of, 29
  physical appearance of, 97–98
  racism of, 34, 51, 166, 208
  religious beliefs in early life of, 24, 31
  timeline of life, 239–245
Bryan, William Jennings, in Scopes trial
  arrival in Dayton, 97–98, 98
  banquet welcoming, 103–104
  on *A Civic Biology*, 160–167, 161
  closing argument of, 104–105, 176,
    197, 202
  day one of, 114–119, 122
  day two of, 127, 130
  day four of, 143
  day five of, 157–167
  day six of, 174
  day seven of, 179–196
  day eight of, 196–202
  after end of trial, 202–203
  in *Inherit the Wind*, 217
  photos of, 98, 156, 163, 174, 183,
    189
  recruitment of, 91–92
  speeches out of court during, 104,
    122
  as witness, Darrow's questioning of,
    181–196
Bryan, William Jennings, political career
  of, 29–37
  in Congress, 31–34
  Malone's work with, 169–170
  photos from, 32, 36
  in presidential campaign of 1896,
    35–37, 45–46, 46, 48–50
  in presidential campaign of 1900, 48
  in presidential campaign of 1908, 48,
    52
  as secretary of state, 51–52, 168, 206
Bryan, William Jennings, speeches of
  "Back to God," 72, 75
  "The Bible and Its Enemies," 76
  on Chautauqua circuit, 54–56
  "Cross of Gold," 35–37, 45–46, 79, 105
  in Dayton, out of court, 104, 122
  development of oratorical skills, 26–37
  "In His Image," 75
  "Is the Bible True?," 82
  last, released after death, 209–210
  "The Menace of Darwinism," 75–76, 78
  in presidential campaigns, 35–37,
    45–46, 48–50
  press coverage of (*See* Press coverage)
  "The Prince of Peace," 54, 55, 71
  radio broadcast of, 208
  recordings of, 50
  religion in, 31, 33, 37, 50–51
  "Science v. Evolution," 78
  at Scopes's graduation, 72–74, 73, 103
  voice in, 31, 50, 208
Bryan, William Jennings, Jr., 92, 157–
  158
Bryan Clubs, 50
Bryn Mawr College, 70
Buddhism, 189–190
Butler, John Washington, 4, 82
Butler Act (1925), 82–87
  Darwin's books as target of, 10
  fine for violation of, 84, 100, 199–200,
    203, 223
  legal challenges to (*See* Scopes trial)
  opponents of, 4–6, 86–87
  passage of, 4, 84–87
  provisions of, 83–84, 128
  repeal in 1967 of, 228
  timeline of, 242, 245
  as violation of religious freedom, 128,
    200

Cain (biblical figure), 181, 191
California Eagle (newspaper), 207

Capital punishment cases, 44-45, 93
Cartoons
    on Butler Act, 83, 85, 86
    on Darwin, 19
    on modern creation vs. evolution
        debate, 230, 231, 232
    on Scopes trial, 95, 120, 136, 175, 194
Cartwright, L.M., 114
Charlotte Observer (newspaper), 209
Chattanooga Daily Times (newspaper), 4-6,
    5, 89, 196
Chattanooga News (newspaper), 107-109,
    119
Chautauqua circuit, 54-56, 58
Chicago
    Darrow in, 37, 41-42
    Democratic National Convention in,
        35, 35-37, 45-46, 46
Chicago Daily Tribune (newspaper), 80,
    80-81, 182
Chicago Defender (newspaper), 107
Child labor, 58, 69
Chimpanzees, 19, 76, 101, 101
Christian morals, 33, 48-51, 231
Church and state, separation of, 225-226
A Civic Biology (Hunter)
    Bryan on, 160-167, 161
    Darrow on, 145-150, 146
    "The Doctrine of Evolution" in, 149
    eugenics in, 166-167, 228
    "Man's Place in Nature" in, 146,
        149-150
    "The Number of Animal Species" in,
        160-162, 161
    number of pages on evolution in, 10
    in origins of idea for trial, 3-4, 8
    "The Races of Man" in, 165-166
    reproduction of pages from, 3, 146, 161
    Scopes's use in classroom, 3-4, 8, 90,
        148-149
    statewide use in Tennessee, 3-4, 87
Civil War, American, 17
Climate change, 234, 235
Closing arguments
    by defense, 197
    by prosecution, 104-105, 176, 197,
        202
Collins, Francis, 232
Commercial Appeal (newspaper), 194, 209
The Commoner (newspaper), 48, 49, 51
Compulsory education laws, 69
Congress, U.S. See House of Representa-
    tives; Senate

Conspiracies, 236
Constitutional amendments
    Eighteenth, 52, 93
    Fifteenth, 51
    First, 221-222, 225-226, 230-231
    Nineteenth, 50, 52, 92-93
    proposed, to ban evolution in schools,
        104
Contempt of court, 174, 177-178
Coolidge, Calvin, 176, 204-205
Corporal punishment, 40
Courthouse, Rhea County, 112, 112
COVID-19 pandemic, 234-235
Creation science, 228-231
Creation story. See also Biblical literalism
    creation of all species at once in, 12-15
    reading aloud of, in Scopes trial,
        114-115
    two versions of, 84, 129, 152
Creation vs. evolution debate
    Butler Act in, 4, 83-84
    changes after Scopes trial to, 224-232
    creation of all species at once in,
        12-15
    Darwin in, 12-15
    evolution as consistent with religious
        belief in, 5-6, 70, 182
    evolution as work of God in, 16, 18
    expert witnesses on, 151-153,
        172-175, 178-179, 197
    jury instructions on, 198
    legends about outcome of, 213-219
The Crisis (magazine), 214
"Cross of Gold" speech (Bryan), 35-37,
    45-46, 79, 105
Cultural differences, 235-236

Daily Telegraph (newspaper), 193-194
Dalhart, Vernon, 213, 213
Darrow, Amirus, 21-22, 25
Darrow, Clarence
    agnosticism of, 41, 44, 186, 191
    autobiography of, 210, 211
    on Bryan's "Cross of Gold" speech, 37,
        45-46, 79
    and Bryan's death, 204-205, 205, 210,
        215
    Bryan's last speech on, 210
    childhood of, 21-26
    Darwin's books read by, 22, 23
    death of, 211, 223
    in Democratic Party, 42-47
    education of, 24-26, 38-40, 68

fifty-five questions for Bryan, *80*,
80-81, 182
health problems of, 92, 211
legacy of, 215-217
McKenzie's friendship with, 159
physical appearance of, 57, 105
political career of, 46, 56
Scopes's friendship after trial with, 212
teaching career of, 39-40
timeline of life, 239-245
Darrow, Clarence, in Scopes trial
banquet welcoming, 105
Bryan questioned as witness by,
181-196
contempt citation against, 174,
177-178
cross-examination of witnesses by,
145-149
day one of, 113-119
day two of, 126-133
day three of, 134-137
day four of, 145-155
day five of, 167-170
day six of, 172-175
day seven of, 177-196
day eight of, 196-202
after end of trial, 202-203
and expert witnesses, 151-155,
172-175
in *Inherit the Wind*, 217
photos of, *94, 106, 127, 156, 170, 183,
189*
pro bono work by, 94, 113
selection of, 92-96
on testimony by Scopes, 151
Darrow, Clarence, legal career of, 40-45,
43
death penalty in, 44-45, 93
fame in, 58, 92-94
labor unions in, 45, 56-58
last cases in, 210-211
Darrow, Clarence, speeches of
on Chautauqua circuit, 56, 58-59
as courtroom lawyer, 44-45, 56-58
in Dayton, before start of trial, 105
development of oratorical skills, 26,
38-47
for political campaigns, 43
religion in, 44
Darrow, Emily, 21-22
Darrow, Jessie Ohl, 40-41, 114
Darrow, Ruby, 114
Dartmouth University, 78

Darwin, Charles, 10-20, *11*. *See also*
Evolution; *specific books*
Beagle journey by, 10-11, 13
A Civic Biology on, 149-150
Darrow's reading of, 22, 23
Dayton descendants of, 99, 101-102,
109
death of, 66
responsibility for Social Darwinism,
64-67
Scopes's reading of, 91
timeline of life, 239
Darwin, Jim, 99, 101-102, 109
Darwinism, Social, 64-67, 71
Darwin's Dry Goods Store, 99, *99*
Dayton (Tennessee), *7*. *See also specific
locations*
and *Inherit the Wind*, 217-218
preparations for trial in, 98-103, *100*
publicity for, as motivation for trial,
6-8, 218
Dayton Progressive Club, 103
Death penalty cases, 44-45, 93
Debs, Eugene V., 45, 56
Decatur Daily Review (newspaper), 43
Declamation contests, 28, 39, 171
Defense lawyers. *See also specific lawyers*
closing arguments by, 197
in day one, 113-119
in day two, 124-133
in day three, 134-137
in day four, 137-155
in day five, 157, 167-170
in day six, 171-175
in day seven, 177-196
in jury selection, 116-121
motion to quash indictment by,
124-133
opening statement by, 142-143
prosecution witnesses cross-examined
by, 145-149
religious freedom missing in arguments
of, 225
selection of, 92-96
strategy of, 142-143, 153
on testimony by Scopes, 151, 153
Defense witnesses
Bryan as, 181-194
expert, 151-155, 158, 171-175, *173*,
178-179, 197
rumors about, 107-108
Democratic National Convention of 1896,
35, 35-37, 45-46, *46*, 79

Democratic Party
  Bryan in, 29-31, 35-37, 48
  Darrow in, 42-47
The Descent of Man (Darwin), 18-20
  in Darrow's childhood, 22, *23*
  human evolution in, 18-20, 65-66
  natural selection in, 67
  popularity of, 60, *61*
  press coverage of, *19*, 20
  publication of, 18
  in Scopes trial, Bryan on, 164
  and Social Darwinism, 65-66
Descent with modification, 16, 53, 226-227, 231. *See also* Evolution
Discrimination. *See* Racism
DuBois, W.E.B., 214

Earth, age of, 128, 143, 187-188, 226-227. *See also* Creation
Edison, Thomas A., 107-108
Editorial cartoons. *See* Cartoons
Eighteenth Amendment, 52, 93
El Paso Herald (newspaper), 209
Elementary schools. *See* Public schools
England, Social Darwinism in, 64
Epperson, Susan, *222*, 222-223, 226, 228, 230
Equality
  racial, 17, 42
  social, 41-42, 64
Establishment Clause, 225-226, 231
Ethics, Christian, 33, 48-51, 231
Eugenics, 64-66, 166-167, 228
Eve (biblical figure), 181, 191-193
Evolution. *See also* Natural selection
  acceptance by public, 233
  acceptance by scientists, 16-18, 60-62, 67, 69, 227
  debate over creation vs. (*See* Creation vs. evolution debate)
  debate over mechanisms in, 18, 62-63, 227
  definition of, 3, 5, 12, 154-155
  descent with modification in, 16, 53, 226-227, 231
  development of Darwin's theory of, 11-15, 18-20
  evidence supporting, 61-62, 77
  expert witnesses at trial on, 154-155, 158, 172-175, 178-179, 197
  fossils in, 11, 61, 226
  as godless, 6, 70
  as God's work, 16, 18
  as hypothesis, 77
  modern developments in understanding of, 226-227
  opponents of (*See* Anti-evolutionism)
  religious belief as consistent with, 5-6, 70, 130, 182, 231-232
  in schools (*See* Public schools)
  Social Darwinism as perversion of, 64-67
  Wallace's theory of, 16
Expert witnesses, for defense, 151-155, 158, 171-175, *173*, 178-179, 197

Fifteenth Amendment, 51
Finches, *13*, 13-14
Fine, for violation of Butler Act, 84, 110, 199-200, 203, 223
First Amendment, 221-222, 225-226, 230-231
First Lessons in Botany (Gray), 15
Fisk University, 86
Fittest, survival of the, 63-64, 71
Flood, biblical story of, 185, 187-188
Fortas, Abe, 221-222
Fossils, 11, 61, 226
Free silver, 33, 46
Freedom. *See* Academic freedom; Religious freedom
Fundamentalists. *See also* Biblical literalism
  on evolution as godless, 70
  legends about victory of, 215
  prayers at trial by, 136

Galápagos finches, 13
Galton, Francis, 64
Gene flow, 227
Genesis. *See* Creation story
Genetic drift, 227
Genetic mutations. *See* Mutations
Genetic sequencing, 227
Genetics, discoveries in, 62-63, 227
Germany, 65, 71, 211-212
Gilded Age, 51, 71
Ginzberg, Louis, 181-182
God. *See also* Creation
  evolution as work of, 16, 18
  in intelligent design, 229-230
Godless, evolution as, 6, 70
Gold standard, 33, 36
Gorillas, 19, 101, 102-103

Gould, Stephen Jay, 227
Gray, Asa, 14-17, 84
Great Commoner, Bryan as, 48
Great Defender, Darrow as, 58
Guilty verdict. *See* Verdict

Haggard, Wallace, 91
Harper's New Monthly Magazine, 20
Hays, Arthur Garfield
    in day one of trial, 113
    in day two of trial, 124-125
    in day three of trial, 135-137
    in day four of trial, 138, 145
    in day five of trial, 157-158
    in day seven of trial, 178-182, *179*
Hell & the High School (Martin), 102-103
Henry, Patrick, 28, 171
Hicks, Herbert, 91
Hicks, Sue, 91, 92, 138, 157-158
High schools, private, 25, 28, 68-69. *See also* Public schools
History education, 234, 235
Hitler, Adolf, 211-212
Holocaust, 211-212
Hooker, Joseph, 12-14
The Hornet Magazine, 19
House Bill 185. *See* Butler Act
House of Representatives, U.S.
    Bryan as member of, 31-34
    Darrow as candidate for, 46, 56
Housing segregation, 210-211
Humans
    classification as mammals, 145-147, *146*, 150, 162-163, 167
    Darwin on evolution of, 18-20, 65-66
    different species of, 17
    fossil record on, 61, 226
    Lyell on evolution of, 61-62
    in Social Darwinism, 65-66
Hunter, George William, 10. *See also A Civic Biology*
Hutchinson, William K., 139
Hygiene, racial, 65
Hypotheses, 77

Illinois College, 28
"In His Image" speech (Bryan), 75
Indiana, Social Darwinism in, 65
Indianapolis News (newspaper), 37
Indictment, motion to quash
    Darrow's argument for, 124-133
    definition of, 124

Raulston's ruling on, 135, *137*, 137-140
Inherit the Wind (film), *216*, 217-218, 223
Inherit the Wind (play), 215-217
Inheritance of traits, 62-63
Intelligent design, 229-230, *230*
"Is the Bible True?" speech (Bryan), 82

Jazz Age, 71
Jefferson, Thomas, 225
Jim Crow laws, 51
Joe Mendi (chimp), 101, *101*
Jonah (biblical figure), 184
Jones, John E., III, 230
Joshua (biblical figure), 184-185
Jury, in Scopes trial, *200*
    announcement of verdict by, 198-199
    excluded from expert testimony, 154, 158, 172, 178-180, 183
    excluded from motion to quash indictment, 125
    Raulston's instructions to, 197-198
    selection of, 115-121, *118*
    and sentencing of Scopes, 223

Keller, Helen, 54-56
Kelly, Gene, 217
Kentucky, anti-evolution laws in, 91
Kenyon, Nellie
    on academic freedom, 234
    on Bryan's death, 206-207
    on Jim Darwin, 109
    on jury selection, 119
    on legacy of trial, 215
    on Raulston, 112
    on Scopes, 110
Kinsman Academy, 38-39, 68
Knoxville Journal (newspaper), 195-196

Labor unions, 45, 56-58
Laws. *See* Anti-evolution laws; State laws
Legends, about outcome of trial, 213-219
Leopold, Nathan, 93, 210
Lincoln (Nebraska), 29-31
Lincoln, Abraham, 17, 22
Literalism. *See* Biblical literalism
Loeb, Richard, 93, 210
Los Angeles Times (newspaper), *176*, 195
Louisville Courier-Journal (newspaper), 76
Lyell, Charles, 18, 61-62

Malone, Dudley Field, *170*
  in day one of trial, 113, 115
  in day two of trial, 125
  in day three of trial, 134–135
  in day four of trial, 141–143
  in day five of trial, 158, 167–171
  in day eight of trial, 201
  opening statement by, 142–143
  pro bono work by, 93–94, 113
  selection for defense team, 93–94
Mammals
  classification of humans as, 145–147,
    146, 150, 162–163, 167
  origins of, 19
March, Fredric, 217
Martin, T.T., 102–103
Massingill, J.P., 118–119
Mather, Kirtley, 182
McGeehan, W.O., 133
McGuffey's Readers, 24–25, *25*
McKenzie, Ben G.
  Darrow's friendship with, 159
  in day two of trial, 125
  in day four of trial, 140–141
  in day five of trial, 157–159
  selection for prosecution team, 91
McKenzie, Gordon, 91
McKinley, William, 46
Memory, 213
"The Menace of Darwinism" speech
  (Bryan), 75–76, 78
Mencken, H.L.
  on Bryan's death, 207
  coining of Monkey Trial nickname, 101
  on Darrow, 133
  in Dayton for trial, 108–109
  on end of trial, 175
Mendel, Gregor, 62–63
Metcalf, Maynard M., 153–155, 167, 172
Miami Herald (newspaper), 76
Miller, Arthur McQuiston, 91
Mississippi, anti-evolution law in, 224
Modernists, 70–71
Money supply, 33, 36, 46
Monkey Trial, 101
Monkeys
  Bryan on, 53, 72, 76, 82, 164
  vs. chimpanzees, 76
  classification as mammals, 145–147, 150
  in Dayton, 100–102
  misunderstanding of Darwin's views
    on, 53, 102, 142
  in Scopes trial, 142, 150, 164

Morals, Christian, 33, 48–51, 231
Morgan, Howard, 143–147, *144*, *146*
Muller, Hermann Joseph, 228
Music, *213*, 213–214
Mutations, random
  in descent with modification, 226–227
  in natural selection, 11–12, 18, 62
Myths, 213–214

Nashville Banner (newspaper), 108
Natural selection
  A Civic Biology on, 150
  debates over mechanisms in, 18, 62,
    227
  definition of, 11–12
  development of theory of, 11–12,
    15–16
  in Social Darwinism, 64–67
  vs. survival of the fittest, 63–64
  Wallace's vs. Darwin's theory of, 16
Natural Theology (Paley), 12, 26
Nazi Germany, 65, 211–212
Neal, John Randolph
  in day one of trial, 113
  in day two of trial, 124–125
  in day four of trial, 138, 142
  in day eight of trial, 199
  on Edison as defense witness, 107
  selection for defense team, 92, 93–94
Nebraska, Bryan in, 29–31
Nebraska State Journal (newspaper), 75
New York Times (newspaper)
  on Bryan's speeches, 54, *55*, 104, 208
  on *The Descent of Man*, 60
  on Scopes trial, 112, 113, 125, 175, 196
New Yorker (magazine), 105
Newspapers. *See* Press coverage; *specific*
  publications
Nineteenth Amendment, 50, 52, 92–93

On the Origin of Species (Darwin). *See*
  Origin of Species
Opening statements, 142–143
Origin of Species (Darwin), 10–18
  in Darrow's childhood, 22
  development and writing of, 10–16
  human evolution in, lack of, 18, 65
  hundredth anniversary of, 228
  length of, 15–16
  popularity of, 60, *61*
  publication of, 16
  reception of, 16–18, 60, *61*
The Outlook (magazine), 60

Paley, William, 12, 26
Pandemic, COVID-19, 234–235
Peay, Austin, 86–87, 88
"Pessimism" speech (Darrow), 59
Philadelphia Inquirer (newspaper), 194
Pickens, William, 106–107
Pittsburgh Courier (newspaper), 86, 208, 211
Plants
　Darwin's theories on, 14–15, 150
　inheritance of traits in, 62–63
Plea, in Scopes trial, 124, 141–142
Political cartoons. *See* Cartoons
Politics. *See* Presidential elections; Religion and politics
Prayers, at Scopes trial
　day one of, 114
　day two of, 123–124
　day three of, 134–137
　day four of, 138
　day five of, 158
　day six of, 171–172
　day seven of, 177
　day eight of, 196, 201
Prendergast, Patrick Eugene, 44–45, 240
Presidential elections
　of 1860, 17
　of 1896, 35, 35–37, 45–46, 46, 48–50
　of 1900, 48
　of 1908, 48
　of 1980, 229
Press coverage. *See also specific publications*
　of Butler Act, 83, 85, 85, 86
　of Darwin's books, 19, 20, 60
Press coverage, of Bryan
　commencement speeches by, 73
　death of, 204–208, 205
　early speeches by, 31–33
　on evolution in schools, 75–76, 79
　leading up to Scopes trial, 104–105
　as presidential candidate, 37
　"The Prince of Peace" speech by, 54, 55
　in Scopes trial, 171, 193–196
Press coverage, of Darrow
　death of, 211
　early speeches by, 43, 59, 105
　fifty-five questions for Bryan by, 80, 80–81
　in Scopes trial, 125, 133, 193–196
Press coverage, of Scopes trial, 120–121
　by Black newspapers, 106–107
　on Bryan, 171, 193–196

cartoons in, 95, 120, 136, 175, 194
on Darrow, 125, 133, 193–196
end of, 201–202, 202
on expert witnesses, 175
on jury selection, 119–121
on Malone, 171
number of reporters in, 105
preparations and lead up to, 98–100, 104–110
on Raulston, 112, 123, 135, 137, 137–139
on Scopes, 110, 113, 122–123, 123, 203
start of, 111–121
Primates, 19, 100–101, 150
"The Prince of Peace" speech (Bryan), 54, 55, 71
Private schools, 25, 28, 68–69
Prohibition, 52, 93
Prosecution lawyers. *See also specific lawyers*
　arrival in Dayton, 97–98, 98
　banquet welcoming, 103–104
　closing argument by, 104–105, 176, 197, 202
　in day one, 114–119, 122
　in day three, 134–137
　in day four, 137–155
　in day five, 157–170
　in day six, 171–175
　in day seven, 177–196
　in jury selection, 116–121
　opening statement by, 142
　resting of case, 150
　selection of, 91–92
　testimony of witnesses for, 143–150, 144
Prosecution witnesses, 143–150, 144
Public schools
　history classes in, 234, 235
　McGuffey's Readers in, 24–25, 25
　religious education in, 6, 25–26, 72, 225–226
　rise of, 24, 67–69
Public schools, evolution in. *See also* Anti-evolution laws; *A Civic Biology*
　in 1860s, lack of, 24–25
　in 1920s, prevalence of, 69
　Bryan's speeches on, 72, 75–79
　current status of, 233–234
　Fundamentalists' opposition to, 70
　as godless subject, 6, 70
　after Scopes trial, 224–226, 228–231
Publicity, as motivation for Scopes trial, 6–8, 218

Punch (magazine), 19
Puppies metaphor, 131

Racial equality, 17, 42
Racial hygiene, 65
Racial segregation, 210-211
Racism
of Bryan, 34, 51, 166, 208
implications of evolution for, 17
in Social Darwinism, 64
in Sweet trial, 210-211
Radio coverage
of Bryan's death, 208
of Scopes trial, 105-106, 114, 124
Rappleyea, George W., 2-9, 9, 113
Raulston, John T.
at Bryan's speeches out of court, 122
in day one of trial, 111-119
in day two of trial, 123-132
in day three of trial, 134-137
in day four of trial, 137-155
in day five of trial, 157-170
in day six of trial, 171-175
in day seven of trial, 177-196
in day eight of trial, 196-201
family of, 111-112
in jury selection, 115-119
mail sent to, 123
photos of, 173, 174, 200
preparation for trial, 111-112
press coverage of, 112, 123, 135, 137, 137-139
sentencing of Scopes by, 198-200, 223
Reagan, Ronald, 229
Religion and politics
in Bryan's speeches, 31, 33, 37, 50-51
common views on intertwining of, 21
in separation of church and state, 225-226
"Religion of secularism" argument, 231
Religious belief
vs. "belief" in science, 235
decline of, 70, 231
evolution as consistent with, 5-6, 70, 130, 182, 231-232
Religious education, in schools, 6, 25-26, 72, 225-226
Religious freedom
Butler Act as violation of, 128, 200
First Amendment on, 221-222, 225-226
Supreme Court on, 221-222, 225-226

Republican Party, 30-31, 43, 46, 229
Rhea Central High School, 6, 89. *See also* Scopes, John T.
Rhea County Courthouse, 112, 112
Riley, Jim, 117-118
Riley, William Bell, 215
Roberson, W.F., 116-117
Robinson, Frank Earle "Doc"
in origins of idea for trial, 1-9
at trial, 115, 149
Robinson's Drug Store, 2
and *Inherit the Wind*, 218
planning meeting for trial in, 1-9, 90, 99, 109
during trial, 101

Salem (Illinois), 24, 72-74, 73
Schools, private, 25, 28, 68-69. *See also* Public schools
Science education. *See also* Public schools, evolution in
current status of, 233-234
after Scopes trial, 224-226, 228-231
"Science v. Evolution" speech (Bryan), 78
Scientific creationism, 228-231
Scientific knowledge
"belief" in, 235
Bryan's speeches criticizing, 54, 59, 76-77
current status of resistance to, 234-236
evolution as accepted part of, 16-18, 60-62, 67, 69, 227
hypotheses in, 77
Scientific method, 77
Scopes, John T.
on academic freedom, 200, 218-219, 225
arrest of, 8-9
at banquet welcoming Bryan, 103-104
on Bryan's death, 205
Bryan's speech at graduation of, 72-74, 73, 103
at Darrow's arrival in Dayton, 106
Darwin's books read by, 91
in day one of trial, 113-119
death of, 223
education of, 89, 91, 212
evolution taught by, 2-4, 8, 89-90, 148-149
and *Inherit the Wind*, 217-218, 223
life after trial, 212-213, 223
mail sent to, 110, 122-123
move to Dayton, 89

other subjects taught by, 3, 89
photos of, 9, 90, 106, 113, 170, 199
physical appearance of, 8, 113
press coverage of, 110, 113, 122-123, 123, 203
recruitment for trial, 1-9, 88-91
in selection of defense team, 92-96
sentencing of, 110, 198-200, 199, 223
testimony at trial by, lack of, 151, 153
timeline of life, 240-246
Scopes, Mildred, 217
Scopes, Thomas, 113, 113
Scopes songs, 213, 213-214
Scopes trial. *See also specific trial elements and participants*
day one of, 104, 111-122
day two of, 123-133
day three of, 134-137
day four of, 137-155
day five of, 157-171
day six of, 171-175
day seven of, 177-196
day eight of, 196-203
dress code in, 111, 114-115
lead up to start of, 97-110
legends about outcome of, 213-219
Monkey Trial nickname of, 101
origins of idea for, 1-9, 88-91
outdoor session of, 178-194, 179, 183, 189
preparations in Dayton for, 98-103, 100
press coverage of (*See* Press coverage)
publicity as motivation for, 6-8, 218
timeline of, 242-245
Secular Union, 41-42
"Secularism, religion of" argument, 231
Segregation, housing, 210-211
Senate, U.S., 34
Sentencing, of Scopes, 110, 198-200, 199, 223
Separation of church and state, 225-226
Seward, William, 22, 39, 42
Shelton, Harry "Bud," 147-148
Silver, free, 33, 46
Slavery, 17, 21-22
Social Darwinism, 64-67, 71
Social equality, 41-42, 64
Social Gospel movement, 50-51
Songs, Scopes, 213, 213-214
Soviet Union, 228
Spanish-American War, 126
Species. *See also* Evolution

as all created at once, 12-15
A Civic Biology on number of, 160-162, 161
Spencer, Herbert, 63-64
Sputnik I, 228
St. Louis Post-Dispatch (newspaper), 93, 196
State Department, U.S., 51-52, 168, 206
State laws. *See also* Anti-evolution laws
on compulsory education, 69
First Amendment applied to, 225-226
Social Darwinism in, 65
The State of Tennessee v. John Thomas Scopes. See Scopes trial
Sterilization, 64-65
Stewart, A. Thomas, 126
in day two of trial, 125
in day three of trial, 135-137
in day four of trial, 138, 142-150, 154
in day five of trial, 158, 170
in day seven of trial, 186, 190
examination of witnesses by, 143-150
opening statement by, 142
selection for prosecution team, 91
The Story of a Bad Boy (Aldrich), 38
Straw man arguments, 53-54
Stribling, Reverend, 135
Sullivan, Anne, 54
Supreme Court, Tennessee, 223
Supreme Court, U.S.
ACLU's plan to take case to, 95, 153
on anti-evolution laws, 220-223, 226, 228, 230, 246
on creation science, 229
on religious freedom, 221-222, 225-226
Survival of the fittest, 63-64, 71
Sweet, Gladys, 210-211
Sweet, Ossian, 210-211

Tariffs, 30, 31, 46
"Teach the controversy" argument, 230-231
Tennessee, Butler Act in. *See* Butler Act
Tennessee Supreme Court, 223
Tennessee v. John Thomas Scopes. See Scopes trial
Testimony. *See* Defense witnesses; Prosecution witnesses
Textbooks, biology. *See also A Civic Biology*
current status of, 233-234
after Scopes trial, 224-226, 228
Textbooks, history, 234

Theories, debates over, 77, 227
Timeline, 239-246
Tolstoy, Leo, 58-59
Tracy, Spencer, 217
Translations, biblical, 152-153
Trump, Donald, 234
Twain, Mark, 51

University of Chicago, 212
University of Kentucky, 89, 91
University of Michigan, 40
University of Tennessee, 87
Ussher, James, 185, 187

Verdict, in Scopes trial, 197-200
   announcement of, 198-199
   defense's views about, 153
   sentencing based on, 198-200, 223
Voting rights
   for Black people, 51
   for women, 40, 50, 52, 52, 92-93
The Voyage of the Beagle (Darwin), 13, 13

Wallace, Alfred Russel, 16, 18
Washington Post (newspaper), 79

Washington Star (newspaper), 120
WGN radio, 105-106, 114, 124
Whipple Academy, 28, 68, 171
White, Walter, 6, 108, 149
White people
   in Social Darwinism, 64, 65-66
White supremacy, 17, 30, 42, 66
Whitman, Walt, 41
William Jennings Bryan University,
   218
Wilson, Woodrow, 51-52, 241
Witnesses. See Defense witnesses; Prose-
   cution witnesses
Women
   Darrow's views on, 21, 40, 92-93
   Darwin's views on, 66
   sterilization of, 65
   voting rights for, 40, 50, 52, 52, 92-93
Working classes
   Bryan's advocacy for, 30, 33-34
   Darrow's advocacy for, 43, 45, 56-58
World War I, 51-52, 71
World War II, 211-212
World's Christian Fundamentals Associ-
   ation, 91